SONGS THAT MAKE
THE ROAD DANCE

SONGS *that* MAKE *the* ROAD DANCE

COURTSHIP AND FERTILITY MUSIC OF THE TZ'UTUJIL MAYA

Linda O'Brien-Rothe

Forewords by Allen J. Christenson
and Sandra L. Orellana

University of Texas Press
Austin

This book is a part of the Recovering Languages and Literacies of the Americas publication initiative, funded by a grant from the Andrew W. Mellon Foundation.

RECOVERING
LANGUAGES&LITERACIES
OF THE AMERICAS

Copyright © 2015 by the University of Texas Press
All rights reserved
Printed in the United States of America
First edition, 2015

Requests for permission to reproduce material from this work should be sent to:
   Permissions
   University of Texas Press
   P.O. Box 7819
   Austin, TX 78713-7819
   http://utpress.utexas.edu/index.php/rp-form

♾ The paper used in this book meets the minimum requirements of ANSI/NISO Z39.48-1992 (R1997) (Permanence of Paper).

LIBRARY OF CONGRESS CATALOGING-IN-PUBLICATION DATA
O'Brien-Rothe, Linda, author.
   Songs that make the road dance : courtship and fertility music of the Tz'utujil Maya / Linda O'Brien-Rothe. — First edition.
      pages   cm
   Includes bibliographical references.
   ISBN 978-1-4773-0109-8 (cloth)
   ISBN 978-1-4773-0538-6 (pbk.)
   ISBN 978-1-4773-0110-4 (library e-book)
   ISBN 978-1-4773-0111-1 (non-library e-book)
   1. Tzutuhil Indians—Music.   2. Tzutuhil Indians—Religion.   3. Tzutuhil Indians—Rites and ceremonies.   4. Folk dance music—Guatemala.   5. Santiago Atitlán (Guatemala)—Religious life and customs.   6. Santiago Atitlán (Guatemala)—Social life and customs.   I. Title.
   F1465.2.T9O33   2015
   305.897'4207281—dc23

                                                                    2014044268

doi:10.7560/301098

Jun ala' xusil prchi'b'ey, pnic'aj rujay, nute'.

Xusil quije' esquina rxin wuchoch.

Ajni'la buen ala' xintzu' nen, nute'!

A boy made the edge of the street move,

and the inside of the house, mama.

He made the four corners of my house move.

How good he looked to me, mama!

—"SONG OF THE YOUNG GIRL WHO SAYS
    GOODBYE TO HER MOTHER"

Quintorina tzrij tak b'ey, cha'

quinsobsaj b'ey, cha'.

I sing with power on the road, so they tell it

I make the road dance, so they tell it.

—"SONG OF THE FRUIT"

CONTENTS

FOREWORD

THE TZ'UTUJIL MAYA PEOPLE OF SANTIAGO ATITLÁN, Guatemala, believe themselves to occupy sacred land, the place of first creation, the navel of the earth and sky, and the very heart of the world. They are fiercely proud of their language, costumes, and traditions. The town is built at the center point where the lower skirts of three massive volcanoes come together to form a rocky and uneven foundation for its winding streets and buildings. In ancient Maya belief, the creation of earth and sky first unfolded when the creator gods raised three great mountains from the primordial sea that once covered the world. Atitecos, as the people of Santiago Atitlán call themselves, echo this belief in their own mythic stories. Despite centuries of pressure by outsiders to abandon their ancestral traditions, sometimes with well-meaning persuasion but often with unthinkable violence, a significant number of them continue to cling to centuries-old ceremonies and ritual practices whose core elements are often directly related to those once carried out by their ancient forebears. This remarkable persistence likely derives in part from their history following the Spanish conquest in the sixteenth century.

The territory now occupied by Santiago Atitlán was once the capital of the ancient Tz'utujil kingdom, one of three great kingdoms in the region (the K'iche's and the Kaqchikels were the others). The bloody invasion of highland Guatemala by Spanish forces was devastating to the political and social structure of the region. Following the destruction of the K'iche' capital and the execution of its kings in 1524, the Spanish commander Pedro de Alvarado inquired if there were any other hostile forces that would hinder the establishment of Spanish power in the region. The Kaqchikels had formed an alliance with Alvarado by this time and they informed him that their traditional enemies, the Tz'utujils who occupied the southern and western shores of Lake Atitlán, could pose a lingering threat. Alvarado sent three embassies to the Tz'utujil capital at Chiya' to negotiate a peaceful surrender. All were killed outright, prompting Alvarado to invade the Tz'utujil region in force, backed by thousands of Kaqchikel and Tlaxcalan allies. The initial attack, which took place across the bay from the royal city, succeeded in breaking up the Tz'utujil defenses. Many of the defenders that survived the initial battle attempted to swim to safety but were massacred in the water by Kaqchikel warriors in canoes. After nearly 500 years, there is still lingering animosity between the Kaqchikels who occupy the northern and eastern shores of Lake Atitlán and the Tz'utujils on the southern and western shores because of the Kaqchikels' complicity in the Spanish conquest.

That evening, Alvarado and his troops spent the night in a maize field and prepared for a siege of Chiya' the following morning. The ruins of the ancient Tz'utujil capital city can still be seen just across the bay from Santiago Atitlán on the crest of a small hill at the base of the volcano now known as San Pedro. But the Tz'utujil rulers had seen enough and realized that the fall of their city was inevitable, particularly in light of the Spaniards' superior weapons and tactics. As a result they abandoned Chiya' and fled into the surrounding mountains. Alvarado sent several captured Tz'utujils to invite the fleeing inhabitants of Chiya' to return to their homes under the promise that they would not be harmed. If they did not return, however, he threatened to continue hostilities, burn their towns, and destroy their maize and precious cacao fields. Within three days the Tz'utujil king, Joo No'j K'iq'ab', presented himself before Alvarado, offering abundant gifts of tribute and promising not to resume hostilities. He commended the Spaniard for his skill in war and noted that until that day, "their land had never been broken into nor entered by force of arms" (Alvarado 1924, 72).

True to his word, Joo No'j K'iq'ab' never rebelled openly against the Spanish authorities, and his successors followed suit. As a result, the Tz'utujil region remained one of the most peaceful in New Spain. The Tz'utujils controlled the rich cacao fields along the southern coast which, at least for a time, allowed them to keep up with the heavy tribute demands of their Spanish overlords. Other highland Maya communities were not as fortunate. Forced labor and exorbitant tribute drove most of them to take up arms again. This included the Kaqchikels. Although they had initially allied themselves with the Spanish forces, they received little preferential treatment and chafed under their oppressive tribute obligations. Their brief rebellion was ruthlessly crushed. Alvarado hanged the last Kaqchikel king, Kaji' Imox, on May 26, 1540. Soon afterward, in the same year, the last of the K'iche' kings, Tepepul, was also hanged after a long period of torture and imprisonment.

In gratitude for his peaceful submission to Spanish authority, Alvarado allowed Joo No'j K'iq'ab' to remain as the cacique of the Tz'utujils at Chiya'. Caciques, the Spanish title for native rulers, were exempt from tribute and labor obligations. Spanish law considered them to be the direct vassals of the Crown, not subject to the orders of local governors or military administrators. Because of this preferential treatment, Joo No'j K'iq'ab' was allowed to use the Spanish title *don*, own and ride horses, display a coat of arms, and possess weapons. He was also recognized as the legitimate ruler of the Tz'utujil people, and his eldest son was allowed to maintain many royal privileges after his death. The grandson of Joo No'j K'iq'ab was don Bernabé, who continued to reign in Santiago Atitlán into the seventeenth century, likely preserving much of the old power structure without serious disruption. Even today, the Tz'utujils consider themselves to be somewhat distinct from other highland Maya groups because their kings were never killed and their ancient communities were never destroyed.

The surprising degree of conservatism in Tz'utujil society and religion in Santiago Atitlán compared to many other highland Maya communities may stem in part from this early colonial political arrangement. Whereas the kings who ruled the major K'iche' and Kaqchikel lineages were tortured and executed at the hands of the Spaniards, and their capital cities burned, Alvarado left the Tz'utujil ruling dynasty largely intact to administer its affairs much as they had done prior to the conquest. The Tz'utujils likely considered this a sign of divine favor and were thus less susceptible to radical shifts in their indigenous worldview. In contrast to the fatalistic acceptance of defeat found in K'iche' and Kaqchikel accounts of the conquest as well as in contemporary myths, most legends told by Atitecos about the arrival of the Spaniards emphasize the supernatural power of their ancient kings and gods in escaping the destruction that befell other highland Maya kingdoms.

For many Tz'utujils, the Spanish conquest was not a catastrophic event that ended Maya culture, but a kind of temporary death followed by rebirth that is not different in kind from other periodic world renewals that took place prior to the conquest and continue to some degree today. For the Maya of Santiago Atitlán, the world is under constant threat of disaster. If the proper rituals are not carried out at the proper time, the world will sink back into the primordial world of watery darkness and endless death. To prevent this horror, the traditionalist elders of the community observe the complex and exhausting cycle of prayers, processions, and ceremonies first established by their ancestors, what the elders call the "ancient word."

Among the most beautiful and eloquent expressions of this ancestral tradition are the songs that Linda O'Brien-Rothe has worked tirelessly for the better part of half a century to record, translate, and study. Her work is what all ethnographic work should be but seldom is—painstakingly accurate in her scholarship but mixed with a profound respect for the dignity and humanity of those who composed the songs described in this book. Linda's interpretation of these songs is sensitive and persuasive, but she also wisely lets her Maya collaborators speak for themselves wherever possible. As a result, we never lose sight of the fact that these are not the bare bones of a dying craft, but the creations of men with blood in their veins who love and cherish their art. Some of the songs that Linda recorded when she began her work are nearly forgotten now, particularly those related to courtship since the rules of young love have changed dramatically over the intervening decades. Those songs related to the ancient gods, such as the Recibos of Rilaj Mam and Santiago, are most often played today by brass and marimba bands as part of *cofradía* ceremonies, amplified to bone-rattling levels from massive loudspeakers so that even communities far across the lake can hear them on the night air. What one misses, and which is rapidly passing away, are the quiet performances of these songs by a single master *ajb'ix* (literally "he/she of the song") to the accompaniment of an old guitar. Partly this is because of the disapproval of Christian institutions such as *Acción Católica* (Catholic Action) and the numerous evangelical Protestant churches that have sprung up in the twentieth century, partly because the younger generations have, until recently, taken little interest in this art, and partly because traditionalist Tz'utujils who tried to maintain their ancient practices have been targeted for murder by horribly misguided factions that for various complex reasons feel threatened by them. As Linda has painfully noted in her conclusion, many of those who were the most passionate about preserving these songs for future generations have since died in the violence, often leaving no living followers. We are fortunate to have their recorded voices and words, eloquently singing to us from their graves the lines that they loved and sought to preserve during their lifetimes.

Soon after the Spanish conquest, the survivors of the various highland Maya lineages desperately attempted to salvage what they could of their ancient cultural heritage. In some communities this was done through dance dramas and songs based on pre-Columbian traditions. The Rabinal Achí is one example, but there were many. I suspect that many of the songs recorded by Linda O'Brien-Rothe have significant elements of form and content that extend into the pre-Columbian past.

Gerónimo de Mendieta wrote in the late sixteenth century that "one of the principal things which existed in this land [New Spain] were the songs and dances to solemnize the festivals of their demons which they honored as gods, as well as to rejoice and find solace. The house of each *principal* thus had a chapel for singers and a place for dances" (Mendieta 1993, 140). Following the Spanish conquest, the highland Maya of Guatemala continued to perform such songs and dances based on ancient precedent (Mace 1970, 55–65). Bernardino de Sahagún complained that because many priests were ignorant of the languages of recently converted people in the New World, they were easily deceived by them. Through ritual dances and festivals, they continued to honor their ancient gods while hiding the practice beneath a thin veil of Christian faith by occasionally shouting out the name of God or some saint. He suggested that such dances were like a "forest or cave wherein Satan had taken his last refuge" (Sahagún 1956, vol. 1, 255). Despite numerous attempts by Spanish authorities to suppress indigenous songs and dance rituals based on ancient indigenous tradition, the Maya of highland Guatemala continued to observe them. Thus Francisco Ximénez observed in the eighteenth century that although dances on Christian holy days originated in stories of the saints translated for the Indians by the first priests, over time the Maya had altered them to worship their own gods:

> The early Fathers gave them [the Maya] certain histories of the Saints in their language, in order that they might sing them to the sound of the drum in place of those that they used to sing in the time of their gentility. Nevertheless, in my experience, they sing these in public only when the priests are there to hear them, but they then, in secret, sing songs that conform to pretty memories of their gentile condition. (Ximénez 1857, 148–149)

Santiago Atitlán is unique in preserving a rich tradition of songs that echo ancestral precedent, although they have certainly been adapted and altered to fit the changing needs of Tz'utujil society. The Spanish conquest and subsequent evangelization efforts crushed such traditions in most other highland Maya communities.

Elsewhere in the Guatemalan highlands, literate surviving remnants of the old royal courts composed histories and mythic accounts of their gods and sacred ancestors in written form using the recently introduced Latin script taught to them by early Christian missionaries. Many of these documents were composed in secret for fear that Spanish authorities would discover them and burn them as they had hundreds of pre-Columbian hieroglyphic texts. The earliest of these early colonial manuscripts, particularly the *Popol Vuh*, were composed as epic poems, structured into parallel phrases and concepts that echo ancient Maya literary forms. Most often the poetic arrangement consists of parallel couplets, although this is by no means the only form present. Such poetry is a marker of elevated Maya speech, and reflects a tradition that extends back to literary forms, concepts, and even phraseology used at the royal courts of the various highland Maya lineages prior to the arrival of the Spaniards (Hull and Carrasco 2012).

By comparing the songs that Linda recorded in Santiago Atitlán with the

Popol Vuh, composed some four hundred years earlier, it is evident that both belong to a common literary tradition that is uniquely Maya. The following section from the *Popol Vuh* contains a dialogue between the creator gods and the first human beings:

"Kixmuquna' na k'ut,	"Look surely therefore,
Chiwila' u xe' kaj.	see the root of the sky.
Ma q'alaj juyub'?	Are not the mountains clear?
Taq'aj kiwilo?"	And the valleys that you see?"
K'ate k'ut ki k'amowanik ri' chire	Then therefore they gave thanks to
Tz'aqol, Bitol.	Framer, Shaper.
"Qitzij wi chi ka mul k'amo,	"Truly two times we give thanks,
Ox mul k'amo,	three times we give thanks,
Mi xojwinaqirik,	[that] we were created,
Mi pu xojchi'nik,	also we were given mouths,
Xojwachinik.	we were given faces.
Kojch'awik,	We speak,
Kojta'onik,	we listen,
Kojb'isonik,	we ponder,
Kojsilab'ik.	we move.
Utz kaqana'o,	Well we know,
Xqeta'maj	we learned
Naj,	far,
Naqaj.	near.
Mi pu xqilo nim,	Also we saw the great,
Ch'uti'n,	the small,
U pa kaj,	its womb sky,
U pa ulew."	its womb earth."
(Christenson 2003b, 158)	

The original K'iche' for "we move" in the previous passage is *kojsilab'ik*. This is a word rich in underlying meaning. In another section of the text, the authors of the *Popol Vuh* wrote that prior to the creation, when the world lay in darkness and silence, nothing moved (*jun ta kasilob'ik*). They stressed that it is movement that characterizes life, whether speaking of the face of the earth, or the humans that perpetuate its life through sacred ritual. I find it significant that in Tz'utujil songs, poets often use the more ancient and esoteric *s'lobik* (the Tz'utujil version of the K'iche' word for "to move") to refer to ritual dance rather than the far more common word *xjowik* (page 44). Sacred dance, like sacred music, is a means of animating the world and giving it a living soul.

The poetic structure of the *Popol Vuh*, mostly based on parallel couplets, but frequently expanding into triplets, quatrains, and even longer sections, is also characteristic of the songs transcribed by O'Brien-Rothe in this book. Consider this brief section from the "Song of Mam":

Xwinkira,	He was created/engendered,
xtz'ijcara	he sprouted,
ala',	the boy,
acha,	the man,
"Cojol Xe Ak'om" ala'.	"The Medicine Place" boy.
Ay ajrojyu',	Oh man of the mountain,
ajrotk'aj	man of the plain
ay ral mutzmul,	oh son of drizzle,
ay ral sajbach	oh son of the hail
majo'n nk'iwa ruk'a'	no one has hands like his
majo'n nk'iwa rkan,	no one has feet like his,
ala',	the boy,
acha	the man

The nature of the parallelism in early writings such as the *Popol Vuh* is virtually identical with Tz'utujil songs, consisting of the symmetrical arrangement of concepts, grammatical constructions, metaphors, and descriptive epithets, rather than rhyme or meter as in most European-inspired poetry. While most of the parallelism in both ancient K'iche' texts and Tz'utujil songs is based on poetic couplets, there are lengthier parallelisms. When this occurs, a technique known as "gapping" is often utilized whereby an expected word or clause is omitted in one line, although it is implied by the parallelism of the series. Thus in the "Song of Mam," the word *Ay* ("Oh") is omitted from the second line of the quatrain but implied by the other three lines. An example from the *Popol Vuh* is found in lines 66–69, where the expected word "four" is omitted from the third line, perhaps to break up the monotony of the list:

U kaj tz'ukuxik,	Its four cornerings,
U kaj xukutaxik,	its four sidings,
Retaxik,	its measurings,
U kaj che'xik.	its four stakings.
(Christenson 2003b, 15)	

What I find perhaps most intriguing in Tz'utujil songs is the use of phraseology and metaphors that are consistent with much older highland Maya texts. One of the most common poetic devices in ancient Maya literature is the use of merismus, the expression of a broad concept by a pair of complementary elements that are narrower in meaning. Thus "sky-earth" represents all creation as a whole. The "Song of Mam" pairs "mountain-valley" to represent the entire face of the earth. It is also a common couplet that is used throughout the *Popol Vuh*. This is a logical pairing that might occur to any poet or songwriter. Other examples, however, seem to be more arbitrary and suggest that the concepts addressed in both are rooted in uniquely Maya modes of thought. For example, in the "Song of Mam" rain is paired with hail, likely to represent all types of precipitation. This same pairing occurs twice in the *Popol Vuh* (lines 5486–5489 and 5583–5584). The couplet that I find most convincing is this phrase from the "Song of Mam": *Xwinkira, xtz'ijcara* ("He was created/engendered, he sprouted"). The same couplet, using the equivalent words in the K'iche' language, appears in the *Popol Vuh* to describe the creation of the world (lines 175–180):

Ta xkina'ojij u tz'ukik,	Then they considered its germination,
U winaqirik	its creation
Che',	trees,
K'a'am,	bushes,
U tz'ukuxik puch k'aslem,	its germination also life,
Winaqirem	creation
(Christenson 2003b, 18)	

The same pairing is used to describe the creation of the first human beings in lines 5540–5541:

Xa pu jun qa tz'ukib'al,	Only also one our germination,
Qa winaqirib'al.	our creation.
(Christenson 2003b, 172)	

The pairing of "germination" and "creation" appears to be a very ancient concept that reflects a uniquely Maya worldview in which creation is tied to agricultural processes. The world germinated, as from a seed, at the beginning of time and continues to grow and die just as crops mature and "die" at harvest time. For the singers of Santiago Atitlán, the Tz'utujil god Rilaj Mam mirrored this process when he was created. This perpetuation of ancient Maya belief suggests that many of the songs performed in Santiago Atitlán may have had their origins in deep antiquity.

This Maya worldview is also expressed in the public ceremonies associated with ritual Tz'utujil songs. At the close of the ceremonial year, now timed to fall during the week preceding Easter in Santiago Atitlán, a group of recently married young men make a pilgrimage to retrieve tropical fruits from the coastal lands that once belonged to the ancient Tz'utujil kingdom. The ripening fruit—cacao, *pataxte* (a lesser grade of cacao), *melocotones* (a large, sweet-smelling, phallic-shaped melon), and plantains—represents the renewal of life at the close of the long dry season, ushering in the rainy season. The fruits are seen as metaphors for both the ancient practice of taking captives to be sacrificed to renew the world with their blood, as well as the taking of wives from their families to bear new life through their future children. When the young men return from the coast, bearing the fruits in packframes on their backs, they sing the "Song of the Fruit," two versions of which Linda recorded and which are transcribed in Chapter 3:

> In these highly symbolic songs the songman sings in the voice of the young man, and in the voice of the fruit itself; the *xul* or cane flute and the drum also speak, all of which are also the voices of the Santo Mundo.

In the song, the fruit describes itself in self-deprecating terms as "poor orphans," singers on the roads that wind through the mountains and valleys. In this respect the "Song of the Fruit" echoes important sections of the *Popol Vuh*. In this text, the cycle of the agricultural year is played out in the form of the Hero Twins, Hunahpu and Xbalanque, who are summoned to the underworld realm of Xibalba where they are taken as captives and ultimately sacrificed by the Lords of Death. Hunahpu and Xbalanque are gods that have power to regenerate themselves and by extension the world itself, just as hard, dead seeds are planted in the ground and subsequently germinate to new life. The text explicitly connects the death and rebirth of the Hero Twins with the life cycle of maize. Before they take the long journey to the place of their deaths, the twins counsel their grandmother:

> "Surely we must go, our grandmother. But first we will advise you. This is the sign of our word that we will leave behind. Each of us shall first plant an ear of unripe maize in the center of the house. If they dry up, this is a sign of our death. 'They have died,' you will say when they dry up. If then they sprout again, 'They are alive,'

you will say, our grandmother and our mother. This is the sign of our word that is left with you," they said. (Christenson 2007a, 160)

Following their death at the hands of the underworld lords, the Hero Twins are reborn—the foundation of Maya myth is this regeneration of life in endless, repeating cycles. The same concept underlies the ritual procession of the young men to the coast (Tz'utujils consider large bodies of water, particularly the ocean, to be portals to the underworld) where they retrieve unripe fruit, much like the unripe maize left behind by the Hero Twins. Following their sacrificial death, Hunahpu and Xbalanque managed to be reborn and the withered maize that they had left behind sprouted with new life:

> Then the ears of maize had sprouted once again, and the Grandmother had burned copal incense before them as a memorial. The heart of their grandmother rejoiced when the maize sprouted a second time. Thus they were deified by their grandmother. She named it Center House, Center Ancestral Plot, Revitalized Maize, and Leveled Earth. (ibid., 188–189)

In Santiago Atitlán, when the fruit arrives in town it is greeted by grandmotherly post-menopausal women who wave clouds of copal incense smoke from braziers over the fruit to empower it to ripen. The wording used in the *Popol Vuh* text, I believe, is directly related to the words of the Tz'utujil "Song of the Fruit." When Hunahpu and Xbalanque first appear after their deaths, it is as poor orphans dressed in rags, who despite their shabby appearance are wondrous performers who sing and dance:

> And on the very next day, they appeared again as two poor orphans. They wore rags in front and rags on their backs. Rags were thus all they had to cover themselves. But they did not act according to their appearance when they were seen by the Xibalbans. For they did the Dance of the Whippoorwill and the Dance of the Weasel. They danced the Armadillo and the Centipede. They danced the Injury, for many marvels they did then. (ibid., 180)

In the Tz'utujil "Song of the Fruit" (which appears in Chapter 3), the fruit describes itself in song much like the description of the Hero Twins in the *Popol Vuh*:

> We are poor,
> we are wandering orphans.
> They see us as lost, so they tell it.
> This is what I sing on the road, so they tell it.

In both the *Popol Vuh* and the "Song of the Fruit" the word that is used for orphans is the same, *meb'a'*. Both the Twins and the fruit are truly orphans. In the case of Hunahpu and Xbalanque it is because their father died in the underworld before they knew him. In the case of the fruit, it is because the young men of Santiago Atitlán cut them away from their mother trees and took them as captives. Despite their circumstances, both the Twins and the fruit are singers and dancers that are desired by their captors who gather to greet them in large numbers. Here is the version in the *Popol Vuh*:

> At length they arrived before the lords. They pretended to be humble, prostrating themselves when they came. They humbled themselves, stooping over and bowing. They hid themselves with rags, giving the appearance that they were truly just poor orphans when they arrived. . . . Thus they began their songs and their dances, and all the Xibalbans came until the place was overflowing with spectators. (Christenson 2007a, 182)

In Santiago Atitlán, the young men bearing the fruit from the coast are met by the highest dignitaries of the town, including the mayor, his counsellors, the heads of all the *cofradías* and throngs of people. Traditionally, the fruit represents the promise that the world will be reborn and life will continue. Despite the humble appearance and self-deprecation characteristic of the Hero Twins as well as the fruit, it is all an act and Atiteco singers know it very well. The Maya recognize that beneath the outward shabbiness lies the greatest of all hopes—the renewal of life itself.

Linda mentions in Chapter 2 that one of the few singers who "still improvises his song texts and plays on the five-string guitar in the old way" is José Cua Simaj. I'd like to add just a brief personal note on one of my experiences with don José. In 2007 I accompanied him to conduct a brief ceremony at the place where the wooden body of Rilaj Mam was first carved from a *tz'ite* tree located high in the mountains east of town. José brought along with him a young man who was eager to learn the old songs. The two of them carried a large drum and a well-used guitar to play as part of the ceremony. The purpose of the pilgrimage was to visit a sacred cave near the tree stump to present offerings to the Mam and petition him to help a friend who was having health problems. The "cave" turned out to be a small hollow in the ground less than a foot deep and perhaps two feet wide beneath an outcrop of rock. In Tz'utujil worldview, any opening into the earth is a portal to the other world where gods and sacred ancestors live. These may be accessed through ritual prayer under the proper conditions. It is believed that if one's heart is pure, powerful men and women can open these portals wide and step into the other world. Atitecos lament that there are few if any left who have the power to do this anymore.

The hole was partially blocked with old candle drippings, incense wrappings, and the torn fragment of a woman's skirt. The latter was likely used either in a petition to win the woman's heart, or to curse her for some offense. José swept these aside and laid out approximately three dozen burning candles in colors corresponding to the four cardinal directions (white, yellow, red, and dark purple) in the ground just in front of the shrine. The light from the candles, along with copal incense smoke, is believed to feed the gods and sacred ancestors in the otherworld and give them strength to hear the prayers offered to them. After the ceremony José and his friend played the guitar and drum for a few minutes before José sang the song of Rilaj Mam in his strong, confident voice. I'm sure that he has sung the same song a thousand times or more over the years, though with some creative variations as befitting an artist who is comfortable with his material. But I have never heard him sing when it didn't seem to come from the innermost cords of his soul rather than from his throat. It is always as if he were singing it for the first time.

José has the habit of closing his eyes and lifting his chin during the most powerful parts. At the end of the song, after the last note had been uttered, he continued to incline his head upward with eyes closed and lips parted for a few moments as if to make the sound pause in the air before dissipating back into silence. In Tz'utujil belief, the living carry their ancestors with them in their blood, including all their memories and all their experiences. Traditionalist Maya singers and *ajq'ijab'* (ritual specialists) stress that they do not learn the words to their songs and prayers by hearing them from others. They simply "remember" them from the ancestors that reside in the blood. When the words are repeated, they are not perceived as the product of a single voice, but rather the combined voices of generations of ancestors singing from the blood. For traditionalist Atitecos, to hear these songs is to resurrect the dead and give them a voice. With the encouragement of Linda's Tz'utujil collaborators, we are able in some measure to hear those voices as well.

Allen J. Christenson

FOREWORD

LINDA O'BRIEN-ROTHE HAS WRITTEN a unique and important book that provides a detailed in-depth study of the role of music and dance in the contemporary culture of the Tz'utujil Mayas of Santiago Atitlán, Guatemala. This group retained, until recent times, much of the ancient musical tradition of their ancestors.

O'Brien-Rothe is very qualified to present this study. She obtained her doctorate in ethnomusicology at UCLA and has resided and worked for a long period of time in Santiago Atitlán, the largest Tz'utujil town, located on the southern shore of Lake Atitlán. During her early years there she was a member of the Catholic Maryknoll Sisters and later she returned to the town as a practicing ethnomusicologist. The focus of her research was on traditional music and dance as performed in the system of *cofradías*. She participated in *cofradía* rituals, which were the main vehicle for continuing the old ways.

When I was conducting research for my 1984 book, *The Tzutujil Mayas: Continuity and Change, 1250–1630*, I saw her recording prayers and songs in the *cofradías* of Santa Cruz and San Juan. This proved difficult due to the ever-present background noise from people talking, praying, imbibing, and incensing. Her task required much patience to achieve successful recordings. We also saw each other over the years at UCLA, and during this time I received two cassette tapes from her entitled "Songs of the Face of the Earth," which were published by Ethnodisc and which contained music obtained during *cofradía* celebrations. O'Brien-Rothe is also an award-winning ethnomusicologist, having received a Grammy nomination for her LP recording of the band of San Lucas

Tolimán, a Kaqchikel town located on the southeastern shore of Lake Atitlán.
She has also published several articles on Maya music.

The methodology used in her research on Tz'utujil music involved working
closely with several "songmen" and translators. She collected as many songs
as she could and gradually acquired a significant body of music. She includes
texts of these previously unrecorded songs in both Tz'utujil and English in this
volume. Her book is a labor of love, an intimate perspective of an ancestral musical tradition not found anywhere else. Her long-time relationship with songmen and others in Santiago Atitlán gives her an insider's view that has allowed
her to enter a closed world and to preserve the essence of a tradition that no
longer exists today in the same way.

O'Brien-Rothe also shows that Tz'utujil songs and rituals performed in the
recent past can be linked to the ancient Maya tradition. She deciphers the
meanings and values that are expressed in contemporary Tz'utujil songs and
dance and reveals the relationship of the spirit-lords to the physical landscape
as they interact with each other and with the living. Her research on songs and
dance opened up a path for her to explore Tz'utujil cosmology and to realize
that recent practices were part of a widespread system of ancient Maya thought.

In her first chapter she describes the Tz'utujil world where spirit-lords and
Nawals rule over specific domains of nature. Many of these spirit-lords are associated with statues of the Catholic saints (*santos*) located in the church and
cofradías. It was the Nawals who were said to have created Old Mam, the Guardian of Santiago Atitlán, and who provided models of conduct in the Santo
Mundo (the earth) and in actual life. Prayers and *costumbres*, or rituals, are
used by the living to call forth the spirit-lords and Nawals. The Tz'utujil world,
like that of the ancient Mayas, is characterized by a cyclical perspective, with
time repeating the past, but in new variations. It is the *cofradías* that provide
the setting and resources for the acting out and continuation of the old ways.
These *cofradías* date back to the sixteenth century but did not become the focal
point for the reworking of the ancient ways until after the Spanish clergy left
Santiago Atitlán in the seventeenth century.

Old Mam, who was created by twelve townsmen to be the guardian of morality in the town, is the one who created songs and dance. A key point O'Brien-
Rothe makes is that movement in the form of dance serves as an agent of
change that brings about the renewal and continuation of the Santo Mundo
and progress toward Nawal status for living people. When the living dance,
they reenact the dancing of the Nawals at the first creation. When the statues
of the santos are danced, it incites them to dance themselves, thereby animating and renewing the cosmos. Another more violent form of movement is compared to that of childbirth in which the Santo Mundo tears apart, allowing Old
Mam to be reborn. This is similar to the way the ancient Maya Maize God is

pictured on pottery, being reborn from the carapace of a turtle that represents the earth.

"Songs of the Road" are the largest category of songs O'Brien-Rothe has collected. These songs are said to "open up the road" and guide each person's steps on it in the current cycle of time. The more one dances on "the right road," the more one becomes like the Nawals, and the more favorable becomes one's relationship with them. Dancing on the road is also important in maintaining the cyclical nature of the cosmos because dancing initiates the labor of the Santo Mundo so that she can give birth to Old Mam. Roads are also mentioned in the *Popol Vuh*, the ancient book of the K'iche' Mayas, in which the roads are understood to be alive. For the Tz'utujils the road signifies space in the physical world as well as the process by which one becomes a Nawal. The road represents the path of one's life, one's destiny. Mam is also the guardian of the road. Examples of the texts of songs illustrate these concepts and the codes of behavior.

The poetics of the songs and their relationships are compared to K'iche'an literature, particularly to the *Popol Vuh*. O'Brien-Rothe finds many parallels between the songs and poetic passages of the *Popol Vuh* and suggests that parts of that book may originally have been sung. Unlike Tz'utujil songs, the *Popol Vuh* passages appear to lack extended symmetry and regularity, but she states that this may be due to the fact that some lines that were repetitive were not written down in that work.

Her last chapter contains an analysis of the musical form and style of the "Songs of the Nawals." She shows that the playing technique and the construction of the guitar used by songmen suggests that some of the roots of Tz'utujil songs can be found in the guitar culture of mid-sixteenth to mid-seventeenth century Spain. She discusses this style of music, which in the forms of songs has until now been undocumented. She concludes that Tz'utujil songs are unique examples of the survival of the *guitarra española* and of the song form popular with it.

O'Brien-Rothe also discusses the dance pieces called the "Recibos of Old Mam," more formal musical compositions from which the song melodies are derived. From the melodic motives of the Recibos flow the Songs of the Nawals, which contain the belief system and the cultural codes left by the ancestral Nawals, and for this reason she calls them the "Great Book of the Old Ways." The chapter ends with a discussion of the playing style, technique, and repertoire of the Tz'utujil guitar.

The original material presented in this groundbreaking book is a fundamental contribution to the field of Mesoamerican studies. O'Brien-Rothe states that the body of Tz'utujil music contained in this volume may constitute the oldest and largest body of oral K'iche' sung literature in existence in recorded form. The old ways have been almost extinguished in present-day Santiago Atitlán, which makes her efforts all the more important. Without her patience, dedication, and perseverance, the material presented here would have been entirely lost. Actual recordings of the Tz'utujil songs and prayers are presently available in the Ethnomusicology Archives at UCLA and will also be made accessible on the internet. Now traditional Tz'utujil music can be studied by many, and it can be sung again by the Tz'utujils themselves when they once again become interested in the old ways of the Nawals.

Sandra L. Orellana

ACKNOWLEDGMENTS

I EXTEND MY GRATITUDE TO Matthias Stöckli and Alfonso Arrivillaga Cortés who, as part of the *Centro de Estudios Folklóricos* of the University of San Carlos de Guatemala, urged me to write about my research and offered me the opportunity to return this small but unique part of Guatemala's vast cultural riches to its people in published form. To Dr. Stöckli I owe immense gratitude for his constant encouragement and critical commentaries on the work. Thanks to Johannes Wilbert, professor emeritus of anthropology at the University of California at Los Angeles, who was an invaluable guide during my original research and who facilitated the grant from U.S. Aid to International Development that made it possible. Wilbert later encouraged me to undertake the writing of this book to make available the cultural treasures that I was fortunate to be able to document, in "the hope that your work will come to stand as a genuine and lasting testimony to one of the noblest spiritual cultures ever to have graced American soil. . . Your efforts may indeed have captured a late echo of a fading heritage. All the more serious your responsibility to preserve it for posterity."

Thanks also to Raymond Scupin, director of the Center for International and Global Studies; chair, Department of Anthropology and Sociology of Lindenwood University, and editor in chief of the *Journal of International and Global Studies,* for his guidance and encouragement and for publishing the first version of "The Poetics of Tz'utujil *B'ix* and Their Relationship to K'iche'an Literature." Gratitude is due as well to Peter Furst for promoting and facilitating the publication of this work.

Among the many others who provided opportunity and assistance during the original fieldwork were the Maryknoll Sisters community, especially Sr. Mildred Fritz; Fathers Ramon Carlin, Thomas Stafford, and Robert Westerman of the Oklahoma Catholic Mission in Santiago Atitlán; and at UCLA's Institute of Ethnomusicology, Mantle Hood, Peter Crossley-Holland, and Jozef Pacholczyk; Robert Stevenson of the Department of Music, and Henry Nicholson of the Department of Anthropology. I am grateful to Aaron Bittel, director of the UCLA Ethnomusicology Archives, for his advice and help in accessing my field collection. Thanks also to Sandra Orellana and Allen Christenson for dialogue about the work, both friendly and scholarly, and for their helpful forewords, and to Bret Nelson for his interest and useful suggestions.

It is not possible to thank by name the many persons in Santiago Atitlán who contributed to this research. Among them were the Tz'utujil songmen, several of whom did not survive the violence of the civil war, especially Diego Cua Simaj, Antonio Quieju Culan, and José Sosof Coo'. Thanks also to the great prayer-maker Nicolás Chiviliu Takaxoy, to translators and informants Diego Pop Ajuchan and Nicolás Coche Sapalu Damian, Juan Ajchomajay Set, Diego Reanda Sosof, Juan Ajtzip Alvarado, Juan Mendoza Lacan, and Gaspar Culan Yataz. Many thanks are due to the family of don Miguel and doña Bertha Méndez de León: María Mercedes, Rita, Douglas, and Edwin, for their continuing friendship and hospitality during my time in Santiago Atitlán over the years. I also thank Vincent Stanzione, Andrew Weeks, and Susanna Carry for their invaluable company during my research in Atitlán in 2011, made possible by a grant from the City of Los Angeles Department of Cultural Affairs.

Thanks to my husband Peter for his interest and support, for his pen and ink drawings, and for persistently challenging my ideas, theories, and style, and to Rilaj Mam for finding Peter for me. Thanks also to Edward S. Ruiz for valuable technical assistance, and to my daughters Katherine and Sarah, who have patiently listened to me talk about Guatemala all their lives. I am forever grateful.

INTRODUCTION

A Personal Note

Because ethnographic writing unavoidably conveys the ethnographer's ideal-
izations, biases, self-deceptions, and prejudices—which Steven Feld calls a "dialogue of sensibilities implicated in encountering and depicting a people and
place" (1990, x)—it seems important to explain that I entered cart-before-the-
horse into the field of ethnomusicology, doing fieldwork first and only later
seeking to learn how to do it, and that I went from bringing a message I wanted
to impart, to becoming the one who got the message. Feld goes on:

> This dynamic creates numerous ironic mysteries for an author, and no less for the
> people who are trying to figure out what the author is up to. But in the end an eth-
> nographer's accountability for depiction is more than an accountability for repre-
> sentation; it is an accountability to other human beings whose lives, desires, and
> sensitivities are no less complicated than his or her own. (ibid.)

This, then, is a work of accountability to a people who trusted me to document an important tradition that they regard as originating at the beginning
of the present era of creation, and that has become all but lost in the intervening forty years.

The story begins on a June day in Guatemala City in 1966, a day on which
Father Ramon Carlin was not particularly happy. More than anything, he had
always loved to hear his congregation sing gustily at Mass, but in spite of all his
efforts to encourage his Tz'utujil flock in Santiago Atitlán to find their voices,

most of them didn't sing, and those who did sang without enthusiasm.[1] He had translated *Kyrie eleison* and *Gloria in excelsis Deo* into Tz'utujil and set the words of other hymns to the new music for Mass that was coming out of Mexico.[2] He had a hunch what the problem was: they could not relate to the music because it was too different from their own tradition. But so far no one could tell him what—or even if—Tz'utujils had their own vocal music that might be adapted for use in church. And it was all made more upsetting by the constant reminder of how well the people sang in Pedro Mendoza's Iglesia Centroamericana,[3] a Protestant church that blasted hymns day and night from their newly installed, crackly, tinny loudspeakers.

All of this was on the mind of this priest from the diocese of Oklahoma, who since 1964 had pastored the Catholic Mission of Oklahoma (which he named MICATOKLA[4]), as he was on his way to a workshop in Guatemala City. During the closing discussion he listened to others at his table describe the problems confronting them at their missions. Finally he said, "I am looking for someone who could find out if my people have any music that could be used for Mass." It was my good fortune to be there, and I told him that that "someone" he was looking for could be me.[5] The situation in Guatemala was complex, and I was still emerging from a sheltered life of certainties at home and later in the convent. At home, the 'ultimate questions' had certain answers, but all other questions were open for discussion, evaluation, and criticism. We were not a typical Irish Catholic family—our ties to Irish culture had vanished after a century and more in America. My mother was a nonpracticing Methodist, and my father a devout Catholic, a radio engineer with a degree in physics, a deep interest in theoretical musicology, and a very active creative streak. When I was eighteen I joined the Maryknoll Sisters, a liberal American missionary community that held great appeal for me: the sisters wore habits that were more modern than the usual weird, starchy medieval ones, and joining them provided a way to "see the world" while doing good works. To my surprise, I later discovered that it was founded by a Smith College classmate of my paternal grandmother. I spent the first eleven years in a secluded monastic setting in the woods overlooking the Hudson River, where the natural beauty of the surroundings was complemented by the surpassing richness of the liturgy that graced our lives with its sublime drama. We sang renaissance polyphony and the Gregorian chant repertoire of the *Liber Usualis* to the rhythms of the seasons of the church calendar. A small group of us studied the chant at Pius X Institute of Liturgical Music under dom Joseph Gajard, OSB, then the choirmaster of the Benedictine monks of Solesmes, France, whose research and dedication had restored the ancient sacred music and promoted its revival. I felt, as Emily Dickenson put it, that "beauty crowds me every day." I did not realize then that this intense experience of a symbol system expressed in sacred ritual and its music would prepare me in a very deep way for my encounter with the ritual and music of the Tz'utujils.

Thanks to Maryknoll, I learned to apply the open-minded values of my parents to international humanitarian issues. Maryknoll's goal was to bring the Catholic faith to the supposed unenlightened in the most distant parts of the globe, and fifty years of global experience had also somewhat enlightened its own darkness.

I was pleased to be sent by Maryknoll to Guatemala in 1965, but could not begin to comprehend what was going on there. Marjorie Melville (then Sister Marian Peter) picked me up at the airport when I arrived. I was profoundly influenced by her during my initial and all too brief involvement in her work of teaching social justice and political activism to university students through the *Cursillos de Capacitación Social* (Workshops in Social Consciousness) that were offered at the *Centro de Capacitación Social* called *"El Crater"* ("The Crater").[6] A few months later, still mystified by the sociopolitical realities of Guatemala, I was still not ready to accept her invitation to join this movement. I had been assigned to the teacher training program (*Magisterio*) at Colegio Monte María, an American-style elementary and secondary school in Guatemala City, where I taught for two years. Colegio Monte María was dedicated to the promotion of social justice, inspired by the hope of awakening the consciences of the daughters of the elite with the goal to effect top-down change in a deeply unjust society. I learned much about Guatemala in that atmosphere, and began to understand the part my own country played in mandating its policies and maintaining its oppressive regimes. I saw the role of the Catholic hierarchy that upheld the system of oppression and institutionalized violence, especially evident in the self-aggrandizing and ignoble behavior of the archbishop of Guatemala, Cardinal Mario Casariego, who harshly reprimanded us and all priests and nuns for working for peace and social justice when "they ought to stay in their convents and pray."

Some of the students of Colegio Monte María went on to hold key positions of influence in Guatemala, and in my classroom were the future wife and the sister of successive presidents. Some, like Yolanda Colóm, made heroic personal sacrifices in the cause of peace and justice in Guatemala, even giving their lives like anthropologist Myrna Mack, who was murdered for promoting the values we taught.

Convent life was stifling at Monte María, so often after school I took the bus and explored Guatemala City. Always a hound for anything musical, I found and bought old, possibly ancient terracotta whistles and rattles that the Maya peasants dug up in their cornfields, mostly broken and caked with mud and hidden under a counter or in a dusty box in one of the many tourist shops on Sixth Street in downtown Guatemala City. In the library of the *Instituto*

Guatemalteco-Americano I found original phonograph discs of rural Guatemalan music recorded by Henrietta Yurchenko for the Smithsonian Institution in the 1940s. At the *Instituto Indigenista de Guatemala* I became friends with its director, Maestro José Castañeda, who encouraged my interests in indigenous music and pointed me to available resources about the music of the Guatemalan Maya. At that time I found no reference to songs among the Maya of Guatemala, but only a statement that the Maya of Guatemala do not sing.[7]

After two years at Monte María I was ready for a change. I wanted to stay in Guatemala, so I began to take philosophy classes at the University of San Carlos to earn a degree equivalent to my MA in philosophy, hoping to secure a teaching position there. At that time the Maryknoll Sisters had discontinued wearing the habit and I was now in street clothes. A few months later in Santiago Atitlán I learned that this seemed like suspicious behavior to the secret police, who thought that I was working incognito with university students. Together with a distant relationship (through my brother's marriage) to the politically well-known Colóm family in whose home I often stayed, and my association with Maryknoll (which was considered "leftist" because it championed human rights), I had been placed on a "police list." The fact that I had been shopping around for topographical maps of the Maya area as part of my study of musical instruments from archaeological sites added evidence to their suspicion. I was told by Maryknoll's superior John Breen not to leave Atitlán. Only later when Maryknoll Father William Woods was killed, and Maryknoll Fathers Tomas and Arthur Melville and Blase Bonpane, Maryknoll Sister Marjorie Melville, and others were expelled or fled for their lives from Guatemala, did I understand how serious this was. In the 1980s several of my personal friends and associates in Atitlán—traditional musicians, singers of the old songs, my translators and informants, and those most closely associated with MICATOKLA— would be the first targets of the murderous violence of the military. In 1981 Father Stanley Rother, who joined the mission when I was there in 1968, was murdered in the mission house in Atitlán.

And so I jumped at the chance that Father Carlin's invitation presented because it would put some needed distance between me and Maryknoll, would not include direct proselytizing, and would allow me to do something unrelated to the political and economic situation. After all, I thought, music is innocent and neutral, and I hoped my work would be helpful in some way to the Tz'utujils. It was naive, however, to believe that the project of discovering or promoting traditional music was politically neutral or innocuous.

It was idyllic to live in the amazing beauty of Santiago Atitlán, surrounded by the kaleidoscope of moving colors worn by the people in their traditional dress when they gathered at the open market, with the changing skirts of the Volcano San Pedro and its halo of clouds rising over the blue of Lake Atitlán ever dominating in the background. I could hear marimbas playing somewhere nearby almost every day, often in front of the sixteenth-century church with its colonial achitecture and remnants of the monastery's cloister garden and statues of the saints. It was a privilege to work and live with the mission staff and share the friendship they extended and their patience with a young renegade.

It is not my desire to be an apologist for the church, nor to justify my own association with the Catholic missionary effort that has been responsible for many mistakes arising from its own ignorance, blindness, and a sometimes crude disregard for the value of indigenous cultures. At the same time my intimate involvement with the people and the programs of the church in Atitlán gave me a certain positive perspective on the interaction between the Atitecos (as people from Santiago Atitlán are commonly called) who followed the traditional "Old Ways," and the Tz'utujils who became part of the movement called *Acción Católica* (Catholic Action).[8] MICATOKLA was clearly dedicated to the promotion of education, the development of self-reliance, the alleviation of suffering, and the liberation of the poor. Rather than direct proselytizing, the Oklahoma priests developed programs that addressed the needs of a people who were enslaved by poverty and in imminent danger from the tidal wave of violence threatening to overcome Guatemala.[9] It was a privilege to work with these courageous men and women.

The music project assigned to me for Father Carlin's Mass failed to achieve the intended result. After considerable effort I discovered some traditional songs and I applied myself to the task of developing music for Mass, but the militantly conservative and rabidly antitraditionalist parish leadership, the *Catequistas* , were not about to admit any kind of traditional Tz'utujil music into the church, and my own initial efforts at composing in the style of the "Songs of the Nawals" were summarily rejected:

> Later, without duplicating any of the melodies exactly, but imitating the style of the recorded pieces, I set music to the words of the *Kyrie eleison* in Tzutuhil: *Kajawal Dios, tpoknak kawach*. I played and sang this for Tzutuhil friends who responded with amused approval. But my demonstration of it to the *Catequistas*, a conservative group of Catholic Tzutuhil men who are in charge of the teaching of doctrine and the regulation of Church functions, was received with silent horror.
>
> Finally a spokesman protested: "This music is not for Church. It is bad music. It has bad words. The young men sing it to girls with evil intentions. If we sing this in Church, passersby will say that now the Catholics are singing bad songs in Church."
>
> There could be no argument against their strong feeling. The failure of this experiment led me to conclude that music which would appropriately express the religious sentiments of the Indians would have to be composed by them. It also

taught me that there was something powerful and profound to be learned about the Tzutuhil "Songs of the Face of the Earth." (O'Brien 1975, 3–4)

Later I reflected:

Several educational projects initiated in the last decade among the Tzutuhil-Maya of Santiago Atitlán, Guatemala, have been oriented toward innovation rather than perpetuation of traditional indigenous forms. Many of these programs have failed to reach their proximate and ultimate goals owing to the impropriety of some innovation the educator has introduced, the implications of which he does not, however, understand. (O'Brien 1976, 377)

I was not to be discouraged, however, and in hopes of developing composers from the indigenous community I invited interested persons to form a band of marimba and other instruments, to whom I attempted to give basic music education:

Unfamiliar with the combinations of instruments popular in other village ensembles, and unsure of the preferences, tastes, and talents of the proposed group, I procured a variety of familiar instruments for this orchestra: cane flutes, *chirimías*, six-string guitars, a Guatemalan harp, a four-and-one-half-octave box marimba, a bass drum, and a slit drum. (ibid., 381)

But the orchestra that was formed as a result also failed to produce the composers that I hoped for. The most musically gifted and enthusiastic among them, Diego Reanda Sosof, who was also the mentioned cantor, had already been taught to read music and play the harmonium. I worked with him and he began to compose, but he left suddenly to join the guerilla forces and was later killed. The Orquesta Atitlán Tzutuhil became a popular group and was hired in and out of town for fiestas for several years, until its members began to fall to the fear and violence of the civil war in Guatemala.

One day I surprised the orchestra by arriving early to rehearsal. They were playing a piece I hadn't taught them or heard before. To my astonishment they acted embarrassed and apologized profusely. When I questioned them I learned that it was a ritual song for a local deity called "Old Mam." I still didn't understand their shame and pressed for an explanation. Then they told me that in exchange for becoming part of *Acción Católica* they were taught that they had to abandon everything associated with their traditional religion, including its music. So much for my simple ideas of the neutrality of music. I began to see that I was associated with a movement that caused cultural impoverishment, and to understand why there were no musicians among the *Acción*

Católica community. This realization shook me to the foundations of my missionary work.

Gradually I realized that I was far more interested in the traditional music itself than in the mission's project of developing music for the Catholic Mass. In my purist idealism I also objected to some of the mission's policies, judging them harshly and with little real comprehension: the attempt to make the weaving cooperative's products commercially viable by imposing American tastes in color and textural consistency ("It's not smooth enough") on traditional Maya textiles was offensive to my personal artistic sensibilities. In an effort to improve the economic level of local indigenous farmers, the mission (through an agricultural cooperative) was promoting the planting of cash crops instead of the traditional corn. By then I understood from my studies of the Maya that the "holy corn" was the divine substance of human life and sustenance for them. And then I heard a Tz'utujil maize farmer give us his reason for declining to join the mission in this project:

> I went into my field, and the Spirit of the Corn said to me, "Are you going to abandon me? If you abandon me, *I will abandon you.*"

This had a deep impact on me. Should we dare to try to uproot or replace what was clearly holy in the lives of others? Yet I could see that hunger and oppression were unholy, too.

Something else was wrong. The majority of the Spanish-speaking Ladinos[10] were Catholics. The deep social problems in the Ladino community were easy to see: families of a single mother with several children of different fathers, all of whom were absent; violent and abusive behavior, including murders; exploitation and degrading treatment of the Tz'utujils; robbery, betrayals, infidelity, and so on. In contrast, the Tz'utujils who lived by the Old Ways appeared at least to me to live in harmony with nature and to have a high degree of social order among them. I tried to imagine what could possibly motivate them to be converted to Catholicism.

I had seen their public rituals and wanted to know more about traditional beliefs, but we were prohibited by church policy (a policy that Carlin lamented but was constrained to follow) from visiting the *cofradía* prayer-houses lest we give the impression of approving of a religion that was not Catholic. Reflecting on all of this, it seemed the Tz'utujils of *Acción Católica* might be more attracted to embrace the benefits of association with the mission than to "conversion," finding there some possibility of a future that might enable them to overcome their disempowerment in an unjust society. Through the education they received from the mission they were made aware of the impending threat of violence and of the urgent necessity to prepare themselves to survive it.

I felt I was in an impossible position. I was a Catholic, and the mission's efforts to dispel ignorance and starvation and protect the indigenous community from exploitation were clearly good works. But there was no longer 'one way, one truth' for me. I found myself there, and I also knew I wanted to experience *their* way, and if doom was coming for the Tz'utujils, I hoped I might be able to document and preserve whatever part of their cultural treasures I could before it came: the music, and the rituals of the Old Ways that were its context. I saw this as a "good work" I could do: to affirm the personal worth of a people who were regarded as inferior by legitimizing their view of the world as it was expressed in the oral traditions.

In 1969, after two years as part of the Oklahoma Mission, I left it and the Maryknoll Sisters' community and returned to the United States to study at the University of California at Los Angeles Institute of Ethnomusicology under Mantle Hood. I wanted to acquire the tools I realized I would need to approach the study of Tz'utujil music in a systematic way. But I was not motivated by the desire to pursue a career in academia, nor was I interested in becoming a "wannabe" Tz'utujil. I had simply been amazed to find that here was a living liturgy, vibrant and complete with all the elements of beauty and symbolic ritual behavior that I had experienced at Maryknoll's liturgies. I wanted to know what this other symbol system was, and what view of the world it expressed, especially in musical ritual behavior. I realized then that my experiences had equipped me to approach this, and I was passionate about the discovery that lay ahead. What Clifford Geertz said about coming to understand one's informants resonates with my motivation at that time:

> whatever accurate or half-accurate sense one gets of what one's informants are, as the phrase goes, really like does not come from the experience of that acceptance as such, which is part of one's own biography, not of theirs. It comes from the ability to construe their modes of expression, what I would call their symbol systems, which such an acceptance allows one to work toward developing. . . . more like grasping a proverb, catching an allusion, seeing a joke—or, as I have suggested, reading a poem—than it is like achieving communion. (1983, 70)

During the next six years I returned to Atitlán during the summer months, school breaks, Holy Week, and at every other available opportunity. I chose to focus my research on the traditional music performed in private contexts that was unavailable for the public to hear, mainly the songs. My underlying interest, as I expressed it in Mantle Hood's graduate seminar, was to discover how music functioned in the context of ritual:

> I have chosen to draw what is possible from an array of disciplines through exploration of aspects which prove relevant to my personal matrix within ethnomusicol-

ogy. I am motivated by a strong predilection for the exploration of man's percep-
tions of his relationship to the universe. My choice of related disciplines grows out
of a substantial exposure to the consideration of this question from four distinct
viewpoints: the normative sciences, religion, philosophy, and highland Maya culture. It is the pursuit of the above question which leads me to ethnomusicology. Its
breadth, however much the result of the ambiguity of its fundamentals, permits a
creative approach to problems. The choice of ethnomusicology as a field relates to
my personal preference for music as a creative expression and an aesthetic pleasure. Further, musical behavior of different peoples, both creative and aesthetic, is
an aspect of the perception of the nature of the universe: the question with which I
am concerned. (O'Brien 1972a, 12)

I recorded what they told me, and how I felt about it, what my informants
said. I went fishing in the stream of their experience, and for a specific kind of
fish. I wanted to be enriched by them and to try to understand it in their terms
and describe it in mine, to know what they wished to tell me plus what I could
interpret myself. Geertz says he tried to get at what a person is in the culture
he was studying not by imagining himself as one of them, but by "searching out
and analyzing the symbolic forms—words, images, institutions, behaviors—in
terms of which, in each place, people actually represented themselves to themselves and to one another." I was looking for beauty, the beautiful that was beneath the surface. It started with an experience-distant agenda: to forward the
practical aim of developing music for church, "to produce an interpretation
of the way a people lives which is neither imprisoned within their mental ho-
rizons, an ethnography of witchcraft as written by a witch, nor systematically
deaf to the distinctive tonalities of their existence, an ethnography of witchcraft as written by a geometer" (Geertz 1983, 57–58).

Research in Santiago Atitlán

Santiago Atitlán is the largest of the towns on the southern shores of idyllically
beautiful Lake Atitlán, which lies 5,125 feet above sea level amid the volcanos
of the southwestern highlands of Guatemala. The town is situated on the western slope of the Volcano Tolimán, on a broken lava terrace that rises in some
places to 900 feet above the lake. It is a place of breathtaking natural beauty
overshadowed by the imposing presence of the Volcano San Pedro that domi-
nates the Bay of San Pedro. Of its 40,000 residents reported in a recent census,
the percentage estimated to be Tz'utujil Maya was 98 percent. The Tz'utujil language belongs to the larger family of K'iche'an languages.[11]
Santiago Atitlán has five *cantons* or neighborhoods, each divided into ir-
regularly shaped blocks made up of house compounds or *sitios*. In 1965 each

Lake Atitlán, showing the Bay of San Pedro where Santiago Atitlán is located. Viewed from San Jorge la Laguna, 1968.

The Volcano San Pedro viewed from the church in Santiago Atitlán, 1968.

A *sitio* or family compound in Santiago Atitlán in 1970, viewed from above.

sitio had one or more *ranchitos*, which are one-room buildings with an earthen floor, walls of two or three feet of stone surmounted by corn canes lashed together, and a roof of thatch. No access by vehicle was possible to any place in town except the central plaza and a short way further along the edge of the lake. One walked the town on narrow and very rugged dirt paths that often required climbing around or over large boulders. Most *sitios* had a small stone building used for a steam-bath or *temescal*; a vegetable garden for chiles, onions, and tomatoes; and often some coffee trees, chickens, and a turkey that gobbled loudly at passersby, usually causing amusement and laughter between the walker and the inhabitants of the *sitio*. The road to town from the Pacific coast and another from Godinez were unpaved and barely passable for cars, and were especially treacherous in the rainy season, as I often experienced driving my friend Father Tom Stafford's four-wheel drive Automula. The estimated population at that time was 14,000, of whom a small percentage were Ladinos. Less than 6 percent of Tz'utujils over seven years of age were literate, and less than 40 percent of males and 10 percent of females had any speaking knowledge of Spanish.[12] Escuela Mateo Herrera, a public elementary school, educated about 500 students, mostly Ladinos. The few Tz'utujil children who attended the school usually did not continue beyond second grade because of their limited Spanish and the inhospitable atmosphere.

A *sitio* in Santiago Atitlán in 1970.

A single launch brought tourists across the lake from Panajachel every day around 11:30 a.m. and returned three hours later. In an open outdoor market in the central plaza, Tz'utujil women sat on the ground with their produce spread out on cloths or in baskets. Some sold textiles and finely embroidered articles for the tourists. One day a week loudly squealing pigs announced their arrival as they were led on leashes to the butcher's stands. The plaza was dominated on the southwest side by the sixteenth-century Catholic church, and next to it the Catholic Mission, where tourists often stopped in to visit with the Americans. When I arrived (bringing with me the town's first piano), the mission had five priests (one of whom was finishing research in anthropology), a nurse and her assistant, and two Montessori teachers.[13] The mission staff grew and changed and volunteers came and went. Only one other American lived in a rented cottage on the outskirts of town.[14] At that time there were seven or eight Protestant churches in the town.

Santiago Atitlán had already become the focus of ethnographic study. Foundational work had been done a decade earlier by E. Michael Mendelson. In 1965 Bill Gray Douglas was finishing his research on illness and curing, and anthropology student John Early was at the mission completing his research.[15] In the next few years Sandra Orellana published her ethnohistorical work on Atitlán in the late pre-hispanic and colonial eras, Joseph Gross described kinship structure in his dissertation, and Douglas Sharon published his research on local shamans. These and the later work of Robert Carlsen, Allen Christenson, Vincent Stanzione, and the fine ethnomusicological study of a closely related community by Sergio Navarrete Pellicer, among others, have provided me with a deeper understanding of the Tz'utujil world that has been essential to this study of traditional songs and dance.

In the late 1960s young people from the USA began to come to town and stay for the summer months or longer, adding new influences and values. Unfortunately these were not always of a positive nature, like introducing LSD to the Tz'utujils who befriended them.

Returning as a scholar and now independent of the church, I had the advantage of established friendships among Tz'utujils and Ladinos, and a basic familiarity with the *cofradías*. The *cofradías* (literally "confraternities" or "brotherhoods") are a religious organization whose members practice the traditional Old Ways of the Nawals, the revered ancestors. Atitlán's twelve *cofradías* are responsible for carrying out calendric and other rituals and customs, and the *cofradía* celebrations, customs, and rituals are the context for most traditional music.

I went first to the principal *ajcun*,[16] Nicolás Chiviliu Takaxoy, a lion of a man, whose greatness of spirit and intelligence drew the respect of all who lived by the Old Ways and gained him a position of leadership in the community. He was the *alcalde* (headman) of the *cofradía* San Juan. I asked him to help me learn about the Old Ways, explaining that I wanted to write them down in a book so they would not be forgotten. I was wary of the effect that my former association with the church might have on my welcome because of a history of conflict, at times violent, between the church and its *catequistas*, and the followers of the traditional religion, as Mendelson recounts in his 1965 account, *Los Escándalos de Maximón*. I was certainly expecting something less than a warm reception. His response was otherwise: "The truth has two parts," he said, "the words of JesuKrista and the words of the Nawals. Those who listen only to the *padres* have half of the truth, but you have come searching for the other half." No doubt my work in forming the Orquesta Atitlán Tzutuhil helped to pave the way as well. After that he facilitated my research however he could, kept me informed of the times of rituals and celebrations, and gave me a place in the *cofradía* to sit on the mat with the *tixels*, the women officers of the *cofradía*. I spent many intensely enjoyable and amazing hours with them, sharing in the ritual censing, drinking, dancing, and smoking the Thrifty Drug store Owl Cigars that I always brought with me from the United States. These were especially popular with the women, who would drop them down the neck of their *huipil*, the woman's blouse that also served as a big pocket, to smoke them later. For the rituals of Holy Week in 1974 I was given a ceremonial *huipil* and a shawl,

Nicolás Chiviliu Takaxoy,
ajcun, watches the Baile
de la Conquista, 1970.

and was invited to participate in the ceremonies of the deity Rilaj Mam or Old
Mam, as the *rox tixel* (third *tixel*), the place of honor, the central place, among
the *tixels*.

I recorded as much music as I could in the *cofradías*: prayers and chants for
various rituals, healings and other petitions, the music of marimbas, harp, guitar, violin, and songs, which were already becoming rare in that context. Amid
the noise of conversation and the chanting of prayers in the *cofradías* the songs
were rarely sung, but rather were played very simply on the guitar. Having discovered the songs, the task I set myself before all others was to find traditional
singers and record them. My principal guide and informant, Nicolás Coche
Sapalu Damian, was a young man who followed the Old Ways and who had
experience as a research informant by working for Douglas Sharon, Sandra
Orellana, and others before me. He was the most helpful in leading me to sing-

ers and arranging recording sessions in their homes or in the *cofradías*. As part of Carlin's staff I had learned the basics of Tz'utujil grammar and vocabulary and become comfortable in simple conversation in Tz'utujil, but was not always up to the challenges in the contexts of research. Nicolás was an orphan and owned no land, and this situation made it nearly impossible for him to marry or to become a fully initiated member of the *cofradía* system. He took the alternative that was open to a person in his situation and began to study with an *aj-cun*, in hopes of finding his path in this vocation. Before he could realize this hope he lost his life in the military violence.

When a singer performs in the semiprivate setting of the *cofradías* for a ritual or a prayer, it is often a matter of a solo guitar playing in the background of the ordinary noises of a small group of people talking softly, and amid a prayer-maker's softly chanted prayers. In the private setting of the singer's home a quiet environment was more likely, and the singer was usually more comfortable and motivated to "do his best" without the competition from others, and he could sing as long as he wanted. Singers were highly motivated to be re-

A songman in the *cofradía*. Painted for the author by Miguel Chavez, 1968.

corded once they became aware of what the recorder was and after hearing themselves in the playback. They knew this tradition was slipping away and that I was making a copy that could last. Once my interest in the songs became known it was easy to find singers who were eager to be interviewed and recorded. No doubt the payment I was able to offer them was a great motivator.

After a recording session the verbal contents of the tape were transcribed in Tz'utujil and translated into Spanish. Most of this work was skillfully done by Diego Pop Ajuchan, who had been trained and recommended by Ramon Carlin as an experienced translator, and who had a facility for writing in both languages. After transcribing the Tz'utujil texts from each recording, he made a written Spanish translation. Later we listened again together to the recording, while he translated aloud into Spanish what we were hearing on the tape. As we went along I compared this spoken Spanish with the written one he had done earlier. Frequently we stopped and replayed to check the accuracy against the Tz'utujil. This method gave plenty of opportunities for questions about obscure passages of text. Although Diego was a member of Catholic Action, his pride and enthusiasm for explaining the Old Ways to me was a great asset. During our conversations I gained many basic insights into the meaning of the songs and of the traditions from his explanations, and was able to add to my understanding of Tz'utujil ritual language and develop a simple lexicon. Most of the Tz'utujil texts in this book are his transcriptions, with some corrections of obvious mistakes and omissions. Diego transcribed without much punctuation or capitalization, and without versifying the poetic texts. I have added as little punctuation as possible to avoid adding meaning that is not in Diego's translation. I have added versification that follows the musical phrases and the singers' pauses. The English translations are mine, using Diego's Spanish as a guide.

Most of the recordings in my collection, which is housed at UCLA's Ethnomusicology Archives, were made using a Nagra III recorder and an Electrovoice 666 microphone on Scotch 202 ½″ magnetic tape. Original recordings of songs discussed in this book can be found at the University of Texas Press website (www.utpress.utexas.edu/index.php/books/obrien-rothe-songs-that-make -the-road-dance). For a complete list of these recordings, see the Audio Files of Recorded Examples on page 197.[17]

The "Songs of the Road" ("*B'ix rxin B'ey*")—the songs that make the road dance—are part of the larger body of "Songs of the Nawals" ("*B'ix rxin Nawal*") or "Songs of the Ancestors."

CHAPTER ONE

The World of the Tz'utujil Maya

THIS IS A STUDY OF TRADITIONAL SONGS of a Maya community in the southwest highlands of Guatemala. As a work of ethnomusicology it explores several aspects of a particular genre of musical behavior, but ultimately it is also a contribution to the discussion of the nature of time in a Maya cosmos, a question that has long been central among scholars of both ancient and contemporary Maya. The context for this study was the town of Santiago Atitlán, about which Robert Carlsen observes: "a defining characteristic of Post-Columbian Santiago Atitlán is a distinct and identifiable continuity with the pre-Columbian past" (1997, 5).

Tz'utujil sacred texts and ritual behavior make clear their belief that, at the beginning of the present creation, ideal cycles—of astrological, agricultural, and human natures—were set in motion by the gods and ancestors. In this cosmology, time begins when the astrological revolutions are set in motion, and thereafter unfolds in repeating cycles in which the original models are replicated in nature and by the actions of people. It is the actions of humans that cause the Santo Mundo (the Holy World) to be re-created in a form that can be described as a variation on a perduring theme.

A central concern for this community, which is traditionally dependent both on local subsistence agriculture and on the naturally occuring produce of nearby coastal lands, is the fertility of the Santo Mundo. Ways of behaving that guarantee the continued fertility of the Santo Mundo are transmitted by songs and dance that were received by the ancestors from the Maize God at the beginning, "the root of time." The energy generated by their musical behavior is an agent that guarantees both the constancy of the Tz'utujil customs (the Old

Ways), and the viability of a myriad of metaphorical variations of the original act of creation. Without the Old Ways the road of the ancestors would be lost, the order of the cosmos would fail, and the Santo Mundo would fall into chaos and darkness.

The textual style of the songs places them with the oldest surviving highland Mayan literature, to which they make a unique and significant contribution. The study of Tz'utujil songs adds new insight into the creative function of dance, also an important currency of exchange between gods and men for the ancient Maya. The songs reveal the Santo Mundo as the womb that gives birth to the Maize God when dancing initiates her labor.

The musical style of the songs can be traced to a dance form originating in Spanish sixteenth-century guitar practice, as can other known survivals of sixteenth-century Spanish music in highland Maya communities. The contents and contexts of the songs contribute contemporary ethnographic detail to the classic Maya myth of the creation of the Maize God.

Linda Schele, in a view that has reached consensus among scholars, describes a system of understanding the nature of the Maya cosmos through five basic ways of looking at the world:

> [their] concept of the fivefold structure (the four directions plus the center) of material and spiritual space; the vitality of their belief in the importance of the ancestors; the Maya one-in-many principle of divinity; the reciprocal nature between sacrifice and nurturing that binds humanity to the gods; and the understanding that people were made from the divine and life-sustaining substance maize. (Freidel, Schele & Parker 1993, 58)

The World of Spirits

The oral literature of the Tz'utujils—prayers, ritual speech, origin stories, and songs—depicts a geospiritual or geomythical cosmos, animated with spirits both human and nonhuman who have power over specific domains of nature. The world, that is, the cosmos, is called "World-Face of the Earth" (*Mund-Ruch'lew*) or "Santo Mundo" (Holy World) or "Mountains-Plains" (*Jyu-Tkaj*). It is described as a living body on whose back the forests grow, whose nose can be seen in the shape of the mountains, who carefully carries the lake like a basin of water, and whose flowering body labors like a woman in childbirth to bring forth corn. The Santo Mundo includes the Pacific piedmont that along with Lake Atitlán forms a flat rectangle floating within the sphere described by the path of "Our Father the Sun" ("*Ndta' K'ij*") or "Lamp of Saint Bernardine" ("*Lambra Marnadina*"). The five directions include the center point of the Santo Mundo, and "the four corners" of the rectangular Santo Mundo that lie at the intercardinal direction points described by the positions of the sun at sunrise and sunset during the solstices.[1] The hemisphere through which Our Father the Sun travels in the day is the world of the living, and the hemisphere beneath the earth where he goes at night is the underworld of the dead and the spirits of darkness. His passage across the sky is divided by sunrise, zenith and sunset, and to mark each one Our Father the Sun is honored by the playing of the slit-log drum called the *c'unc'un* in the *cofradías* while they pray "Three times holy are you, three times you give us food."[2]

The area of the central plaza is the center, called "the Heart [literally, the Navel] of the Face of the Earth." There stands the sixteenth-century church and, in the center of the plaza, a stucco-covered cross, both oriented approximately to the four intercardinal directions. This is a cosmos that is organized by four roads that come from these four corners and meet in the center, the "Heart of the Face of the Earth." Where the roads meet is "a place of power where this world and the spirit world collide; a place where communion and transformation are possible, and where the gods and ancestors are present" (Keller 2009, 147). The vertical column of the cross points toward the zenith of the sky and the nadir of the underworld, visibly marking a physical and spiritual center and the axis that connects sky and underworld. The church is considered to be the real center, the heart of "our mother corn, our money."[3]

A complex pantheon of nonhuman spirits, the *jawal*, is described by Bill Douglas as a pyramid including the Spirit-Lords (*Ajaw*) who rule over specific domains of the natural world; guardians (*chalbeij*) of specific locations in the natural world; and Spirit-Lords (*Rujawal, Rusantil,* or *Rudiosil*) of a specific class of objects in the natural world such as in *Rujawal ixim,* the Spirit-Lord of corn (1969, 68–73). The songs and prayers indicate that the Spirit-Lords of nature are manifestations of San Martín, the great Spirit-Lord of the natural world:

> The spirits that inhabit the Santo Mundo would seem to form a hierarchy under the highest Lord, San Martín. Each group of spirits belongs to a specific place in the geographical world, which is its proper sphere of activity and its dwelling. The hierarchical order of spirits in the world corresponds to the geographical order. In concrete terms, the higher on the mountains or in the sky is the residence of the spirit, the higher in the hierarchy is his power. In this system the physical and the supra-physical are analogs. (O'Brien 1975, 47)

In Tz'utujil thought, all the parts of the physical universe are inhabited or guarded by spirits who control the weather, plants and animals, subordinate spirits, and one's destiny. These spirits of nature, who are called "The Company of the World," are embodied in statues and artifacts arranged on the altar of the *cofradía* San Juan in two groups. Those on the left side, near the bundle of San Martín, are the spirits in charge of the affairs of men: crops, rain and weather, tools, trade, and so forth. The right side of the altar is reserved for the spirits of the affairs of women: weaving, childbirth, and rearing. A wooden box, similar to that containing the Martín bundle, hangs on ropes from the rafters on the far right. It is called "the cradle" (*cusul*), and contains sacred objects used in the rituals for women. This box, to which the leader of the women members of the *cofradía* San Juan (the *xo'*) has the key, is referred to in shamans' prayers as "the umbilicus of the world, the heart of the world, the source of the life of men." In the *cofradía* San Juan, the powers of the mighty and transcendent spirits of the generation of life and the cycles of nature are focused (ibid., 44–45).

These Spirit-Lords, the "Martins," control the forces of nature from the sky and the sacred mountains that surround the lake, the volcanoes San Pedro, San Lucas, Cerro de Oro, and Atitlán. Among them are the Ángeles. From the Spanish word for "angels," the Ángeles are spirits who inhabit certain trees associated with specific places of special power and tradition on the Face of the Earth. Many Spirit-Lords are associated with one of the statues of Catholic saints in the church and in the various *cofradías*. These richly clothed and colorfully repainted statues of the saints, the "Santos," have taken on the identities of old native deities, often because some detail of the symbols on the figure suggest a certain domain. Bill Gray Douglas explains: "San Pedro is thus seen as the Spirit-Lord of domestic fowl in Santiago Atitlán, since he is represented with a rooster" (1969, 74). Some of their names, like Dio's, JesuKrista (Jesus Christ), and Mriy Dolors (Mary of Sorrows), and a host of other names of saints and angels, have been assimilated from Catholicism. Others have the names of the friars who first established themselves in Atitlán in the sixteenth century.

High in this pantheon, perhaps at the apex of a pyramid of spirits, is Dio's. While this name is clearly from the Spanish word for God (*Dios*), I prefer to use the orthography my translator often used, which includes the glottalized vowel o', to clearly distinguish this greatly acculturated deity from the Christian God. There are several statues of Dio's under various titles such as *Dio's Titixel* (Grandfather God), *Dio's Padre* (Father God), and *Dio's Divina* (Divine God).

Spirits known as the *Nawals*, the "Old Ones" or "Ancient Ones," form a specific group of ancestors-become-gods who figure in Tz'utujil origin stories as the original fathers and mothers who caused the enigmatic trickster deity Old Mam, or simply Mam, to become their guardian spirit.[4] The Nawals were taught what are called "the customs" (*costumbres*) or the "Old Ways" by Old Mam, and then passed them on to the Tz'utujil people. The term *Nawal* is also used in a general sense to describe all of the ancient Spirit-Lords, the Martíns, the Marías, the Santos, and the Ángeles.

A continual operative economy exists between the living people and the Nawals, who live on and inside the mountains to the west of town, in which the Nawals respond favorably with good weather for growing corn, health, fertility, and good luck or destiny in exchange for sacrifices or offerings understood as nourishment for the Nawals, such as music, dance, prayers, food, liquor, incense, tobacco, and candles. The origin stories tell how the Nawals provided models of conduct in the Santo Mundo. Their names, such as Marcos Prophet (*Marcos Rujuch)* and Maria Spindle (*YaMriy Bitz'b'al*), reveal them as the original models of prophets, weavers, corn-growers, healers, merchants, musicians, warriors, midwives, childbearers, and other traditional roles in Tz'utujil society.

The relationship of exchange between the spirits and the people can be discerned from the words of a prayer in which the Spirit-Lords, the Santos, and the Nawals are invoked. The central currency of this exchange is movement: the prayer-maker awakens the ancient spirits by offering the sacrifice of burning incense, candles, and tobacco—sacrifices that are consumed by fire—calling them by name and reminding them of their great power. Finally the prayer-maker tells them he has cradled them and danced them, and now is making them move and stand up and use their "great hands and feet" to do what is asked of them.

One example of this is the following prayer recorded in the *cofradía* San Juan in August of 1971. Nicolás Chiviliu Takaxoy, the most revered and powerful *ajcun* in Atitlán for many years, had been engaged by visitors to the *cofradía* to pray for them. He was at that time the *alcalde* or head-man of the *cofradía* San Juan. We had known each other since 1967, when I came to Atitlán,[5] and on this occasion his warm approval and support of my project of documenting the rituals and music facilitated my reseach. I had been invited by him to attend the *cofradía* when I wished to, and to record what took place there. Because I was present, my name was also included in the prayer.

Excerpt from a Prayer of Nicolás Chiviliu Takaxoy, *ajcun*[6]

don Juan Martín, don Diego Martín	don Juan Martín, don Diego Martín
Pascual Martín, Nicolás Martín	Pascual Martín, Nicolás Martín
Yo'l Wa'y, Yo'l K'an	Giver of Corn, Giver of Yellow Corn
Mund, Ruch'lew	World, Face of the Earth
Rjawal jyu'	Spirit-Lord of the mountain
Rjawal tk'aj	Spirit-Lord of the plain
Rjawal che'	Spirit-Lord of the trees
Rjawal c'am	Spirit-Lord of the vine

Ay Rjawal gloria, ay Metzmul
    ay Cb'a' rkan
	Oh Spirit-Lord of glory, oh Drizzle
	    oh Earthquake

ay Queypa', ay Sakba'ch	oh Lightning, oh Hail
Ja nya'ana jab, Ja nbnawa sajbach	oh You who drop rain, You who make hail
Ja nbanwea rayo	You who make lightning
ay Juan Martín, ay Prancisco	oh Juan Martin, oh Francisco
ay Jacobo, ay Marcos.	oh Jacobo, oh Marcos.
Ay Dio's ek'a, Dio's ewekan	Oh Dio's your hands, oh Dio's your feet[7]
extz'bula, exnatala	you are seated, you are long remembered
ex te'ej, extitexel.	you are mothers, you are fathers.
Ay pagr mío, pagr Juan	Oh my father, father Juan
Dio's JesuKrista	Dio's JesuKrista
San Juan Bactist, San Juan Comalapa	San Juan Bautista, San Juan Comalapa
ak'a, awkan	your hands, your feet
alojden Ángel	you carry it [*in your arms like a baby*][8] Ángel
Ángel, apajken	Ángel, you carry it [*in your hands carefully* *like a basin of water*]
Nedta Dio's, JesuKrista	Our Father Dio's, JesuKrista
. . . .	. . . .[9]
Rey Monarc, Rey Matecsum	King Monarca, King Matecsum
Rey Matectan, Rey Matectne	King Matectan, King Matectne
Rey Saq'uixo'l, Rey Samaner	King Saq'uixo'l, King Semanero
Rey Pastor.	King Pastor.
Exco' pjuyu', ptk'aj	You are on the mountains, on the plains
Quensil, quenyic	I make you move, I stand you up [*so you* *can work*]
ek'a, awkan	your hands, your feet
Ajaw Galist Martín, Grabiel Martín	Lord Galisto Martín, Gabriel Martin
Pagr mío Dio's.	my Father Dio's.
Extz'bul, exnatal	You are seated, you are long remembered
ex Dio's JesuKrista	you [*plural*] are Dio's JesuKrista

chwach lomlaj esiy, lomlaj
    escañ
	before your great chairs, your great
	    benches

Dio's JesuKrista.	Dio's JesuKrista.
Ex Rjawal	You are Spirit-Lords

ctz'ej echi', cab
    ek'a
	flowers adorn your mouths, sweet as honey
	    your hands

capot ek'a.	hooded capes are your hands.[10]
Exaj Ruch'lew	You are of the Face of the Earth
Ay Dio's	Oh Dio's
pnek'a xwinkirwa ley	in your hands law was conceived

pnek'a xwinkirwa justis.
Xuyaca, JesuKrista
Jesús xba pgloria, Krista xba
  pgloria
Dio's Ángel, Divino Padre Sacapulas
Santuario, San Pelip, Dio's JesuKrista.
Xek'etej, xemosej

lomlaj Mund Ruch'lew Señor.
Pnak'a xcanajcwara'
ay roxe' k'ak', ay roxe'
  ya'
ay roxe' che', ay mar, ay alagun
ay cbeljuj volcan, ay cbeljuj cchuc . . .
ay cbeljuj Pral, ay cbeljuj
  K'elba'l
ay cbeljuj K'ak Che',
  ay cbeljuj Salina
Awxin tet Dio's, awxin tet
  nute'
María Sabela, María Elena
María Magdalena, María Lucía
María Candelaria, María Chiantla
María San Lorenzo, María
  Guadalupe
Exco'la, exnatala . . .
chwach Rudiosil, chwach rmetr.

Tzir c'a xinyuc wa jun or, media or

Esant'il, chwach elibr
Dio's JesuKrista
Dio's, xeme'al, xewlec'wal
. . . .
Per bar nk'c'utuwa, Dio's?
Por ese wenkir, xwenkircana Patron
  Santiago
xwenkir Santiago Tz'utujil
Santiago Pop
Santiago Españ, Santiago de Roma
Santiago Jacobo, Santiago Felipe

in your hands justice was conceived.[11]
You left it, JesuKrista
Jesus who went to glory, Krista who went
  to glory
Dio's Ángel, Divine Father Esquipulas
Santuario, San Felipe, Dio's JesuKrista.
You embraced them carefully, you carried
  them
great World Face of the Earth Lord.
In your hands it stayed
oh [you] the root of fire, oh the root of
  water
oh root of the trees, oh sea, oh lake
oh twelve volcanoes, oh twelve . . .
oh twelve Volcanos San Pedro, oh twelve
  Places where Nawals Visit
oh twelve Hills where Nawals Greet Each
  Other, oh twelve Salt Marshes.
They are yours Dio's, they are yours, my
  mother
Maria Isabela, Maria Elena
Maria Magdalena, Maria Lucia
Maria Candelaria, Maria Chiantla
Maria San Lorenzo, Maria
  Guadalupe
You are remembered, you are . . .
before your Spirits, before your great
  distance.[12]
Here then[13] I stand you up for an hour,
  half an hour
your Spirits, before your books
Dio's JesuKrista
Dio's, your daughters, your sons
. . . .
But where shall we ask, Dio's?
That is why Patron Santiago was conceived,
  created
why Santiago Tz'utujil was made
Santiago Pop
Santiago of Spain, Santiago of Rome
Santiago Jacobo, Santiago Felipe

Santiago de Galicia.	Santiago of Galicia.
Cano'cana rok'a	Your hands stayed with us
María Andolor, María Agost	Maria de Dolores, Maria Asunción
Oh Dio's JesuKrista.	Oh Dio's JesuKrista.
Canojcana rjawal, rwenekil	You left your lordness, your person
benbal justis, benbal orda.	doer of justice, maker of order.
Pnek'a c'a, pnewkan, c'a	In your hands, in your feet, then
xek'etej c'a,	you embrace them carefully like a baby,
Ay Dio's	oh Dio's
xek'etej c'a	you embrace them carefully like a baby
Mund	Mundo
xek'etej c'a j	You embrace them carefully like a baby
Ruch'lew	Face of the Earth
q'uin Pagr Antonia, San Gaspar	with Padre Antonio, San Gaspar
San Martín, San Baltazar,	San Martin, San Baltazar
Dio's Ángel, Juan Santa Cruz	Dio's Ángel, Juan Santa Cruz
Krista Salvador	Krista Salvador
. . . .	. . . .
Ndta don Juan Martín, don Diego	My father don Juan Martin, don Diego
Martín	Martin
Pascual Martín, Rey Martín	Pascual Martin, Rey Martin
Nicolás Martín, Gabriel Martín	Nicolás Martin, Gabriel Martin
Pagr San Juan, Rajaw Pastor	Father San Juan, Lord Pastor
Rajaw Samnera, Rajaw Copral	Lord Semanero, Lord Caporal
Rajaw jyu, Rjawal tk'aj	Lord of the mountains, Lord of the plains
Rjaw Mund	Lord of the World
Rjawal k'an, Rjwal sak	Lord of the yellow corn, Lord of the white corn
Rjawal echaj, Rjawal much'	Lord of the herbs, Lord of the *chipilin*[14]
Rjawal tz'lam, Rjawal pixnac'	Lord of the leaves, Lord of black nightshade

[8.71.4, item 39][15]

"Song of the Spirit-Lord of the World" ("*B'ix rxin Rajau Mund*")

The traditional songs are called *b'ix* (pronounced "beesh"), and one who sings them is called a songman, an *ajb'ix* (pronounced "ah-beesh"). Songman Diego Cua Simaj sang the following "Song of the Spirit-Lord of the World" that develops the picture of the Santo Mundo. It is a salutation to Our Father the Sun and other Spirit-Lords of earth and sky, who are invoked under the many names of these multiple powers and manifestations that exist in the Santo

Mundo, among them San Martín, Green-Mountain World, Dio's Padre, Lamp of St. Bernardine, Dio's JesuKrista, and Manuel de JesuKrista Salvador.

The expressions of respect and gratitude that Diego offers to the spirits of the Santo Mundo hide a reverential fear of the same spirits who he knows can protect him from grief and harm, but can also abandon him and cause him to "lose his luck" as a consequence. "Song of the Spirit-Lord of the World" contains a keen awareness that people walk, move, plant, cultivate, and so forth on the *back* of the Santo Mundo—a delicate but unavoidable situation for which he apologizes.

The subtext of his gratitude for being allowed to stand and walk on the back of the Santo Mundo is a confession of his past offenses. He admits them to avert their ill consequences by begging pardon, and he also defends his own behavior by pointing out that all animals do the same thing. He thanks Lamp of St. Bernardine for the gift of light and the present day, the fruits of the earth, and his own life which he compares to the sprouting of a seed, a comparison that is deeply imbedded in Tz'utujil vocabulary, where birth and life are understood as analogs of the sprouting and growth of corn. He is especially grateful for the great guardian deity of Atitlán, Old Mam.

The Tz'utujils feel an ever-present threat of disease and trouble and even death that can be caused by spells and witchcraft. When these things befall you or someone you know, it is possible that an enemy who wants to cause harm has hired a witch to send these evils upon you. In songs and conversations this might be expressed as thorns a witch has put into the person's belly or in their path, or as being pushed by an unseen force into a ravine. On another occasion Diego claimed to be a witch himself.[16] Here he says he hopes Father Dio's will protect him from witchcraft:

if someone puts thorns
if someone puts brambles
if someone pushes me into a ditch
if someone pushes me into a ravine
In your hands, in your feet you keep me, Father.

In his comments after the song, Diego identified it as directed to the sun as "Lamp of St. Bernardine" or "Our Father in Heaven." The title "Lamp of St. Bernardine" comes from details of a statue in the church that depicts the fifteenth-century Franciscan Saint Bernardine of Siena, who is commonly represented holding a sign in the shape of a sunburst. Thus the sun acquired the name "Lamp of St. Bernardine."[17] A conversation between Diego, a traditionalist, and Gaspar Culan Yataz, a young man who had embraced Catholicism, reveals something of the personal conflict created by the new liberal brand of Catholic Action of the Catholic Mission of Oklahoma. For Gaspar, who struggled because of the conflation of the cosmic deities with Catholic saints, Diego's traditional position is tempting, but difficult. Gaspar was my translator on this occasion:

DIEGO: This is the music of the Lord of the World, of Our Father in Heaven, because it is about all of them.
GASPAR: Who is "Our Father"?
DIEGO: Lamp of Saint Bernardine.
GASPAR: Then I will write down "Our God (Dio's) who is in heaven."
DIEGO: Yes, Lamp of Saint Bernardine who is in heaven, in the sky, who is circling around us.

"B'ix rxin Rajaw Mund"
Diego Cua Simaj, songman

"Song of the Spirit-Lord of the World"[18]

Rex Jyu' Mund
Rex Jyu' Ruch'lew
nkobye'na c'a, nawc'axaj.
Nkpalbej, nkobina chwach
    Ruch'lew Dio's

Green Mountain World
Green Mountain Face of the Earth
we will be regretful later,[19] you hear us.
We have to stand, we have to walk on the
    Face of the Earth Dio's

Dio's Lambr Marnadina
atc'o pciel, atc'o pglor.

Dio's Lamp of St. Bernardine
you are in the sky, you are in glory.

Mund Ruch'lew, nokawc'axaj,
    Tierra.
Mil doscientas, trescientas pas
    nkaya'
chchaxe' chawach a.

World Face of the Earth, you hear us,
    Earth.
Maybe two hundred, three hundred steps
    we take
up and down you.

Ay Dio's, ay Mund
ay Mund
nka'ja che' chawij, entons
    nawc'axaj Dio's.

Oh Dio's, oh World
oh World
you lend us the trees on your back, and
    you hear us, Dio's.

Dio's
nawc'axaj, Ruch'lew.
Po voluntad de Dio's
siquiera nkaban gnar año mil
    nuevecientos setenta y uno.
Xtacuy kil, xtacuy kama'c.

Dio's
you hear us, Face of the Earth.
If Dio's wills it
may we live through the year
    nineteen seventy-one.
Pardon our sins, pardon our faults.

Ay vez jun sba psamaj
ay vez jun xba pnegos.
Cada kasuert ay'on
    Lambre Marnadino
atc'o psiel, atc'o pgloria.

Dio's Padre, Dio's Reino
ruq'uin cielo, ruq'uin gloria.

Naya' rabendicion, naya'
    rainstrumentos
con bona santa voluntad Dio's.

Naya' kcxilway, naya' kichaj

naya' kimunil, ay'on kic'aslemal.

Nicjar ciel
    nic'jar gloria
yo'l ak'ij, yo'l ak'or.

Dia jueves
meltiox Ta'
meltiox Lambr, meltiox Marnadina
meltiox Ndta', meltios
    Nute'.

Ach'bon Mund, ach'bon

    Ruch'lew
c'ola ajward, c'ola santinel.

C'ola testig, c'ola ajront
c'ola alwsiles, c'o mayores,
Nc'astana, nmayjana.

Ta' nc'ay pk'ij, ta'
    nc'ay chak'a'
ay Dio's SuKrist, jc'anen, Ta'

Sometimes one goes to work
sometimes one goes to do business.
Each one has his luck[20] that you give
    Lamp of St. Bernardine
you are in the sky, you are in glory.

Dio's Father, Dio's King
in the sky, in glory.

You give us your blessing, you give us
    your instruments
with good and holy will Dio's.

You give us our tortillas, you give us our
    herbs
you give us our fruit, you give us
    our life.

You divide the sky in the middle
    you divide glory in the middle[21]
giver of sunlight, giver of the *atol*.[22]

Today is Thursday
thank you Father
thank you Lamp, thank you Bernardine
thank you my Father, thank you my
    Mother.

You took thought of us, World, you took
    thought of us
    Face of the Earth
we have a warden, we have a sentinel.

There is a witness, there is a watchman[23]
there are *alguacils*, there are *mayores*,[24]
He [Old Mam] walks around, he trots
    around.

Papa [Old Mam] watches by day, papa
    watches by night
oh Dio's JesuKrista, and I, Papa

jc'anen Dio's, quinpalbej
quinchcalbej, Mund.

Ml rkal nuchi', ml quinwyina

pr pnak'a enc'owa', Señor
pnak'a . . . .

Pr y Dio's
exc'ola,
     Exjsoc
Dio's, Exajquiypa
Exajmutzmul, Exajcb'artan.

Ncsol nejitz Mund
ncsol nejitz Ruch'lew.

Anen, Dio's, quin majcuna . . .
quinc'astana chwach ak'a
chwach k'ejkum Mund
mec'ola ajward,
     mec'ola ajchjenel.

nwok'ben nway . . .

Pero Dio's
quinwajo', Ndta'
quinwok'ej Mund Ruch'lew
. . . .

Nacuy lomlaj kil, nacuy lomlaj kama'c

ay Mund, ay Ruch'lew.

Nca'y k'ij, nca'y
     chawij
pc xri'l chic k'ij.
Manaque'x Dio's.
. . . .

and I Dio's, I stand
I am watchful, World.

Should I cry out, should I really
     scream
in your hands am I, Lord
in your hands . . . .

Because Dio's
you have always been there,
     you have been the Lightning-Men
Dio's, you have been the Mist-Men
you have been the Rain-Men, you have
     been the Earthquake-Men.

You loosen and spellbind the World
you loosen and spellbind the Face of the
     Earth.[25]

I, Dio's, I sin . . .
and I think in the night
in the darkness of the World
perhaps the warden is here,
     perhaps the guardian is here.

I have cried for a tortilla . . .

But Dio's
I want, my Father
to cry to the World Face of the Earth
. . . .

You pardon our great faults, pardon our
     great sins
oh World, oh Face of the Earth.

The sun watches, the sun watches over
     your head
because day has come again.
Do not change it Dio's.
. . . .

Nbij ndta', adta' babosad nqueban

pr awq'uin tet Señor
. . . Lambr Marnadina
Manuel de Jesus de Krista Salvador.

Pre pnak'a' c'alwa', Ndta'
alojden,
apajken.

K'an acorona, sak acorona

k'an espina, sak espina
achpon ctz'e'j, achpon
    gloria.

Todo del mundo awxin Ndta'
todo del mundo señor awxin Padr Rey.

awxin Ndta' . . .
awxin cab, awxin cxilway

awxin lok', awxin canel
awxin rexwach, awxin
    tuja'

awxin pujuy . . .

Selwir pnak'a xlaxa' pujuy.
Awxin much', awxin chaj

awxin. . . , awxin xcoy.

Pr y Dio's
pr y bar nokexque wal?
Mani kpalben Ndta'
nokacuy c'a Mund
nokacuy c'a Ruchlew

My father talks, your father talks
    nonsense[26]
but with you Lord
. . . Lamp St. Bernardine
Manuel de Jesus de Krista Salvador.

Because in your hands, my Father
you carry it in your arms like a baby,
you carry it in your hands carefully like a
    basin of water.

Golden is your crown, white is your
    crown

golden rays, white rays[27]
in your hands the flowers,[28] in your hands
    the glory.[29]

The whole world is yours my Father
the whole world is yours Father King.

yours my Father . . .
yours is the honey, yours the maize
    dough

yours the produce, yours the cinnamon
yours the black corn, yours the
    yellow corn

yours the mottled corn . . .

In your hands the mottled corn was born.
Yours is the *chipilín*, yours the resinous
    pine
yours. . . , yours the tomato.

But Dio's
where do we kneel down?
Since we have stood [on you] my Father
pardon us then World
pardon us then Face of the Earth

prc Dio's JesuKrista
msc mejor quej, msc mejor wacax
chi jun jan, chi jun snic
chi jun chcop c'ola pmontaña Ndta'

chi jun tz'e', chi jun syaw
atrpalben Mund
    atrpalben Ruch'lew.

. . . .
Anen quinwajo' Dio's
quinc'astan jun rat
chnawc'axbej kk'ojom, xul

pr pnak'a, pnawkan Dio's
xul, k'ojom
hoy Ta', hoy Reyna.

Delante Dio's qui' xul
delante Dio's qui' marimp.
Xinlax, xmob cxhwach Ruch'lew

xaya' arsyon npnwa'.
Meltiox chul.

Anen quinwajo', Mund
jun mc'ol, jun yoyon c'ix
mc'ol ljun yoyn tucan
mc'ol ljun quinrumin chawach jul
mc'ol ljun quinrumin chwach siwan

pnak'a', pnawkan anyo'n
    Ta'.
Pr mlay anen
Dio's, tya'ta rzon
mna wewaj, mna colbej c'a
    Dio's.

Wawe' c'olwa' tentacion bel c'siwan
y jc'anen, Ndta', xinwc'axaj tzij
xinwc'axaj consej c'in powr.

because Dio's JesuKrista
even the best deer, even the best bull
or a fly, or an ant
or an animal on the mountain my Father

or a dog, or a cat
is always standing on you World
    is always standing on you
        Face of the Earth.

. . . .
I want Dio's
to enjoy myself a while
so you can hear our drum, our flute

because in your hands, your feet Dio's
is the flute, is the drum
today Father, today King.

Before Dio's the flute is sweet
before Dio's the marimba is sweet.
I was born, I sprouted on the Face of the
    Earth
they sang birth prayers over me.
Thank you dear.

I want, World
if someone, someone puts thorns
if someone puts brambles
if someone pushes me into a ditch
if someone pushes me into a ravine

in your hands, in your feet you keep me
    Father.
But I hope
Dio's, you will speak to me
do not hide, do not conceal yourself
    Dio's.

Here there is temptation and the ravine
and I, my Father, heard the words
I heard the teaching from a poor man.[30]

Anen, Dio's	Me, Dio's
xinrsiq'ij, xinruchol pruchoch.	they called me, they talked about me in their house.
Pnak'a bnon, w nute'	In your hands they did this, my mother
pnak'a bnon, w nxenyor.	in your hands they did this, my lady.
Xta'k nsic'xic	They sent to call me
iwir, ay Ndta', el diez y ocho de Agosto	yesterday, oh my Father, the eighteenth of August
xenuc'axajc' wawe'.	I heard them here.[31]
Xatnpalbejc' Mund	I set foot on you World
xatnmalbejc' Ruch'lew.	I set foot on you Face of the Earth.
Enmonta equ'e' wamig chwij	I brought my two friends with me
psant Igles, psant empl.	to the holy church, to the holy temple.
Ewinkirsan Mund	They were engendered World
enwinkirsan Ruch'lew	they were engendered Face of the Earth[32]
Manuel de Jesus, Lambre Marnadina	Manuel de Jesus, Lamp St. Bernardine
en el cielo, en la gloria Dio's.	in the sky, in glory Dio's.
Pnak'a Dio's	In your hands Dio's
pnaplbal c'ow solic.	in your stopping place is unbinding from spells.[33]
Content ranm, content rucupx	My soul is glad, my heart is glad because
xutak nsic'xic.	they sent me a message to come.
Xery'a' volt pwuchoch	He came by my house
"Nanjo'xc' chwara?"	"What do they want with me?"
xinu'l pch'coj nway	I just came home from earning my food
Dio's.	Dio's.
Xinpeta, Ndta'	I came, my Father
camic content wanm	now my heart is content
día jueves el diecinueve de agosto	Thursday the nineteenth of August
mlay Ndta', tia'a bendicion	I beg my Father, give your blessing
pnwa'.	upon me.
[8.71.14, item 91]	

Diego's song requires a note to explain how Tz'utujils classify musical instruments. Diego sings "I want, Dio's, to enjoy myself a while so you can hear our drum, our flute," and then "before Dio's the flute is sweet . . . the marimba is sweet." However, he is playing the guitar, not the drum, the marimba, or the flute, and yet he seems to call it "our drum" and "our flute." Other data I collected clarifies that musical instruments belong to one of two classes. The first class are instruments regarded as feminine and that are played by striking or plucking with the hands (that is, "hands that discipline or caress a woman"). The shape of feminine instruments apparently contributes to this classification, as in the guitar (feminine curves), the drum (membranes), and the marimba (breast-like gourd resonators that are called *rutzum*, "its breasts").[34] These may all be called by their specific names, or by the general term for feminine instruments, *k'ojom*. The second class, masculine instruments, are phallic in shape and are played by blowing with the mouth, such as the traditional cane flute (*xul*), the chirimía, the clarinet, and the trumpet.

As mentioned, instruments have specific names as well: *ctar* (guitar), *k'ojom* (drum), and *mrimp* (marimba). *K'ojom* can also serve as a generic term for any instrument or for instrumental music, and this is Diego's meaning in the song. A male/female pair consisting of a large double-headed drum (*k'ojom*) and a cane flute (*xul*), is the principal ensemble that heralds the arrival of the processions that go through the town announcing calendric or other rituals of the Old Ways. Sergio Navarrete Pellicer found a similar paradigm for musical instruments in a closely related highland Maya group in Rabinal, Guatemala (1999, 87).

Duality and Metaphor in the Santo Mundo

In Maya cosmology divine beings, human life, time, space, and events are dual phenomena, as Tedlock says, "complimentary rather than opposed, interpenetrating rather than mutually exclusive" (1996, 59). Navarrete Pellicer also found that this duality characterizes a broad way of thinking and perceiving in Rabinal. "Pairing is a cognitive strategy used to order the world and society; all categories of hierarchy, gender, and genre operate in dualities" (1999, 87). Duality is a pervasive mode of perception that is expressed by Tz'utujils in the pairing of names and attributes of spirits as well as in the poetic structure of the ritual language of their prayers and songs. Duality can be found in calendric rituals, as in the equinoctial rituals of Holy Week where the central roles are played by the complementary deities Old Mam and JesuKrista, in whom Vincent Stanzione convincingly recognizes the Hero Twins of the K'iche' primal myth, the *Popol Vuh* (2003, 47). Similarly, Tz'utujil courting songs embrace human sexuality as a metaphor for the fertilizing power of the rains.

In this cosmos, time itself is not simply linear as in western thought, in which "now" is a moment between a past that is gone and a future not yet arrived. Maya time endlessly repeats the past but in new ways, as a theme returns in a musical variation, and as alliteration repeats sounds in the lines of parallel verse. So it is not surprising to find that the return of a theme in multiple variations is the governing structure in Tz'utujil traditional songs in the patterns of their texts and of their melodic themes.

At the heart of this organizing concept is a duality called *jaloj-k'exoj*. This duality is well described by Robert Carlsen, who explains "*jal*" as the change manifested by a thing as it evolves through its life cycle, and "*k'ex*" as the process of the replacement of the old with the new. Like the corn that is regarded as the essential substance of human life, *jal* is "change from the outside," at the "husk," from death through birth, youth and old age, and back into death. *K'ex* occurs at the seed and refers to generational change: "the continuity of life, the ancestral origin, a form of reincarnation" (Carlsen 1997, 50). Corn is the model for the cycle of birth, death, and rebirth, giving added significance to the name Tz'utujil, which means "People of the Flowering Corn." Prayermaker Tomás Ajchomajay explained its meaning when speaking of Santiago, the town's patron saint:

> [He is] really Santiago Apostle Tz'utujil. He is a "Flowering Corn Man" [*tz'u*: flower; *-tujil* or *-tojil*: corn], a real "Flowering Corn." Some people say "Flowering Son [Ear] of Corn."[35]

Tz'utujil children are frequently recognized as the reincarnation of their ancestors, often of their grandparents (Carlsen 1997, 51; Stanzione 2003, 176). An example of this expectation was shown in 1968, when Father Stanley Rother arrived from Oklahoma to serve in Atitlán and, finding no equivalent for "Stanley" in Spanish or Tz'utujil, he chose to be known as Francisco. This led to his identification by the traditionalists as the reincarnation of the Nawal APla's (Francisco) Sojuel.[36] Similarly, the actions of the Nawals are repeated when the people follow the Old Ways so that the spiritual essences of the Nawals are reembodied and manifested in the living. The same central concept that informs the Tz'utujil cyclical perception of time generates the repeating patterns of behavior of rituals and customs.

The *cofradía* system is the principal organization that functions to guarantee the continued and faithful practice of the Old Ways of the Nawals. The system was established in the sixteenth century by the early friars as a means of facilitating the teaching of the new Catholic faith. Originating in the guild system in Spain, the *cofradías* evolved into religious confraternities responsible for the characteristically elaborate Spanish celebrations of the feast days of the saints and the mysteries of the Catholic faith. To both prosyletize and simplify their task, the friars organized the Tz'utujils into eight or ten *cofradías*, each with its own chapel or prayer-house under the patronage of a saint or mystery, such as St. John the Baptist (*San Juan Baktista*), St. James the Greater (*Santiago*), Saint Mary of the Rosary (*Santa María del Rosario*), Blessed Sacrament (*Santísimo Sacramento*), and Holy Cross (*Santa Cruz*), and each with an official hierarchy of members responsible for the group's activities. Similar organizational units (*chinamits*) existed among the Tz'tujils prior to Spanish contact, allowing the friars to overlay the Catholic celebrations on this existing structure (Orellana 1984, 208).

With the well-documented genius of the Maya for recognizing old themes and patterns dressed up in new clothes, the Tz'utujils retained their deities, now clothed in the trappings of the saints, and saw in the church calendar so closely tied to the agricultural calendar of western Europe, the general cosmic design of the Santo Mundo.

The period of intense Spanish presence in the late sixteenth and early seventeenth centuries in Atitlán was followed by two and a half centuries of relative abandonment by the clergy, during which time the interpretation of Catholic ritual and symbolism in terms of Tz'utujil beliefs and cosmology was uninhibited. This process was facilitated by the aforementioned congruence of patterns in both Maya and Catholic practices, such as the solar and lunar orientation of their calendars and the great number of holy beings in both cults. The statues of the saints in the church and the *cofradías*, of which more than a hundred still remain, were easily identified with the Spirit-Lords of the Tz'utujil pantheon, so that today little remains of the original Catholic or historical identity of the Santos except their names and the calendar dates of their feast days. The primary rituals revolved around the *cofradías* and the church, and were performed by members of the *cofradía* system.

The Presence of the Nawals

The *cofradía*[37] system does more than assign responsibilities for celebrations to one or another group of members. The *cofradía* system also provides the pedagogy, the resources, the religious paraphernalia and accoutrements, and the access to the power and energy of the complex of spirits so that people can follow the "right road" that leads to finally *becoming* a Nawal by having acted like one.

Active *cofradía* membership involves a lifetime process in which one moves through a hierarchy of positions, each of which requires a year or more of the dedication of considerable time and money. Many people who practice the

Entrance to *cofradía* San Juan with child's toy, 1972.

Old Ways are only able to participate in active service in a *cofradía* to a limited degree, and many not at all. The opportunity to enter this path of formal membership, however, becomes available when a man or woman contracts
marriage. During the year surrounding marriage, the initiation fertility rites
described below in the "Third Song of the Road" take place.

Ideally each *cofradía* has fifteen official members or *cofrades* who volun-
teer their services for a year at a time. The head-man or *alcalde* of the *cofradía*
achieves this status of responsibility by lending one of the single-room *ranchitos* on his property to house the *cofradía*'s statues, decorations, and furnishings,
and by assuming the financial and other responsibilities involved in providing a place for the many calendric festivities, all of which include ritual drinking, music, and dancing, sometimes to a songman's guitar, often to a marimba
or two or a violin or harp hired from out of town.[38] There are six male *cofrades*,
and the *alcalde*'s wife, the *xo'* (head-woman), is the leader of the six *tixels* (female members), making twelve in all, re-creating the twelve ancestors of the
origin myth. Indeed, their task is to reproduce the Old Ways handed down by
the twelve who danced and sang when the figure of Old Mam stood up for the
first time.

Prayer-makers and visitors who wish to honor or pray to the Santos are
welcomed by the *alcalde* and the other *cofrades*, usually with a drink of beer

or soda. When a prayer-maker is hired by an individual who is petitioning a prayer, a songman may also be invited to play or sing during the ritual. Money offerings are collected for the running of the *cofradía*, which are not supposed to be pocketed by the *alcalde*. With a dramatic flourish designed to ensure this, bills that are received in payment are placed in the hands or in the clothing of a Santo in the *cofradía*, where they are left on display, maybe as a reminder to clients that payment is expected, as a sacrifice that is likely to encourage a favorable response from the Santo.

Two *cofradías*, San Juan and Santa Cruz, have a special priest attached to them who is responsible for the rituals of the *cofradía*'s patron Santo. These are the *nabeysil*, the rain-priest of the *cofradía* San Juan, who serves in a lifetime position, and the *telinel*, the one designated to reconstruct and carry the figure of Old Mam, an annual position of service to the *cofradía* Santa Cruz. Other *cofradía* positions include the players of the large two-headed drum and the cane flute (a single person may do both, as was the case during my research), who function at most of the public festivals; the *Sacristanes*, a group of men responsible for the music of JesuKrista, which is composed of the surviving liturgical Latin chants and very old Latin hymns; and the guitarist-singers, the *ajb'ix*, or songmen.

The *cofradía* is the place where *cofrades* also gather to socialize. After spending many hours listening, watching, and participating in these *cofradía* rituals, one gets a growing sense that the Nawals are their alter egos, the hidden identities of these people who live by the old customs, who are themselves more or less faithful simulacra of the first men and women. When I was attempting to enter the world of the Tz'utujils and understand it more than superficially, I found I had to allow appearances to dissolve, and try to see through them as transparencies that allowed both ordinary and divine dimensions to be perceived. With this mindset, things seemed to expand in time and space like the multiple images created by facing mirrors. The people truly live in the presence and assume the forms of "the great hands, the great feet" of the Nawals.

Over and over again I experienced how acutely songmen felt the presence of the Nawals in the place where they were singing. The Nawals came, attracted by their songs, the "Songs of the Old Ones." A typical experience was an evening with songman José Sosof Coo'.

On that evening in July of 1972 my translator Diego Pop Ajuchan took me to visit the songman José Sosof Coo'. He seemed proud to introduce me to a songman he considered to be among the very best. On arriving at his *sitio* we were led by a young boy to a small *ranchito* set apart from the others in the family compound. It was furnished with three small, colorfully painted chairs and a table on which we placed our offerings of candles, cigars, and drinks. José was already there tuning his guitar, and seemed glad to welcome us. A few children

José Sosof Coo', songman, 1972.

José Sosof Coo', songman, 1972.

hung around just outside the door listening, watching and giggling. After introductions, nothing could be done until the appropriate sacrifices were made to please and feed the Nawals. A single glass of *cuxa*,[39] the clear and powerful homemade cane liquor—the *cofradía* favorite—was poured by José and passed to me. Knowing the custom already, I drank it all except the last bit which I poured on the earthen floor as a libation for the Nawals, then returned the glass to him. Diego did the same with the glass he received from José, and finally José drank and made his libation. Then José placed and lit our offerings of yellow and white candles on the earthen floor, saying, "For Old Mam." We each lit one of the cigars I had brought so the sweet smell of tobacco would rise to the noses of the Nawals. Most songmen would not begin without such offerings, because the songs open the portal that effectively connects this world with the invisible world of spirits who must be honored. Answering my question, José explained that the songs call the spirits, and they come as soon as they hear the music. I sensed some anxiety behind his explanation, and thinking in terms of my experience of benevolent and helpful Catholic saints, I questioned José why the Nawals' presence might not be completely favorable. He said with some emotion that the spirits would be angry and even dangerously vengeful should they respond to the call of their music and find nothing for them to eat when they got there. As David Friedel found, the present-day Maya "view these direct exchanges with the supernaturals as dark and dangerous adventures" (Freidel et al. 1993, 130). This kind of "divine economy," in which sacrifices are offered to the ancestors and other spirit beings in return for their favorable intervention in the lives of the people, I found to be a central component of Tz'utujil Old Ways.

CHAPTER TWO

The Dance and Songs of the Nawals

Old Mam Creates the Recibos

The story of the creation of dance and songs by Rilaj Mam is contained in the Tz'utujil origin myth, of which many versions are told with variations in their details. A more complete version appears below, but briefly: In the very beginning of the present creation, twelve heroic male ancestors were merchants who traveled out of town to what is today Antigua Guatemala, where they sold fish from the lake and cacao and other produce that grew on the tropical coastal lands that belonged to the Tz'utujils before the arrival of the Spanish. After some unfavorable experiences, these men agreed that they needed a guardian who would protect their wives and maintain their marital fidelity while the men were away. Conscious of the operative principle of the dual nature of things, we can read this metaphorically, with "wives" as "the fruit- and corn-producing power of the Santo Mundo," and "marital fidelity" as "its faithfulness in fertility." Thus the ancestors were searching for a practical guardian on one level, but for one who was also the Spirit-Lord of corn and of the fertilizing rain on the other.

When they met to discuss a solution, the youngest among them, APla's Sojuel, suggested they look for a tree who might be willing to take on these responsibilities, a tree that had a living Spirit within it. They agreed, and went off separately, searching and striking the trees with their machetes until APla's found one, the *tz'ajtel* (*palo de pito* in Spanish), that cried out when it was struck.[1] They asked it if it were willing to be the guardian and Spirit-Lord they needed, and it agreed. So they carved a figure from the tree, but it was not yet fully alive. Instead, it was weak and floppy and could not stand up by itself. Asked what should be done, the figure told them to bring a *marimba de tecomates*, a marimba hung with gourd resonators, to play at its reception celebration. It should be a great festival with food made of corn and with cane liquor to drink. They did as asked, and at the celebration the figure of Rilaj Mam ("Old Mam" or "Old Grandfather") came fully to life, stood up, taught them his music, and danced. This is the same moving, the "standing up" that means the "summoning of one's power," that is addressed to the Santos and Nawals in the prayer of Nicolás Chiviliu on page 21: "I make you move, I stand you up [so you can work]."

At the festival of reception, Old Mam taught them to play the instruments, to sing the songs, and a dance, all related to—or part of—two sets of three musical pieces called the Recibos, or "Reception Songs." These are the three Recibos of Old Mam and the three Recibos of Santiago. From the melodies and style of these formally developed pieces, the textual content and musical style of the "Songs of the Old Ones" (*B'ix rxin Nawal*) that are discussed here were derived. The Recibos are most often heard as instrumental pieces played on marimbas for dancing. They are also called *sones*.[2]

At the fiesta of Old Mam the first men and women drank, danced, played instruments and sang, and were taught the *costumbres*—the old customs or "Old Ways" of doing things. At this event they acquired their language and the "wise thoughts" of the Nawals, all of which they passed on to their descendants. They understood that as long as the Old Ways should continue to be respected and practiced, they would ensure that the Spirit-Lords of the Santo Mundo would remain in harmony with the people, and that the People of the Flowering Corn would continue to flourish on the fertile, corn-producing Face of the Earth. If the Old Ways should be neglected, despised, or abandoned, chaos would certainly ensue. As Vincent Stanzione says:

> Everything the Nawales did the people of Atitlán would come to imitate in order to become perfect models of the past, in order to stay in harmony with their "Nawal" ancestors and their ways. These Nawales were also magicians, day-keepers, canoe builders, mat makers, hunters, and "curanderos" but deep in their hearts they were merchants. . . .
>
> These Nawales were beings who existed between two worlds. . . . They were so perfect, it is said, that any human who acted like them would in fact become one of them and in so doing walk in the sandals of the gods. These Nawales were created by the "Old Couple," "TiTie-TeTixel," "Great-Grandmother–Great-Grandfather," so that humanity would have something to model itself upon. (2003, 21)

The Song of APla's Sojuel ("*B'ix rxin APla's Sojuel*")

Few songmen are now left in Atitlán, and the Old Ways are fast disappearing. In 2011, José Cua Simaj[3] was the only one I could find who still improvises his song texts and plays on the five-string guitar in the old way. In his poignant song that follows, he expresses the sadness felt by those who still follow the Old Ways of the Nawals, because, as he says, "It's gone, boys."

"B'ix rxin APla's Sojuel"
José Cua Simaj, songman

"Song of Francisco Sojuel"[4]

Kinxjow anen, kinxjow anen
    chpam jaw son
kinxjow anen, kinxjow anen
    chpam nctar, chpam jaw q'joom.

I want to dance, I want to dance to
    to the sound of the *son*
I want to dance, I want to dance to the
    sound of the guitar, to sound of
    the drum.

Ja k'awa kna'ooj, ja k'a

    kitziij cqtiit, cqawma'.

These are their wise thoughts, these
    are the
    words of our grandmothers, our
      grandfathers.

Ja k'awa na'ooj, ja k'awa
    tzojb'al xuyakna alaa',
xuyakna acha', MaPla's Sojuel.

These are the wise thoughts, this is the
    language[5] you left boy,
you left man, Francisco Sojuel.

Ay nawal alaa', ay nawal acha'
ay nawal alaa'
ay nawal alaa', ay nawal acha'.

Oh old boy, oh old man
oh old boy
oh old boy, oh old man.

Kinxowna' anen je chpaam je xuul,
    je chpaam je' q'joom.
Ja k'awa na'ooj, ja k'awa'
    tzojb'al
    xuyaa'kna ala',
    xuyaa'kna achaa', nawal alaa'
    MaPla's Sojuel.
Ja k'awa na'ooj, ja k'awa
    tzojb'al
    ja k'awa, aleey.

I want to dance to the sound of the flute,
    to the sound of the drum.
This is the wise thought, this is the
    language
    the boy left,
    the man left, the old boy
    Francisco Sojuel.
This is the wise thought, this is the
    language
    this is, dear.

Nqo b'ison taa', nqo b'ison Sojuel
    ay nawal alaa'.

We are sad, grandfather, we are sad Sojuel
    oh old boy.

Ktixjoow k'a YaLoor
ktixjoow k'a YaTuun
ktixjoow YaMri'y B'itz'b'al
ktixjoow nutee', naj b'ey ixoq.

Maria Dolores dances
Maria Antonia dances
Maria Spindle dances
my mother, the first [woman] on the road
    dances.

Ay YaMri'y Cervantes, ay YaMri'y
    Tiquir
ay YaMri'y YaTuun
ktixjoow alii', ktixjoow ixoq
    ktixjoow YaTuun
YaCheep Bitz'b'al.

Oh Maria Cervantes, oh Maria
    Small Heddles
oh Maria Antonia
my mama dances, the women dance
    Antonia dances
and Josefa Spindle.

Ja k'awa na'ooj, jak'a tzojb'al.
    Xtu b'a k'a a'ii'.
Nqo b'ison taa', nqo b'ison ned'ta.
Na b'isooj alaa'. Nanataj alaa'
ay nawal acha'.

This is the wisdom, this is the language.
    It's gone, boys.
We are sad grandfather, we are sad father.
The boy is sad. We remember you boy
oh old man.

Ay nawal alaa', ay nawal achuul
ay nawal alaa'
ay nawal alaa', ay nawal acha'.

Oh old boy, oh old handsome
oh old boy
oh old boy, oh old man.

Ja k'awa' kna'ooj, ja k'awa
    knataan
xke'[ban] chwach Ruch'leew.

This is their wise thought, this is what is
    remembered
[of] what they did on the Face of the
    Earth.

Xpet YaMri'y B'itz'b'al, xpet Makox
    Ruujuuch'
xpet YaMri'y Tik'ir, YaMri'y
    Saaleem
YaMri'y . . .

Maria Spindle came, Marcos
    Rujuch' came
Maria Small Heddles came, Maria
    Jerusalem
Maria . . .

Qoxjow ixoq, qalkaalt'; qoxjow
    qaaxoo'
qoxjow permecer
ay nawal alaa', ay nawal acha', MaPla's
    Sojuel.

Let's dance, women, *alcalde*; let's
    dance xo'
let's dance first *cofrade*
oh old boy, oh old man, Francisco
    Sojuel.

José Cua Simaj, songman, 2012.

Ay nawal alaa', ay nawal acha'
meltyox chaw taa', meltyox chaw alaa'
meltyox chaw acha'.

Oh old boy, oh old man
thank you father, thank you boy
thank you man.

Ja k'a awa atziij, ja wa' k'a
    ana'ooj
meltyox chaw ta', meltyox chaw alaa'
meltyox chaw Sojuel.
Ktix joow k'a alaa', ktix joow k'a acha'
Xuya kana ruutziij, xuya kana
    rna'ooj.

These are your words, these are your
    wise thoughts
thank you father, thank you boy
thank you Sojuel.
Dance boy, dance man
You left your words, you left
    your wisdom.

Ja' k'awa ja'ooj, ja k'awa
ja k'awa na'ooj, ja k'a wa
    ruutziij
nawal alaa'.

These are your wise thoughts, these
these are your wise thoughts, these are
    your words
old boy.

Ay MaXwaan Ko'wa', ay Mam alaa',   Oh Juan Cua, oh Mam boy
ay nawal alaa' ay nawal acha'.   oh old boy, oh old man.
[2.2011.15, item 5]

Dance, Movement, and Songs: The Divine Currency of Sacrifice

Dance and song were created together, and only when the dancing and singing began did Old Mam quicken with life and power and join in, dancing
and teaching his songs.[6] Dance and song are in some way identical, as is illustrated in some Mayan languages in which the root *b'ix* (also *b'iix*) means both
to dance and to sing. In the languages (including Tz'utujil) in the group called
"greater K'ichean," *b'ix* means both "song" and "to sing" (Kaufman and Justeson 2003, 748).

The celebration for Old Mam was the event in which the people acquired
the Old Ways, the ways of living with each other in harmony with the Santo
Mundo and the world of spirits. In his study of dance in ancient Maya civilization, Matthew Looper provides an example from the highland Maya of
Chiapas, who also trace the elements of their practical, technical, social, and
spiritual culture to an original celebration. He identifies such highland Maya
festivals, that is, the complex of music, song, intoxication, and dance in which
technological knowledge is fused with spiritual awakening, as the catalyst that
fosters the development of civilization:

> The discovery of the skills required for a proper festival is the pivotal event in the
> acquisition of culture. It suggests the meaning of dance among the Maya as an im-
> age of civilization, as well as a means of achieving harmony between the commu-
> nity and the gods. (Looper 2009, 223)

The importance of dance and movement in this relationship between the
community and the gods is evidenced by the extensive vocabulary for movement and dance in Tz'utujil oral literature. No fewer than nineteen separate
entries for the word "move" (*mover, moverse*) describe the different types of
carrying and moving in the *Diccionario Tz'utujil*, and fifty-five different entries
exist to define *llevar* ("to carry," "to hold") (Perez Mendoza and Hernandez
Mendoza 1996, 648–649, 655). Allen Christenson's K'iche'-English dictionary
has twenty-three variants of "move" or "hold," which (as will be shown later)
are closely related (Christenson 2003a).[7] The Tz'utujil word for "dance" (noun)
and "to dance" (verb) is *xajoj*, but when *sobsaj* and *slob* (*silob*) occur in songs and
prayers, they were also often translated as "dance."[8] *Slob* denotes simply "move"
and also "move as in a temblor."

The usage of these words in Tz'utujil oral literature communicates that certain kinds of movement possess the power to effect change in cosmic events like wind and rain, the fertility of corn, animals and humans, and in one's personal life, especially in marriage and childbirth. During prayer rituals, prayer-makers sometimes took the figure of the Santo from its place in the *cofradía*, held it and rocked it or danced with it to stir the Santo, or perhaps to give him pleasure and lull him or her into a good mood for paying attention to the petitioner. In this way dance and song function as offerings or sacrifices for the Santo to enjoy and approve. The petitioners hope that the Santo is persuaded by the dancing and rocking movements and by the prayers and songs, to become erect and join in, just as Old Mam did at the beginning. In an obvious parallel to human sexuality, dance and music make the Old Ones stand up, come to life, and take the action that is being asked for.

Tz'utujil ritual behavior makes it clear at every turn that a function of this human/divine economy is a reciprocity in this agency of dance: the dancing of the living reenacts the dancing of the Nawals at the first creation, and when the statues of the Santos are danced, it incites them to dance again and thus renew or revive and fertilize and animate the Santo Mundo. The spirit of all-out excitement of that first fiesta with Old Mam is not forgotten when a marimba comes to play Mam's Recibos in the *cofradía*, for an important celebration. The *cofrades* and *tixels* and others of the *cofradía* community spend many hours drinking, talking, dancing, giving ritual speeches, and engaging in general revelry.

No one could do this like Nicolás Chiviliu. Near the beginning of my research I asked him about the songs and wrote the following in my field journal. As my comments in parentheses show, I didn't then understand that *before* meant "at the beginning" or "before the creation of Old Mam," nor did I understand the extent of the meaning of the word *music*:

"Before, no one knew this music," says Nicolás (something that seems to be untrue because Bertha remembers the [Recibos] before the [1950s]). I think he may have misunderstood me, or maybe he meant that some of the *sones* were invented then and others not. Maximón told him to play, but Nicolás protested, "I can't play; I don't know your music."

And as he told me this part of the story he played an imaginary violin and sang a melody I didn't recognize. "That's what I played, and he was happy and he danced, like this." Then he danced around in a circle, facing inward, on one leg, the other lifted up in front and bent at the knee, then he did the same on the other leg.

"That's how he danced, and very happy he was, and he taught me seven *sones*. All the people know three of these, but there are seven. I am the only one who knows them."

I asked, "Will you sing them for me?"

"Come here Friday when I will have a marimba and I will play for you, but not in the cofradía Santa Cruz" (which will have a marimba then, too) "because *mucha gente allí para escuchar. Aquí poca gente* ("because there will be too many people there to hear. Here just a few people.")

"At what time on Friday?"

"At 5 pm. Here."

So I said I would be there. He then told me the names of the *sones*, of which I can remember "María Guadalupa, San Miguel, Santo Lvario" and I can't recall the rest. He said I would need to bring the requisite candles and incense. This was his answer when I asked if he couldn't sing them now for me: "No, you don't do this *así, no más* (just like that). But you must bring the necessary things."

"What do I need?"

"You need four packages of *esterlinas* (white candles); four yellow candles of one pound; six small yellow candles and a pound of incense."

When we arrived, Chiviliu[9] greeted and welcomed us. The marimba was playing in fine style. We sat down, and I went up to Chiviliu and explained that these were my American friends and that we had brought beer. He thanked us, and we all began drinking bootleg *cuxa*, <u>pink</u>! When I asked "Is this *cuxa*?" (since it is usually colorless) he said it was.

"But it's pink . . ."

"*Jai bol*" he said ("High ball")! Then Chiviliu asked me if I was ready to record, as he had promised to show me the old music. Then he went and stood near the marimba and told them to play the first "*son*" of Maximón. I recorded, and he began to dance, and dance as I have never seen anyone dance before. He danced in "*son*" style, but swayed and bowed, threw out his chest like a toreador, twirled, danced backwards and forwards, jumped several times with both feet together, and generally got carried away by the music and the dance. Everyone watched him perform, and he was in fine style.

After the other two *sones* with explanations (recorded) he said we must dance one. So they played a "*son*," and I danced with him. Then Andy and [his wife] Linda began to dance, and they all loved it. After that dance, Chiviliu, whose wife had just come in, took me over to where his wife sat on the floor and said, "Now you dance with her," which we did. Then Chiviliu asked Andy to dance with him, and they really ripped it up together, dancing apart and together, bump and grind and both transported with the whole scene. (O'Brien 1972b)

Prayer-makers and singers constantly praise the Nawals for their "great hands and great feet," an idiom of speech that means a person has strength, ability, and power. In their great hands and great feet the Nawals carry the Santo Mundo and all it contains, holding it carefully like a basin full of water, or rocking it and carrying it carefully as one carries a baby. Some lines from the above prayer of Nicolás Chiviliu illustrate this:

alojden Ángel	you carry it in your arms like a baby, Ángel [*sometimes translated "you rock it"*]
apajken	you carry it in your hands carefully like a basin of water
Quensil, quenyic	I make you move, I make you stand up [so you can work]
Xek'etej, xemosej	You embraced them carefully, you carried them
lomlaj Mund Ruch'lew Señor. Pnak'a xcanajcwara'	great World Face of the Earth Lord. In your hands it stayed

Pnek'a c'a, pnewkan c'a
xek'etej c'a, ay
   Dio's
xek'etej c'a
   Mund
xek'etej c'a j
   Ruch'lew
	In your hands, in your feet, then
	you embrace them carefully like a baby, oh
	   Dio's
	you embrace them carefully like a baby,
	   World
	You embrace them carefully like a baby,
	   Face of the Earth

A particular Santo may be repeatedly reminded that the prayer-maker has held, rocked, carried, embraced, and danced him or her in the past. This is especially clear in the prayer of midwife Andrea Quilal Takaxoy addressed to San Nicolás, the Spirit-Lord of childbirth, for a client expecting a child.

Dancing the Bundle of San Martín

Until this time I had only heard songs sung by men. I asked friends and singers several times whether women sang but their answers were vague, like "Well, women don't know how, but a woman could if she knew how," or "Women can sing (*torij*)[10] to a baby." So I asked Chiviliu if women sang and told him I wanted to record songs sung by women. He then asked a midwife, Andrea Quilal Takaxoy, to allow me to accompany her to a ritual for a woman who was expecting a baby.

Midwife's Prayer and "Song of San Martín" ("*B'ix rxin Martín*")

I met Andrea and her client at the *cofradía* San Nicolás, the Santo who is the Spirit-Lord of childbirth. The single room of the *ranchito* had an earthen floor spread with pine needles, a few benches along the walls and a table in front of them. On the east side of the room was an altar or shelf that extended from wall to wall, covered with cloths of various colors and with several statues of Santos among which San Nicolás with his crown of yellow and gold was the most prominent, occupying the central position. All were clothed in elaborate costumes, with capes and gowns of satin and velvet, edged with fringes of gold or silver, some with headdresses. Some had *quetzal* bills (Guatemalan currency) that had been stuck between their fingers by petitioners. On the north end of the altar was a wooden box that, as I would later see, contained a "Martín bundle." About the size and shape of a baby, the bundle was wrapped in a typical locally woven tie-dyed cloth that hid its secret and powerful contents. The whole place was greatly ornamented and perfumed by tin cans full of flowers, and copal incense that rose from a censer made of a perforated coffee can.

I took a place to the side while Andrea lit the yellow and white candles brought by her client and placed them on the floor in front of the altar. While her client stood beside her, Andrea chanted a lengthy prayer. Then she took the Martín bundle from its box, held it in her arms like a baby, rocked it and sang a *B'ix rxin Martín* (Song of San Martín). The following lines are from her prayer and song.[11]

Midwifes' Prayer and "Song of San Martín" (*B'ix rxin Martín*)
Andrea Quilal Takaxoy, midwife

First Daykeeper, First of the Daylight
First Healer, First Doctor. . . .

Great Corn-dough Man, great Water Man
great are your hands, great your feet.
I will rock you in my arms, I will carry you carefully in my hands like a basin of
  water
your Spirits, your Souls
. . . .
I rock you in my arms, I carry you carefully in my hands like a basin of water

amid a thousand prayers, before a thousand confessions
amid a thousand b'ix, before [a thousand] songs
I rock you in my arms, I carry you carefully in my hands like a basin of water.

You carry in your arms, you carry in your hands
the yellow crown, the white crown
the yellow thorn, the white thorn, as they say.[12]

You hold it in your arms, you carry it in your hands
before the yellow lance, before the white lance,[13] as they say

I rock you in my arms, I carry you carefully in my hands like a basin of water
I will sing to you, I will enchant you with song[14] in the place where you were
    raised up
in the place where you were born
in the place where you appeared, as they say.

I moved you, I roused you for an hour, half an hour.
Truly I rocked you in my arms
truly I carried you carefully in my hands like a basin of water, as they say.
Oh Martín, as they say.

[*Singing:*]

Ay Martín Martín Martín Martín	Oh Martín Martín Martín Martín
ay Sale Sale Sale Sale Martín	Oh King King King King Martin[15]
ay Martín Martín Balbe Martín	oh Martín Martín Balbe Martín
ay chole Martín Martín Martín	oh dear Martín Martín Martín
Nicolás Nicolás Martín	Oh Nicolás Nicolás Martín
ay Balbe Balbe Martín chole chole	oh Balbe Balbe Martín dear dear
Martín	Martín
ay Martín Martín Martín	oh Martín Martín Martín
ay Sabe Sabe Martín	oh Venerable Venerable Martín
Ay Nawal ali ali ali K'poj	Oh Ancient mama mama mama Maiden
ay Nawal ali ali Xten	oh Ancient mama mama Woman
ay quinsobsaj, ay quinyuk'uj	oh I make you dance, oh I rock your
ak'a, awkan	hands, your feet
ay Martín Martín Martín	oh Martín Martín Martín
Ay Sale Sale Sale Martín	Oh King King King Martín
ay rxin ixok, alic'wal	oh you of the woman, the daughter
ay Martín Martín Martín	oh Martín Martín Martín
ay ali K'poj, ay ali Xitan	oh mama Maiden, oh mama Woman
Jac'awa' Ixok, Nawal Ixok,	This is the Woman, the Ancient Woman,
Nawal K'poj Martín	the Ancient Maiden Martín
ay Martín Martín Sale Martín	oh Martín Martín venerable Martín

Sale Martín	venerable Martín
ay Martín Martín Martín	oh Martín Martín Martín
ay nute' María Martín	oh my mother María Martín
Ay Martín ak'ij, ay Martín awalxic awalxic	Oh a Martín-day, oh Martín when you were born[16]
lomlaj ek'a, lomlaj ewkan Martín	great your hands, great your feet Martín
ay don Juan don Dieg Martín	oh don Juan don Diego Martín
don Juan don Pascual Martín	don Juan don Pascual Martín
jac'awa' ame'al, jac'awa'awlic'wal	this is your son, this is your daughter
Lomlaj ak'a, lomlaj awkan Martín	Great your hands, great your feet Martín
lomlaj alojden lomlaj atnpajken	truly I carry you in my arms, truly I carry you carefully
lonle' chwach Adiosil, lonle' chwach Asant'il Martín	rock-a-by before your Spirit, rock-a-by before your Soul Martín
ay apost San Nicolás	oh apostle San Nicolás
Ay Nawal Ali', ay Nawal K'poj	Oh Ancient Mama, oh Ancient Maiden
ay Nawal Ala' ay Nawal Xtan	oh Ancient Boy, oh Ancient Woman
Ay Nawal Awu'k Xtan	Oh Ancient Skirt Woman
ay Nawal K'poj Xtan, K'poj ali'	oh Ancient Maiden woman, Maiden mama
ay Nawal Ali', ay Nawal Xtan,	oh Ancient Girl, Ancient Woman
ay Martín Martín Martín	oh Martín Martín Martín
Ay catnsic'ij, ay catnb'ixaj	Oh I call you, oh I sing to you
ay ak'a, ay awkan Martín	oh your hands, oh your feet Martín
ay nute' María ali'	oh my mother María mama
ay nute' María don Juan	oh my mother María don Juan
Ay Sale Sale Sale Martín	Oh King King King Martín
ay Sale Sale Sale Pascual	oh King King King Pascual
ay Sale Sale Balver	oh King King Balver
ay cholit chloit cholit	oh dear dear dear
Ay Nicolás, ay ak'a' y ay awkan	Oh Nicolás, oh your hands and oh your feet
Ay Nawal Ixok, ay Nawal K'poj	Oh Ancient Woman, oh Ancient Maiden
ay Nawal Ali', ay nawal aleton	oh Ancient Girl, oh ancient lullaby
y ak'a, ay awkan Martín	oh your hands, oh your feet Martín
ay *dgo dgo* Martín Martín	oh *dgo dgo* Martín Martín[17]

Ay don Pascual, ay don Balver	oh don Pascual, oh don Balver
ay don Chale Martín	oh don Chale Martín
ay ak'a, ay awkan	oh your hands, oh your feet
ay Nawal Ali', ay Nawal Xtan	oh Ancient Mama, oh Ancient Woman
ay Nawal Ali', ay Nawal K'poj	oh Ancient Mama, oh Ancient Maiden

Ay ak'a, ay awkan Martín	Oh your hands, oh your feet Martín
ay ak'a, ay awkan Pascual	oh your hands, oh your feet Pascual
ay ak'a, ay awkan	oh your hands, oh your feet
ay ak'eten caja real	oh in your hands is the royal box[18]

Ay awkan, ay Adiosil, ay Asantil	Oh your hands, oh your Spirit, oh your Soul
ay rwa' k'a', ay rwa' awkan	oh your hands, oh your feet
ay rwa' achi'ipil, ay rwa' amakam	oh your little finger, oh your thumb

Ay rapalebal, ay rchcalebal Martín	Oh your dias, oh your table Martín
ay rapalebel Jyu'	oh your dias of the Mountains
ay rapalebel Tk'aj	oh your table of the Plains
ay Ajutzmul, ay Ajmayew	oh Rain-Men, oh Mist-Men
ay ak'a, ay awkan Martín	oh your hands, oh your feet Martín

Ay ndta' Pascual Martín	Oh my father Pascual Martín
ay ndta' Balber Martín	oh my father Balber Martín
ay Adiosil, ay Asant'il	oh your Spirit, oh your Soul
ay ak'a', ay awkan	oh your hands, oh your feet

Lomlaj ak'a, lomlaj awkan Martín	Great your hands, great your feet Martín
jac ame'al, jac awlic'wal Martín	this is your daughter, this is your son Martín
ay xatrlojdej,	oh I carried you in my arms,
ay xatrpajkej al día pjun	I carried you carefully on this
martes sant	holy Tuesday
ay ak'a, ay awkan Martín	oh your hands, oh your feet Martín
Ay Balber Martín, ay Chaler Martín	Oh Balber Martín, oh Chaler Martín
ak'a', ay awkan	oh your hands, oh your feet
ay ncattz'u'jan, ay ncatmujana	oh you drop rain, oh you give shade
ay chwach Adiosil, ay chwach Asant'il	oh before your Spirit, oh before your Soul
ay nctslob, ay ncatk'ajana	oh you move, oh you ring like bells

Ay mlay ak'a', ay mlay awkan	Oh I long for your hands, oh I long for your feet

Ay mlay ach'ipil, ay mlay amakam	Oh I long for your little finger, oh I long for your thumb
ay mlay rwa' Adiosil, ay mlay rwa' Asant'il	oh I long for your Spirit, oh I long for your Soul
ay xatnlojdej, ay mlay xatnpajkej	oh I carried you in my arms, oh I wanted to carry you carefully like a basin of water
ay xatnb'ixaj, ay xatnturij	oh I sang to you, oh I lullabied you
Ay mil orasion, ay mil conpesion ncattzubexa nactyecbexa Martín	Oh a thousand prayers, oh a thousand confessions to look at you to wait for you Martín
lomlaj ak'a, lomlaj awkan atrxin jyu', atrxin tk'aj	great your hands, great your feet you of the mountains, you of the plains
atrxin . . . , atrxin potrero atrxin leyan	you of the . . . , you of the pasture lands dear
ay Adiosil, ay Asant'il	oh your Spirit, oh your Soul
Lomlaj ak'a', lomlaj awkan don Juan don Diego don Martín	Great your hands, great your feet don Juan don Diego don Martín
lomlaj Ediosil, lomlaj Esant'il don Pascual Martín	great your Spirits, great your Souls don Pascual Martín
[7.72.78, item 366]	

The language of these examples of ritual speech and song paints an extensive metaphor that compares childbearing with the rebirth of Old Mam, the Lord of corn and rain. The quickening of a child in the womb and the rocking of a baby are like the sprouting of a seed of corn which points to the quickening of Old Mam and his emergence from the womb of the Santo Mundo. The vocabulary suggests something that moves slowly, like the rocking of a baby in the arms, but the fertility songs tell that the Santo Mundo can also move violently, rending and opening up to allow Old Mam to return from the underworld during the spring equinox rituals of *Semana Santa* (Holy Week). This suggests a parallel between the twentieth-century Tz'utujil rituals and the classic Maya genesis myth in which the womblike earth is represented as the carapace of a turtle that opens up to allow the emergence of the Maize God. This parallel is even more clearly expressed in the "Song of the Fruit" on page 144.

Rocking the Cradle of the Marias

By August of 1971 I had heard several prayer rituals that *ajcuns* performed for people who came to the *cofradía* for healing, protection, and other needs. Often there were a few other people in the *cofradía* with whom I could sit and listen, but I usually felt it was inappropriate and obtrusive to record these private, sacred events. So I decided to request a prayer ritual for myself from Chiviliu. I was single, and so I asked him for a prayer to find a husband. That evening I wrote in my journal:

> *Tuesday, September 1972*: I asked Chiviliu if he knew how to sing the old songs, and he said yes. I asked if he would sing for me someday, and he said he would. I asked what day, and he said "We'll see."
>
> He asked me what I was doing here, and I told him that I wanted to know about the customs and about the old music. I told him I used to be a nun but not anymore. I don't have a husband and want to ask Mam for one. He said "Oh, yes, you will get one, we'll ask Rilaj Mam to get you one and he will."
>
> He told me then that when [E. Michael] Mendelson was here, after his time was up, Chiviliu told him to stay longer.
>
> "But he kept saying to me, before he left, 'But AKlax, What am I going to do? I don't have a wife.' And so he asked for a *costumbre* with Mam to get one, the same *costumbre* I'll do for you," he said. "Now he's married," he said, "and has children. He lives in France."
>
> Later he asked me when I would come back to Atitlán. "Next year," I said, to which he replied "With your husband." (Earlier we talked about my thesis and he told me he has a copy of *Los Escándalos de Maximón*.)[19] (O'Brien 1972b)

Chiviliu had told me what to bring for my prayer: candles, white and yellow; a bottle of cane liquor called *guaro*; money as an offering to the Santo to be placed in the hands or the clothing of the statues. The candles were lighted and placed on the floor before the Santos. A few *cofrades* came and some others from out of town who were waiting for a prayer ritual of their own. *Guaro* was passed around in a single glass from which we each drank, leaving the last drops to pour on the ground for the Nawals. There was plenty of time to chat, drink, and smoke while preparations were made for the prayer with incense and candles.

For the prayer I was invited to stand in front of the altar, beside Chiviliu. The prayer invoked many Santos, principally Old Mam, sometimes addressing him as "don Pedro," a title with two meanings that express his dual nature as a trickster: he is the good St. Peter the Apostle, and also the cruel and ruthless Pedro de Alvarado, envoy of Cortés, whose memory remains in the oral tradition identified with the force of evil.[20]

After about half an hour of chanted prayer, Chiviliu directed me to the chest of the Marías, which he rocked with his hand like a cradle (*cusul*) or a hammock (*warbal*) as he began to sing the following song.

"Song of the Rocking Cradle"

"B'ix rxin Cusul, Warbal"	"Song of the Rocking Cradle"[21]
Nicolas Chiviliu Takaxoy, ajcun	
AUDIO FILE 1	

Ay nute' María yana yana yana	Oh my mother María dear dear dear
lalale lalali lalali	*lalale lalali lalali*
Ay María aleyana aleyana nute'a	Oh María mama mama my mother
a lala lala li	*a lala lala li*
	[*at this point the c'unc'un begins to play*]
lala lala lali	*lala lala lali*
lala lala lali aleyan	*lala lala lali* mama
Xpet stranger, aleyana	A foreigner came, mama
ay María María Sabela	oh María María Isabela
ay María Candelaria	oh María Candelaria
ay María Dio's	oh María Dio's
[*spoken:*] ay atSanto, ay Alanel	[*spoken:*] oh you are a Santo, oh Creator
ay Alc'walanel	oh Engenderer
Dio's JesuKrista.	Dio's JesuKrista.
[*singing resumes*]	[*singing resumes*]
lala lale lale lala	*lala lale lale lala*
ay yan, ay nute'	oh dear, oh my mother
ay cusul, ay warbal, cha'	oh cradle, oh hammock, as they say
ay sak, ay c'aslemal, ay raxwinkil.	oh light, oh life, oh wise judgment.
[8.71.4A, item 40/077]	

Some more semi-chanted prayers followed, after which he opened the cradlelike chest and took out an ancient-looking backstrap loom. He touched it to each of my shoulders, and presented it to me to kiss. Then he took out a square of dark red velvet cloth to which three small heads (which looked like cherubs, probably from broken statues) were sewn, representing the Marías. Below each was a small pouchlike bag that represented a womb. This cloth was placed over my head while prayers were said. He stopped often to explain to me what these items were, and then more prayers followed, the whole thing taking perhaps two hours.

On one of my return trips to Atitlán,[22] as I walked from the dock up into town I happened to meet Chiviliu, who greeted me warmly. Right away he asked me, "Did you find a husband?" I had been studying at UCLA, and in my visit during Holy Week I had gotten no chance to talk with him. Nine months had passed since I spoke to him last. Only when he asked me that question

The *cusul* or cradle of womens' blessings in the *cofradía* San Juan. Illustration by Peter Rothe.

did I make the connection between the prayer ritual and the fact that I had, indeed, found a husband. "Yes, I did," I replied with delight. Chiviliu smiled broadly and said, "*Y se llama Pedro?*" (And his name is Peter?") "Yes," I replied, "*se llama Pedro.*"

Dancing the Wind-Men and the Rain-Men

In 1972 the threat that the traditions of the Old Ways were being lost was already keenly felt. Not even a single marimba in Atitlán knew how to play the Recibos and was willing to play for the *cofradías*. I was also told that the local marimbas wanted more than the *cofradía* could pay, but the one from Totonicapán charged less. In my field journal for June 1972, I wrote down the following conversation with a *cofrade*:

A cofrade and I converse in cofradia San Juan. He is concerned that the marimba they have hired can't play the proper music—the Recibos—for the San Juan ritual:

COFRADE: Tomorrow night San Martín will dance with the Nabeysil.

[*The Marimba de Totonicapan plays a cumbia "Vas a bailar conmigo"*]

LINDA: "The Deer Dance?"

COFRADE: Yes. I am thinking, what music they will play? . . . But the band, well, they can't play the music for San Juan.

LINDA: Tell me about the "Dance of the Deer and the Jaguar."

COFRADE: The band doesn't know the "Dance of the Deer and the Jaguar." The tune for the jaguar is special. They don't know it. They are from Totonicapán. Here we have [a celebration for] San Juan, too [as they do in Totonicapán]. And there is a dance. But only with the right "*son,*" none other. So there is a "*son*" of San Juan, and there is a "*son*" of the jaguar, but only the bands from Atitlán know it. They don't know it because they are from Totonicapán.

Dance with me. (I dance.) (O'Brien 1972b)

To enter the *cofradía* San Juan is to step into the arboreal shadows of the fragrant Flowering Santo Mundo, a spiritual sanctuary, a visual riot of symbols that together create a supersensual shrine of the mystery of every kind of life. Your step is fragrant with the pine scent that rises from the crushed needles

The altar of the Santos and the boxes containing the sacred bundles in the *cofradía* San Juan. Illustration by Peter Rothe.

The *c'unc'un* in the *cofradía* San Juan. Illustration by Peter Rothe.

that cover the earthen floor, and above you a network of crisscrossed poles supports a multitude of hanging breast-shaped cacaos, huge phallic melons decorated with strips of shiny colored paper, coastal fruits and flowers, stuffed coatimundis,[23] and other small animals, all in a thickly hanging bed of green lakeside succulents. This place is the locus of power of the preeminent nature deity San Martín and his many emanations: the Mist-Men, the Rain-Men, the Wind-Men, the Makers of Thunder and Clouds, and the Spirits of fertility (the Marías, the Midwives, the Weavers, and the Childbearers). This *cofradía* houses them, secreted in two bundles that lie inside wooden chests, San Martín on the left and the Marías on the right side of the altar. Dimly lit with candles and perfumed with the sweet smoke of wax and copal incense, a statue of San Juan Bauktista, the Spirit-Lord of wild animals, stands in his central place on the altar with a flag and a book on which lies a small figure of a lamb that has been painted as a jaguar. The colorful flower-painted wooden chest of the Marías swings gently on ropes that encircle it and hang from the rafters. Several other statues and images of Santos on the altar stand surrounded by tinsel decorations and paper flowers and real flowers. As your eyes adjust to the dim light, you can discern a stack of deerskins with their bony white antlers wrapped with colored ribbons, and perhaps one of a mountain lion, on a corner table ready to be donned by the dancers who will transform themselves into the animals to honor the five directions of the Santo Mundo on the days of solstice and equinox in the "Dance of the Deer and the Jaguar." Underneath another table lies the *c'unc'un*, the large slit-log drum of Our Father the Sun.

In this *cofradía* the rain priest, the *nabeysil*, also known as the "First Mover" or "First Dancer,"[24] will summon the Spirit-Lords of winds when he puts on his rainmaking shirt to dance with the sacred Martín bundle, while the *alcalde* dances behind him with the bundle of the Marías. The rainmaker has a permanent commitment involving lifelong celibacy.

> This 'sil', this 'movement,' is exactly what the Nabeysil does as he cradles the Martín bundle in his hands and arms like a precious newborn child and rocks it back and forth to the male-female-sound of the 'kunkun', 'split log drum', while lightly dancing through the sealed-off room of the Cofradia San Juan. As the Nabeysil dances the world transforms into that which is beneficial for the Tz'utujil people who live within it. . . . Of all the costumbre in Atitlán this dancing of the Martín bundle is by far the most protected, private, and perhaps sacred. (Stanzione 2003, 283)

A passage from my field journal tells of my experience of this ritual in 1972:

> Friday I went to the cofradia San Juan and saw the deer dance, then danced with the *xo'* (alcalde's wife, i.e. Chiviliu's). She was so dignified and they (the *tixels*) all liked my skirt which is made of a *corte* from another town.
>
> After I arrived and was invited to sit down by the *juez*, Chiviliu came in. I gave him a cigar I brought from the states and he lit it, grabbed another from me and gave it to Mam, after which he lit the second one (his own) and gave it to Mam because the first one went out. About four times he changed cigars with Mam. (This Mam has a mask made by Nicolás Coche; it's not the old Mam in the cofradía Santa Cruz). Then I said to Chiviliu "Are you going to dance with me?" and he said "You dance with my wife." So I danced with her—a two-step, very nice—to the music of the marimba band from Totonicapan, mostly cumbias with an occasional '*son*', which the Atitecos like much better.
>
> After dancing I sat down with the ladies and the second tixel's husband asked me to dance. I said I was tired and so the second tixel asked me to dance with her. I said ok and she said "*Vamos a bailar bien nosotros*" ("We are going to dance really well") and we did! From 9:30 to 11:30 I danced every dance but one, with her or her husband. It was great fun. She wears shoes, and her husband dresses in *pantalón*.
>
> Later I sat down on the bench and Chiviliu and his wife returned after about an hour's absence, and the deer dance started and was performed about 11:00, and again at 11:30. Then at 12:00am they closed the windows and doors and the *nabeysil* and Chiviliu did the San Martín dance. They took something from the San Mar-

The *nabeysil* dances with the San Martín bundle on June 24th. Illustration by Peter Rothe.

tín trunk that looks like an old style home-woven shirt: white, long like a huipil. The nabeysil wore it and danced. Behind him danced Chiviliu with the lamb statue (about 12" long, on a book) holding it in a cloth. Chiviliu followed the nabeysil's dance steps, which were the same pattern as the deer dance, bowing in the four directions and always returning to the center, while the *c'unc'un* played. Then they went back to the trunk of the woman's blessings and got the cloth with the three Marias which the nabeysil carried, and the two crosses with colored ribbons which Chiviliu carried, and went through the dance again with the *c'unc'un*. After that (maybe ½ hour's worth of dancing) they put them back on the altar in the middle, and the party and dancing to marimba music went on. There was much drinking of cuxa and beer. I left with Joe Gross about 1:30am. (O'Brien 1972b)

Diego Chavez, *nabeysil*, 1972.

Rousing San Martín and the Spirit-Lords of Rain with Song

In August of 1972 the region of Lake Atitlán was suffering from a severe drought. It was well into the rainy season—but there was still no rain. The corn crop was suffering, and some of the black beans were lost. Everyone was talking about it and hoping for rain. Some said the Nawals were angry at the people for their forgetfulness of the old customs.

During that time I was invited to record the songs of Antonio Quieju Culan, an *ajcun* who had once served as *telinel*, the priest of Old Mam whose main task is to carry Mam during the rituals of the spring equinox. I was told he had a great repertoire of songs, which proved to be true. At that time I was renting a room in the home of don Miguel and doña Bertha de León. The daily talk was about the drought, so I was concerned that it *might* rain, because I would be carrying UCLA's Nagra recorder to Antonio's house. So before leaving I asked doña Bertha if she thought it would rain and whether I would need a raincoat. She looked out to the south and west and said, "No. When the clouds are behind the mountains at sunset it won't rain."

Nicolás Coche Sapalu led me through the impossibly confusing tangle of rocky paths to Antonio's house. The usual drinks went around, the candles were lit, and Antonio played and sang with great expressiveness and confidence in his unique style. He told me about his experiences as *telinel*, and after singing several courting songs or "Songs of the Road," asked me what I would like him to sing. I had already collected many courting songs and songs of Old Mam, because songmen always sang them first, so I asked for a Song of San Martín.

"Song of Martín" ("*B'ix rxin Martín*")

Antonio sang a chantlike litany[25] of the Spirit-Lords of nature, some of whom have been given the names of Franciscan saints and of the first Spanish missionaries who come to Atitlán.[26] As the song went on we began to hear the soft sound of raindrops on the thatch above. Gradually it became louder and louder until it was evident that a serious downpour was pounding on the roof. A smile lit up Antonio's face. Nicolás whispered to me excitedly, elbowing me in the ribs, "*Jap! Jap!*" ("Rain! Rain!"). After finishing the song Antonio said, "You see? 'The Song of Martín.' That's why it is raining." The effect on me of a song that coincided with a downpour during a drought was intense. Later I was glad to find the sound of the rain on the roof was quite audible on the recording.

The text of his song contains Spanish, Tz'utujil, and remnants of Latin. Except for the proper names, most of it is not clear enough to translate, and some of it is nonlexical filler. The melodic formula he uses strongly resembles a plainchant formula for singing litanies and psalms, specifically the tone of mode 6, the Hypolydian.[27] The style of singing also resembles that of Gregorian psalmody, in which an extended reciting tone is used for the greater part of the text, while the rhythm of the words dictates the rhythmic pulse. Antonio ornaments the beginnings and endings of lines with formulaic melismatic[28] melodies. Only occasionally is the pattern of the chordal guitar accompaniment interrupted by brief solo guitar passages. He ornaments some lines with a rapid upward glide at the mediant cadence, sounding like "yuh," an octave above the final pitch of *re*. All of this suggests it is a survival of a musical form from a much earlier time, and probably was part of the Latin liturgy taught in the colonial era by the Spanish franciscans.[29] This song appears on audio file 2, and I offer a partial translation.

"*B'ix rxin Martín*"
Antonio Quieju Culan, songman
AUDIO FILE 2

Diego Martín, Diego Martín
Pascual Españ Martín, Nicolás
   Martin

"Song of Martín"

Diego Martín, Diego Martín
Pascal [from] Spain Martín, Nicolás
   Martin

San Juan de Bauktis	St. John the Baptist
Santa Pastorcita, Santa nuestro Señor JesuKrist	St. Shepherdess, Saint our Lord JesuKrist
Santa Salvador en el Mund	Holy Savior in the World
Martín MaGalista,[30] María Sant Ángel	Martín Galisto, Maria Saint Ángel
Santa Juan, Pascualito	St. John, Little Pascal
Ndta' Santa, Dueña en el ciel, Dio's en el Mund	Our Holy Father, Lord in heaven, Dio's in the World
Dio's	Dio's
viene en el Mund	comes to the World
Santa San Pabl, Diego Pascual Martín	Holy St. Paul, Diego Pascual Martín
Reina Martín, Diego Martín	Queen Martín, Diego Martín
Galista Martín, Balver Martín	Galisto Martín, Balver Martín
Ángel Dio's en el Santa Mund	Ángel Dio's in the Santo Mundo
Ángel San Miguel Arkángal *osta suum*	Ángel St. Michael Archangel *osta suum*[31]
Ángel San Rangel la Guarda	Ángel St. Rangel Guardian
Ángel San Refeel	Ángel St. Rafael
Ángel San Martan San	Ángel St. Martin St.
Ángel Dio's Ángeli Mund	Ángel Dio's Ángel World
Don Pedro Maximón, el Dueñ en el Mund Sant	don Pedro Maximón, the Lord in the Santo Mundo
San Simona Pedrina, Apostol Ángel San Pedra	St. Simon Pedro, Apostle Ángel St. Peter
Apostol San Pablo	Apostle St. Paul
Apostol San Andres	Apostle St. Andrew
Apostol AnDolors, San Martín	Apostle Mary of Sorrows, St. Martin
. . . .	. . . .
Ángel esa por toda la vida	Ángel for all of life
. . . .	. . . .
Solo un Dio's Santa el ciel está y de allí Padre Eterno	Only one Holy Dio's is in heaven and also Eternal Father
Santa Pastorcita	St. Shepherdess
Santa Santa *amos* Kri Salvador	Holy Holy *amos* Christ Savior

Kristo kereador el Mundo del todo en el cielo	Christ creator of the World of all in heaven
Somos pecadores, sus hijos está aquí en el Mund	We are sinners, your children are here in the World
Meltiox, Santa	Thank you, Saint
Mano de este humano derecha frente al Dio's Santa	Hand of this right hand before Holy Dio's
A mo-a-e-i al Mund.	*A mo-a-e-i al* World.

[9.72.94, item 424]

Calling the Spirits of the Dead and the Drowned with Songs

The traditional songs may or may not be accompanied by the guitar; likewise, they can be guitar solos without singing. In the *cofradías* people often dance to the strumming of a solo guitar, but they also dance without either instrumental accompaniment or song. Like dancing, all the forms of music that come from the Nawals are the cause of movement and change in the ordinary lives of individuals. In one of the courting songs a young girl tells her mother:

Jun ala' xtzojbej prchi' b'ey	A boy talked by the edge of the street
pnic'aj rujay.	and inside the house.
Jun ala' xusil prchi'b'ey	A boy made the edge of the street move
pnic'aj rujay, nute'.	and the inside of the house, mama.
Xusil quije' esquina rxin wuchoch.	He made the four corners of my house move.
Ajni'la buen ala' xintzu' nen, nute'!	How good he looked to me, mama!

From "Song of the Young Girl" ("B'ix rxin k'jol") by songman Gaspar Yataz Ramirez
[7.22.28, item 170]

My translator told me, "This means that if the boy knows a certain prayer, he can make things move. Her parents won't scold him [for courting their daughter] because he has power, and he can make things move." In the "Song of the Fruit," the young man who participates in the initiation rituals says, "My song makes the road dance." While sometimes dancing to the music of the Nawals may seem to be simply an outlet in which a woman can express her sadness or sing her laments, this release of emotion is only the obvious side of what the lament is doing, since it is also the agent of change in her personal luck that only the Nawals can effect. A striking example of the power of the songs to move the spirits is a "Song of the Drowned."

The Atitecos' fear of drowning has been generated by long and bitter experience, because the gusty south wind called the *xocomil* that comes up suddenly at midday on Lake Atitlán is a peril to unwary fishermen in their canoes. Atitecos regard drowning as an unnatural death that cuts off life too abruptly, with the result that the restless spirits of the drowned are apt to walk about the town, disturbing people and sometimes causing *xbijnim* ("big fright," often referred to by the Spanish word *susto*). *Xbijnim* is feared as one of the causes of illness and distress, both mental and physical.[32] Consequently, Atitecos have considerable fear of the lake and of the "men under the water" who inhabit it, particularly during the midnight hours when the various kinds of Spirits-that-frighten (*Xbinel*) are free to walk the streets of town. The living who approach the lakeshore at any time, but especially at this hour, are in danger of meeting the drowned who will try to lure them to walk too close to the edge of the lake and fall in.

If the body of a drowned person is recovered and properly buried in the cemetery, the threat of the spirit wandering is considerably reduced. The bodies of the drowned are buried facedown to discourage this tendency. The relatives of one who has drowned are very anxious to recover the body and may spend considerable time and money to accomplish this, often soliciting the help of a diviner. Formerly a special cemetery near the church was reserved exclusively for the drowned, but at the time of this research a section of the general cemetery to the west of town had been designated for them.

The Spirit-Lord of the drowned is San Gregorio, whose statue in the church is said to be visited frequently by the drowned. Atitecos tell stories about people who have seen the ghostly forms making their way to the church, where they pass through the locked doors and honor San Gregorio by lighting candles near his statue. The Americans living next door at the mission sometimes noticed the mysterious and inexplicable flicker of candlelight inside the darkened and locked church at night. The statue of San Gregorio is depicted with a conch shell, which signifies his dominion over the lake and his lordship over the drowned, called the "men under the water," the *ajxe'ya*.[33]

The common belief is that there are habitations at the bottom of the lake where a *dueño* or man-in-charge (who may not be San Gregorio), hires the drowned person to work if he has a talent or skill useful to the community of those who live there. This employment is the hoped-for explanation for the disappearance of the body, since it is considered to be a somewhat better fate than being in the lake without finding work there. Informants agreed that the drowned, like the spirits of the dead, can do no physical harm. Some comments were:

> Sometimes I go walking at night. If you meet those who fell into the lake, the drowned, they don't do anything to you.

The dead can't do anything. They are asleep once and for all. . . . They don't do anything. "We won't do anything to you," that is what they say. And "Thank you, much obliged . . ." They don't do any harm. They just *dance*.

If the drowned are encountered in the streets of town during the "bad hours" of the night they are said to look like shadows of people when seen from a distance. They are distinguishable from the dead (*cnumki'*) by an unusual feature: the heads of the drowned are turned backwards on their shoulders. They are also shorter in stature than the dead. The fright that can be caused by looking into the eyes of a Spirit-that-frightens is less likely in the case of the drowned because there is less chance of meeting them face to face:

> They dance backwards, they can only look backwards. They don't look forward like people do. For example, if you meet them on the street, you can put your back against a wall. "Where is he?" they will ask.

Atitecos can defend themselves from the fright the drowned can cause by practicing one of the so-called "secrets." These are traditional formulas for action that are believed to be effective in specific situations. Among the secrets for protection against the drowned is the playing and singing of the *B'ix rxin Ajxe'ya*, the "Song of the Drowned." If one happens to be smoking tobacco as well as drinking *guaro* the protection is even more effective. The sound of their own songs and the pleasing smell of tobacco smoke appease the drowned, who respond by dancing and singing instead of causing fright. An excerpt from an interview with songman Gaspar Petzey Mendoza describes such a situation.

I had been asking Gaspar how he learned to play the guitar, and my questions, coming from the paradigm of western musicology, generated some revealing double entendres and led to the following story about the "Song of the Drowned."

> If you play the "Song of the Drowned," even if they are all around you in the street, and you know how to play it, you can save yourself. . . . The guitar will save you. It can save you.
>
> One time I went with an adventurous friend. Do you know him? His name is Nicolás. They also call him "Walking stick."
>
> Once he said to me, "Go now and get your guitar from your house."
>
> So I asked him, "What for?"
>
> "To play a while in the street. I'll buy you an *octavo* (an eighth of a liter of *guaro*)," he said.
>
> "Oh no, that's too much trouble. Why buy me an *octavo* if you just want me to play the guitar?"
>
> "Just go and get it, even if we only smoke a cigarette together."

"Ok," I said. Then I went to get my guitar and we went together and sat for a while in the street up the hill towards the cemetery. Then he went to get a *cuarto* [quarter of a liter] of *guaro*. We drank the whole *cuarto*, and when we finished drinking he said "Let's go walking."

The town lights went out[34] just then and I said "Let's go back to our houses."

"No, let's go for a walk," he said.

So we went down to Xechivoy, to doña Carmen's.[35] He had half a liter of *guaro* and two beers.

So I asked, "Where are we going?"

He answered, "We're going to go out and drink this in the street." Since I was still quite young, I went with him but I was hesitant and afraid. When he saw I was afraid he said, "Don't be afraid. You have a guitar, and if someone comes along, or we meet anyone, the guitar will defend us."

"Yes, but you need somebody with a little experience," I answered.

"No, that's not necessary," he said.

I wasn't very alert by then, but I noticed that the moon was bright, very bright, just like daylight.

"Play the way you do," he said to me, *clin clin clin* [sound of the guitar]. "Play the 'Song of the Face of the Earth.' Play the 'Song for Inside the House,' the 'Song of the Road,' the 'Song for the Side of the Road.'"

So what could I do? Then he said to me, "Let's sit down over there and have a drink."

So I said, "That's fine."

We sat down there and when I finished playing those songs the drowned came, and they were crying. We saw them from down near the *Administración*[36] and they looked just like people. They came walking down [from the cemetery], hundreds of them, just like all the people on All Saints' Day, they came.[37] So they were coming nearer and we were just looking. They looked like the *Baile de los Negritos*,[38] dancing. But they looked like shadows, like the shadows of people, nothing more. Close by they didn't look like people. They can speak and greet you.

Then Nicolás told me, "Don't give them your right hand, but your left. Don't give them your right hand."

"Alright," I said. But they gave him a chill from *susto* even before they got near us. He caught a chill and was vomiting. He almost didn't escape.

Then he said to me, "Sit on top of me right now."

At first I was so scared that I didn't know what to do, but then I came to my senses and knew what I had to do to defend myself. So I said to myself, "I am going to sit on that boy," and I sat on top of him.

He gave me the *octavo* of *guaro*, but he wouldn't let go of the guitar. The drowned tried—and almost succeeded—to make the guitar go mute. But I had an idea, I remembered a secret "word of wisdom," [a teaching of the Nawals] and

Gaspar Petzey Mendoza,
songman, 1966.

I grabbed the half *octavo* of *guaro* and poured it into the guitar. And the guitar began to sound again [and he let it go].

And the drowned began to cry. There I am, listening to them and they are crying and howling. And I am listening. They are so close now that I can't see them.
I can see that they walk back and forth in front of the stone fences, but only like
shadows, like people's shadows.

Then they said to me "Play our music! Your guitar, play it!" And they sang those
same songs. You could hear them, it went on and on. So when I began to play they
began to dance.

After a while they thanked me for the *guaro* and they left. Then I heard all the
stone fences around me come crashing down. But when we looked later not one
stone had really fallen. Then a large branch of a tree fell into the street. We saw it.
We heard it fall, it was a big one. But no! Afterwards we went to see the branch and
there wasn't a thing in the street. It was just its Spirit, nothing more.

So that is what they did. We saw it. And that's why I say I have tried it. You can defend yourself [with the guitar]. [7.72.1, item 103]

Only on two occasions was a songman willing to sing with words to the "Song of the Drowned" and the "Song of the Dead." They considered it inadvisable to call these spirits by singing their song without having a favor or request to ask of them. A songman explained:

The dead can shake the house in the night and throw stones and dirt, and that's why I don't want to sing it. If they hear that song, they'll come and ask "What do you want?" That is why it can't be sung whenever you please. When I want to talk to them, I talk, but only with the guitar. They will ask "What do you want?" If I sing it they will shake the house. So only with the guitar.

If I sing the words, they will come and shake your room and open your door at night and haunt you. They'll throw rocks and dirt and upset you. You will run out crying "Help! Help!" The other songs are alright to sing, like the "Song of the Road," and the "Song of the Young Girl," but not this one.

Old Mam, or "San Simón" as he is also called, is the Lord of the dead. Nicolás Coche Damian explained:

[NICOLAS:] If you ask a favor you have to go to San Simón first. He is the Lord of the dead. He is the chief, like a policeman. The police give commands. If they say to the people "Go!" they go. He is like a guardian. A guardian and an advocate too, like a lawyer. So he commands. "I will go with you," he says. He goes. Wherever you want, he can go. If you ask him to find a man [who stole from you] he has to find him. "Where is the man?" [you ask]. With a good kick [he says], "Up with you! Go and return the thing you stole!" He talks like this. For example if the dead have stolen something, and you say, "Please, show me where that thing is," San Simón has to show it to you. If a dead person takes a guitar and hides it [and you ask], "Who did it?" If a dead person has hidden it, San Simón comes and says, "Show me that guitar that you hid. If you don't want to I will give you my shoe [i.e., a kick]." That is why they sing, and the dead do nothing. Sometimes I walk at night and they don't do anything. . . .

When you take a cigar with you to the cemetery they don't dance. You just can hear from up there, "Thank you very much, thank you, my son, because you gave me some music." Just a thank you, since you smell like a cigar. For example right now, if one is listening to us he is smelling the cigar. "Oh, thank you very much, you are so kind," they say to you.

[LINDA:] They like it that you are smoking a cigar?

[NICOLÁS:] No, the guitar, when someone is playing, is like the smell of the cigar. They can smell it from the cemetery. It is like a dance. . . . They don't do anything. They just dance.

Four melodies in my collection were played for the "Song of the Drowned." The text below represents the single sung performance that I was able to record.

Songman José Sosof Coo' sang the "Song of the Drowned" as a dialogue between a father and the spirit of his drowned son. It is implied that the father has gone to an *ajmes* (a "man of the table" or diviner who uses objects spread out on a table to communicate with spirits) with a request to talk with his son.[39] An *ajmes* may also function as a counter-witchcraft specialist (Douglas 1969, 159–160). Here José takes the role of narrator of the story, inserting a few of his own comments in the dialogue and a large number of nonlexical syllables that in the text below are in italics. Before singing, José warned me that the Spirit-Lord of the drowned, San Gregorio, is close by (his statue is nearby in the church), and that I must contribute a candle or two before he sang, which I did. Explanations in bracketed italics are the comments of my translator, Diego Pop Ajuchan.

"B'ix rxin Ajxe'ya"   "Song of the Drowned"
José Sosof Coo', songman
AUDIO FILE 3

[JOSÉ:] "San Gregorio is right here. San Gregorio is close by here, in the church. The Spirit-Lord is nearby. You are the hostess here, you are in charge here. If we call them, what shall we give them? You must give a candle. That is the way they are: if we call them but we have no food for them, then what?

Nanani nanana nanani	*Nanani nanana nanani*
ya yan	*ya yan*
ya ya yan	*ya ya yan*
nanani ana nani a	*nanani ana nani a*
nanana nanana	*nanana nanana*
nanani nanana	*nanani nanana*
na nani nana nana nana	*na nani nana nana nana*

[*The father scolds the spirit of his son for having drowned, angrily calling him "mister." He should have taken a path farther from the shore:*]

"Ximbij chawa, a',
na ximbij chawa?
Xabant cuenta awi'
xatbata cawra, tale."
ay ya yana
ay ya yan

"I told you, son,
what did I tell you?
You should have watched yourself
you should have gone over this way, mister."
ay ya yana
ay ya yan

[*The son complains that his father has failed to have food to give him:*]

"Majo'n naban tzra.
Ximba c'a awq'uina
pr majun nway c'a."

"There's nothing to be done now.
I came here with you
but you don't have any tortillas."

[*José tells me the son needs food, i.e., a candle. I light some:*]

"Necesita jun candela."

"He needs a candle."

I ya yai na nana ni ay
anana ananana
ninana aya nanana na

I ya yai na nana ni ay
anana ananana
ninana aya nanana na

[*The son speaks to his father:*]

"Nengan q'uintej jlal."
Na nanana nanana nanani

"I would like to eat something."
Na nanana nanana nanani

[*José explains that his son is hungry, having traveled the road from the world under the water to meet us:*]

"Pc ja' xixinb'ey rbanic."

"Because he has been on the road."

Ni nani nanani
nanani na nanana na
a lala a lala
alala la alala
ni nani nani nana na
na nana yaya nana
nana nana
ya nana nana nana
nana nana nana
Ay a nani a

Ni nani nanani
nanani na nanana na

alala la alala
ni nani nani nana na
na nana yaya nana
nana nana
ya nana nana nana
nana nana nana
Ay a nani a

nanani a   *nanani a*
lalala lalala
lalala lala lalala   *lalala lala lalala*

[*The son tells how it is with the drowned:*]

"Okch'nal a'   "We are naked
jaw kbanic."   this is how we are."

[*The father cries because his son's body has not been recovered, and he fears his fate is ominous:*]

"Ay ximbij chawa, nc'ajol   "Oh I tell you, my son
quinok'a a', quinok'a, quinok'a   I am crying son, I am crying, I am crying
Atet nachcata awc'atzil ta'."   You are no good anymore."

Ay yan nananani a   *Oh mama, nananani a*

"Quinbij chawa a'   "I tell you son
quinbij chawa, quinbij chawa."   I tell you, I tell you."

ay yan, ay yan   *Oh mama, oh mama*
"Ay quinbij chawa, ale,   "Oh I ask you, dear,
pr bar c'a atc'owa' le?"   where are you?"

[*The son explains that there is no fire under the water and it is cold. The heads of the drowned are turned backwards. But because he has "big hands" he has found work there and is not condemned to idleness:*]

"Wawe' xina' tew.   "Here I feel cold.
Inbnak pya' camic,   I am in the lake now,
inajxe'ya' chic.   I am a 'man under the water' now.
Chwij quinc'ay wa'.   I look backwards now.

Pr si xwinkirw nuk'a'."   But my hands were born big."

Nanani nanana nanani a   *Nanani nanana nanani a*
lalala lalala   *lalala lalala*
lalale la lalala   *lalale la lalala*
lalali la lalali la   *lalali l lalali la*
lalali la lalala la   *lalali la lalala la*

lalala la lalala   *lalala la lalala*
lala lala lala   *lala lala lala*
lali lala   *lali lala*
lala lala lala lala   *lala lala lala lala*
lali lala lali lala   *lali lala lali lala*
lali lala lala   *lali lala lala*
[8.72.83, item 388]

Such is the power of the songs left by the Nawals at the beginning of time: they can rouse the spirits to action, almost like Aladdin could bring the genie from his lamp to accomplish his wishes.

CHAPTER THREE

The "Songs of the Road": Texts and Contexts

SONGMEN WERE UNANIMOUS IN REPORTING THAT their music came from the Nawals, and that they learned it not from any other person but from the Nawals, sometimes in their dreams. Stanzione gives fine expression to this idea:

> Mam is also Lord as "Ajawal Ch'ol Tz'iij," "Lord of Ordered Words," "Ajawal B'iix," "Lord of Song." It is Mam who prays and sings through his shamans, midwives, and singers as they let themselves be possessed by him and his inspiration. It is said that the prayer makers and singers are only vehicles through which Mam does his work with himself. Yes, there is Mam on his reed-mat throne and there is the shaman who kneels before him with his client. But at the moment of "ordering words," "Ch'ol Tz'iij," there is only 'One' and that 'One' is Mam; the ancestral being who speaks through the shaman to himself like the Nawales once did at Mam's creation, Nawales who are the very ancestors of the shaman enchanter. It is Mam who orders the world through prayer and song but he does it through the mouths of those who do his bidding here on the face of the earth. (2003, 52–53)

Tz'utujil traditional songs like the "*B'ix rxin Ruch'lew*," "*B'ix rxin Ojer*," or "*B'ix rxin Nawal*" ("Songs of the Face of the Earth," "Songs of Yesterday," or "Songs of the Nawals") are especially relevant in transitional times in the life of an individual and of the community, and have a dual function: one is the didactic function of teaching the deeper meaning of each situation and the correct conduct for it according to the Nawals, and the other is to engage the re-creative power of the Nawals during this specific event or point in time. For the individual, the songs guide the steps on life's road that lead to participation as a full member of the community through service in the *cofradía* system, finally leading to one's becoming a Nawal in the current cycle of time and in the afterlife. Liminal events in the human journey through life occasion the songs, such as courting; marriage with its joys and problems; grieving and lamenting; and times of individual need such as healing, protection while traveling on the road, or communicating with the spirits of the dead. Some songs, especially songs of courting and fertility, are about one's personal life and at the same time about the life cycle of the world of nature, and are commonly related to the agricultural calendar.

Although the songs clearly relate to specific contexts or occasions, they are also sometimes played and sung for pure enjoyment or for the visiting ethnomusicologist's tape recorder, in the hopes of preserving the tradition that is in danger of being lost. The songs I recorded were sung in private or semipublic rituals in the *cofradías*, and in the homes of songmen, except for the first session (described below), which took place in the office of the Catholic mission.

The first songman I met was Diego Cua Simaj. Diego was a neighbor of Juan Mendoza Lacan who was trained at the Summer Institute of Linguistics with Ramon Carlin. Juan was one of the group who met daily to work with Carlin on translations of liturgical and biblical texts. I was in Atitlán with an assignment to find Tz'utujil songs that could be used as a basis for developing music for the Mass in Tz'utujil. Everyone in this circle knew I was seeking songs in Tz'utujil, and that behind it was the authority of an assignment given by Father Carlin. Still my search was yielding no results. No one admitted that they remembered anyone singing in Tz'utujil. Nor could Ladino friends say they knew of Tz'utujil songs. After several weeks, and with obvious misgivings, Juan offered the information that one of his neighbors sang old "street songs" or "songs for the road" in Tz'utujil. He assured me, however, that it was probably not what I was looking for, and certainly not something I would want to hear. Later I understood the elements of fear that must have deterred him and the others: fear of the power of the songs to bring a spirit into the room, to enchant, or to bring us into contact with the unknown realms of the Santo Mundo. Also, these men had made a committment to leave behind everything in the Old Ways that was considered to be inconsistent with Catholic faith. Later, as I became aware of the strong and longstanding opposition to the religion of the *cofradías* by the Catequistas, the ultraconservative Catholic leadership who vehemently opposed the Old Ways, I began to understand his and others' hesitation.

So one November afternoon in 1966, Diego Cua Simaj arrived at the translation office accompanied by two friends who flanked him like bodyguards, all wearing Stetson hats, brims turned down and collars up, looking and acting like characters from a film noir. There is no doubt that they were "creeped out" by coming to the Catholic mission. No doubt either that the promise of payment helped them to overcome their fears.

Diego played twenty-one songs that afternoon, offering a title or a short explanation of the life situation that provided the context or motive of each song, such as: "For a widow who was left with a son and has no one to give food to her or him, and she went to the lakeside to do washing." Songmen often named a song by using such expanded titles or brief stories that identify the motive or context for which a song is played or sung. But outside of the performance situation of making a recording, the context in which a songman plays and sings dictates the content and the corresponding melody, and the listeners need no explanation, even without a sung text. A song for a favorable journey at a prayer ritual for protection while traveling on the road is understood without explanation to be a "Second Song of the Road."

At first Diego played but did not sing at all. When I asked about this, he sang two songs to nonlexical vocables like *"lala lala li,"* and finally three in Tz'utujil. One of the first things that impressed me as I studied the recordings was the number of songs Diego called "Songs of the Road." In that first session in November of 1966, fourteen of his twenty-one songs were called "Songs of the Road." In August of 1970, eight of his twelve songs were "Songs of the Road." They are the most numerous in my collection, including those called "Sad Song of the Road," which are songs of loss and separation, and "Songs of the Road of Rilaj Mam." Of the approximately 280 songs in my collection, 126 were called "Song of the Road." The following are some examples of expanded titles:

Song for opening the road

Of the young man, to court a girl

Of the young man and the girl, about insults and ridicule

The girl's answer

Of the girl who stays in her house

Of the girl who wants to marry

Of the girl who says goodbye to her mother

Of the young man who lost his luck

Of the unmarried man or the unmarried woman

Of the young man who goes to live in the compound of the girl's parents

Of the man who is thrown out of his wife's house

Of the woman whose husband left her, to call him back

Of the couple that fights and reconciles

Sad song of the road

Of the guitar, because a guitar is also called "Young girl"

Of the girl that says "I got you"

Song of the young man who courts a girl who has a split hand

Song about a woman who didn't let her daughter get married. At the age of 18 she died out of envy. The parents didn't like the girl and she died from sadness. There were two or three petitions from boys, and she died.

Song for the woman whose daughter died and her husband, too. She cried with her son in the hammock because there was nobody to give her food, and she went to wash her clothes in the lake. One son was all she had in the world. When the baby cried she made the sign of the cross under his hammock with pieces of pitch pine.

Song for a man who left his woman, and he wanted to reconcile with her playing the guitar in the form of a *son* but he couldn't. He wanted to go by himself but he was afraid, but with the guitar she would hear him outside.

Some "Songs of the Road" tell a familiar story in the form of dialogue and are known by titles such as "They Fought" *("Xqueti' Qui'")*, "Christobal," and "Nicolás and Francisca." The following is a general list of the songs in my collection based on titles and narratives explaining their context and contents:

"B'ix rxin B'ey": *"Songs of the Road"*

rxin b'ey najb'ey: first song of the road, the short one, for walking in the town

rxin b'ey rucab': second song of the road, the long one, for walking far, outside the town

rxin b'ey rox: third song of the road, songs of courting and fertility, including

  rxin c'jol: of the young man

  rxin k'poj: of the young girl

  rxin cotz'ej: of the flowers

  rxin skul: of the fruit

  rxin b'ey tristes: sad songs of the road

"*B'ix rxin Rilaj Mam*": songs of Rilaj Mam

"*B'ix rxin Martín*": songs of Martín

"*B'ix rxin cnumki'*": song of the dead

"*B'ix rxin ajxe'ya*": song of the drowned

"*B'ix rxin Ruch'lew*": song of the Face of the Earth

"*B'ix particular*": private songs for enjoyment

The Road in the Tz'utujil Maya World

The image of the road appears frequently in Mayan literature both before and after the Spanish contact. In ancient Maya myth and iconography the paths of the sun, the moon, the planets, and the spreading Milky Way are roads across the sky, figuring as prominent elements in the story of creation, just as Tz'utujil songs and prayers prominently feature the paths created by the cycle of the sun and the stars. The road as a trail of footprints is familiar in Mesoamerican iconography, as in the *Chilam Balam of Chumayel* from colonial Yucatan, which tells the story of counting and naming the twenty days of the lunar calendar or *uinal* by the footprints of the sun priest as he walked, intimately connecting time and movement in space (Sodi 1964, 28). Munro Edmonson (1986, 50) captures the road as a metaphor of time in a Maya riddle:

QUESTION: What is a man on a road?
ANSWER: Time.

Angela Keller has explored the concept of the road in Mayan language and thought. She notes that in ritual texts

> Maya scribes elegantly developed numerous metaphoric languages between roads
> and time, incorporating the allied concepts of life, obligation, and destiny. . . . All
> collected use examples converge on a ritual sense of *beh* [in Tz'utujil *b'ey*: road] as
> a spiritual thread of destiny and communication between realms. . . . from the Co-
> lonial period to the present *beh* has a relatively stable meaning, integrating life-
> cycle, temporal, and vocational meanings with the image of the physical road.
> (2009, 146)

In the origin myth of the Maya K'iche', the *Popol Vuh*, the road figures importantly several times, as when the Hero Twins are faced with a choice among four crossroads: the red, black, white, and yellow roads that come from the intercardinal directions to the center of the Face of the Earth. The roads are alive, and so Black Road speaks to them, saying: "Me! Take me, for I am the lord's road" (Christenson 2007a, 122). Later the twins plead with the gods for protection and for their posterity: "May there be true, lifegiving roads and pathways" (ibid., 206).

Recent ethnography documents the importance of the road as a metaphor for one's luck in life; it is a road that may be closed but can be opened. Contemporary shamans in Yucatan are said to "open the path" when laying out the cardinal locations on their altar (Freidel et al. 1993, 130). In Atitlán, the road is opened by prayers and songs, especially the "Songs of the Road."

For traditionalists in Santiago Atitlán the road also has deep historical and formative significance, since from before the Spanish contact the Tz'utujils have been merchants or *ajb'eyom* ("men of the road"), whose proximity to and ownership of the fertile coastal lands of the Pacific piedmont connected them to an important Mesoamerican trade route. The lands they once controlled allowed them to trade coastal products in the highlands, such as the highly valued cacao, rubber, dyes, salt, feathers, and produce.

The Tz'utujil world is one in which from its beginning the Nawals' ways of living in the world, the Old Ways, ensured the harmonious interaction between men and nature. If today the people walk in the roads of the ancestors, replicate their lives and faithfully offer sacrifice to them, the deified ancestors will provide for the needs of the people, who will themselves become Nawals both here and hereafter. Speaking of his experience in Atitlán in the 1990s, Alberto Vallejo Reyna recognized the dual levels on which the concept of the road functions in Tz'utujil cosmology:

> These roads refer to a double metaphor, on the one hand the geographic spaces of a territory, mythical spaces full of legend, where nature acquires a sacred significance in each one of its attributes: the lake, the mountains, the volcanos, the rocks, the trees, the springs; they are sacred places, places of entry, of transition, of passage; *pal b'al* they call them in Tz'utuhil, since their principal characteristic is that they put one in touch with the other space, the other territory, the other world, the sacred, the world of the Nawals, of the Santos, the Lords of things, the Spirits of the ancestors and the Maya gods.
>
> On the other hand, the road also refers to the process by which a person can become a Nawal, that is to say, can come to acquire the knowledge of the ancestors, in order to pass through these sacred places and establish communication with the other world, the other space, the other time, that of the Nawals. (Vallejo Reyna 2001, 20–21)[1]

The road, then, is a metaphor that on one level signifies the space of the physical world and all its sacred foci on the Face of the Earth, and at the same time, with typical dualism, the road is the process of becoming a Nawal by which one's life unfolds by following faithfully in the path the Nawals laid out. The songs say, in effect, "Act like this, and so become a Nawal." Songman Diego Cua Simaj tells us that this personal path is also dependent on one's luck:

> Each one has his luck that you give,
> Lamp of St. Bernardine
> you in the sky, you in glory..

If one is faithful to the old customs, but one's "luck is lost," one cries out to the gods and the Nawals:

> Why? Why, Dio's? Why *Mund*?
> Why, Father, Mother, *JesuKrista*?

So the road means the path of life, your journey, your destiny, and your fortune. Songman José Sosof Coo' answered my question about the road this way:

> "Of the Road." It means where we are going to get to with him or her. Also, whether we die or live. We don't know when or where we will disappear. And there is nothing we can do about it. Dio's helps us. Some day there are no tortillas to eat tomorrow. But today there are tortillas. So we call it "Of the Road," we call it "For the Road" and that is why.[2]

Its dual meanings, the ordinary road and the road of the Nawals, are not explicitly distinguished because they are commonly understood as integrated. After a well-accomplished ritual during Holy Week, Nicolás Chiviliu Takaxoy remarked on his satisfaction to the head man of the *cofradía*, "This is the real road!" On another occasion, songman Gaspar Petzey Mendoza told me, "As soon as I got my guitar, I took it into the road."

Old Mam, the Guardian of the Road, Creates Music and Dance

The experience of living in Atitlán was one of a growing awareness of the variety and number of invisible spiritual powers the Tz'utujils sense around them. Spirits both benign and frightening inhabit places, objects, and animals. Some Spirits-that-frighten hide themselves from human gaze in the daylight hours but walk or dance in the streets of town in the darkness, like the dead and the drowned. Some inhabit the bodies of dogs, or disguise themselves to look like dogs and other animals. One Atiteco offered this question as an explanation: "Haven't you noticed there are more dogs in town at night than during the day?" Walking at night with the Tz'utujils rarely felt casual; there was always a sense of the possibility of fright. After some time in this atmosphere, I came to appreciate that, because spirits are constantly around, it is natural to interpret the rattling of your door at night as the response of the spirits that are being called by their song that is being sung inside your house, or to recognize the footsteps you hear circle your house and disappear into the darkness as a visit from Old Mam, the guardian and watchman of Atitlán.

It is hard to imagine a deity more complex and stimulating to the imagi-
nation than Old Mam.[3] His powers are many and very great and he is the em-
bodiment of duality; as the songs say, he is "smart man, stupid man; good boy,
bad boy." His personality is sometimes proud and lordly, sometimes formidable
and even despicable, and his personal manners and behaviour are often offensive, outrageous, and obscene. Two versions of the story of Old Mam's creation
were told to me. Gaspar Culan Yataz told me:

> I don't know for certain if it was before the conquest or after the conquest, that
> is, before the Spanish came or after the Spanish came, but according to what my
> grandfather's father and my grandfather told me, they knew more or less how it
> was. They said that in times past there were twelve men here in Santiago.

Juan Sisay told me that he heard these stories from his mother and that they
are very ancient. The Songs about Old Mam are unambiguous on the topic of
his ancientness:

nawala nawala ala'	ancient ancient boy
nawala nawala acha	ancient ancient man
nawal ala'	ancient boy
nawal acha	ancient man
nawal cap	ancient cape
nawal botín	ancient boots
nawal svetr	ancient sweater
nawal cos	ancient thing
nawal tzebena	ancient laughing one
roca cho nawal	rock since antiquity

Juan began his story by naming Old Mam "Judas," saying, "This explanation of
Judas comes from the beginning."

Later Juan will call Old Mam "Judas Iscariot," the apostle who betrayed Jesus, of which an effigy is made by the Ladinos during Holy Week, then hanged
and burned. According to Gaspar's account, this name for Mam originated
with "the Spaniards" as an attempt to discredit the cult, but is not part of
Mam's real identity. The name Judas is used in the town by members of Christian churches who would like to abolish the traditionalist cult, and by outsiders who are ignorant of the tradition or who regard the ways of the indigenous
people as ridiculous, or associate it with witchcraft. Claiming that Rilaj Mam's
real identity is that of Judas Iscariot identifies him with the devil and the em-
bodiment of evil. Even outside of this story, Juan's position relative to the Old
Ways was conflicted.

"Maximón" is the name by which Old Mam is known most widely outside of Atitlán. This name is predominantly used by nontraditionalists, by the Ladinos of Atitlán, in tourist guides, and in speech or literature derisive of the cult. Some say it means "Mr. Simon" (*Ma-Ximon*) and refers to Mam's dual good/evil identity as the benevolent Simon Peter the apostle, and the malicious conquistador Pedro de Alvarado. Stanzione translates Maximón as "the the knotted one, the bound-up one," because he is tied together with ropes, and is hanged from a tree during Holy Week, suggesting that he takes on the role of a captive who is sacrificed in these rituals (2003, 54). However, Gaspar says that this hanging is a recent introduction, part of the attempt to identify him with Judas, who hanged himself. The point seems important to the understanding of Mam as the Maya Maize God, who dies by dismemberment and is born again on Wednesday of Holy Week; death by hanging two days later would be a second death and rebirth, and indeed may be a recent addition in an attempt to identify him with Judas.

Gaspar continued:

> Before, the town of Santiago was very small. All around were mountains; where the hospital[4] is it was just the mountains, full of trees. All those places where there are chalets now were woods. Well, those twelve men, according to what I was told, were very clever, very smart, we could say they were like prophets or wise men. Their well known business was to take fish from this lake and take them to Pank'an, the old name of Antigua. This means that there was a small town there before Antigua existed, no? As I understand it, it was like Santiago where the Spaniards came later and did harm to the people. So the twelve travelled as usual to Antigua. They took fish; they caught fish here in Santiago and still alive, put them into a box. In a moment they were in Antigua. That is how they tell the story. When they arrived there they sold fish in the market of Antigua, in the market of Pank'an, as we call it.[5] Fresh fish, still alive. They left here walking and they say that they only took— some say—two or three steps. But what I was told is that they took no more than an hour.[6] The old road goes down here between two volcanoes. That road didn't exist before, so they just got to Antigua. Yes, the road was shorter before, so they got to Antigua with fish that were still alive.

These twelve heroes had special powers. Juan said:

> Anything they wanted to do, they could do. They would ask for rain, and they could themselves make rain.

The names of of these heroes and their wives, the Nawals, indicate their specialties. Some of them are:

MaPla's Sojuel (Francisco Rattle Man)

Andrés Pacay (Andrés Pacaya [the edible blossom of the date palm tree])

AXwan Polín (Juan Roasted Beans)

Marcos Rujuch' (Mark Prophet)

MaxCop Coo' (MaxCop Noseplugs, Earrings, or Small Parrot)

Jacobo Coo' Chenen (Jacobo Plow)

Esteban Ajcot (Stephen Eagle Man)

AXwan Quieju (Juan Deer)

AXep Sapalu (José Closed)

AXwan Poklaj (Juan Came from Dust)

AXwan Batzin (Juan Monkey)

YaMriy Quemo' (Maria Thread-Beater)

YaMriy Ch'ejquem (Maria Warp-Beams)

YaMriy Tzitzu' (Maria Small Thread-Beater)

YaMriy Q'uir (Maria Small Heddles)

YaMriy Skaj (Maria Large Heddles)

YaMriy Canon (Maria Serpent or Yellow)

YaXep Bitz'bal (Josepha Spindle)[7]

The discovery of the infidelity of the wife of one of them is told in both accounts. Gaspar says:

> And one time the twelve were going on the road. But they had no knowledge that their wives might do something, like have relations with other men.
>
> After some time the youngest of the twelve said to one of the others, "Listen!"
>
> "What happened?" said the other one.
>
> "Don't you know what is happening?"
>
> "No, I don't know what is happening. Tell me."
>
> "Well, your woman is going with another man."
>
> "Really?"
>
> "Yes, it is true. I just found out myself."
>
> "It's not possible!"
>
> "It's possible!"
>
> "Well what should we do to find out?"
>
> "Well I think we have to find a way to restrain the women so they don't keep on doing this." It was a problem for the men, especially for the youngest of the twelve,

the man who had problems with his woman. Then they went on walking while they carried on this conversation.

"What shall we do? If my woman is doing this thing, you must help me. Because it cannot be that the women continue in this way with us and with other men. For then, what good will we have with the women?" They began to discuss it.

"Very well, we can do something to prohibit the women so they will not have contact with other men, because husbands do not like this," so they say. This was the conversation they had.

Well, they came back from their journey to Antigua and they began to discuss it again. "What are we going to do? One raised his hand, we could say. "Ok, men, you are thinking if we have the ability to do something, let's do it. What shall we do? We have to have something, a soldier, like a policeman or a watchman who will take care, stay here in charge of all the women so they won't keep on doing wrong things."

So they got together for a meeting about these problems. And they said, "Let us build a figure. We are going to give it life. We know we can give it power, and we will give this figure power so it will become a man who will take care of the women."

But since the men, the way they tell it, the men of before were very clever, so they say, and they knew secret things—maybe you could say magic, because there are many people now who know something about magic, it is true.

So they began to look in the mountains and the wild places that used to be all around the town before. And they went, three or two to one place, and three or two to another, and they began to talk to the trees. They spoke to the first tree they found. They greeted it and asked it if it was willing to be in charge of this work. But the tree didn't respond at all. The twelve kept on doing this, but they didn't find anything.

"What are we going to do? The trees don't answer us."

They began to discuss it again, and the youngest of the twelve said, "It's not possible that there is not one tree that will respond to us." So he went all alone in that direction, east of town, as the old men used to say. He went looking for trees, almost to the top of the volcano. Here we must remember that the town was quite small. Finally he got to the place we call *Xe'cjol Ak'om* ("The Place or Root of Medicine"). Maybe it was a place where people used to find medicinal herbs, it's close by, over there by the big hill, northeast of town. And there he found a tree, a big one, so they say. He spoke to it and asked if it would do the job.

And they say the tree answered: "It's fine, with much pleasure! I am here to carry out this task."

And so he went back happy to his companions: "I have found a man who wants to do the job."

So they began to discuss it. "Very well, get your tools and bring food and we will find out if it is true."

This time the first among them spoke to the tree, to test the word of the youngest, asking if it were willing to carry out this task, and the tree answered "Very well," accepting. So they cut it down. According to the way they tell it, with each blow of the axe some words were heard. A blow, some words; who knows how many blows fell on the tree? And then the words stopped.

José Sosof Coo' sings the answer for us:

Corent tz'ku' sc'an rxin nc'ajol	Forty chisel-blows withstood my young man.
Utz c'ara', acha, nawal ala'.	It is good, man, ancient boy.

Juan added some details about this part:

So then he answered that he was in agreement. The figure spoke with them. But all this was done in the clouds, it was raining hard, and with all the customs that they do, candles, incense on all sides. This is what they did. Of a particular tree they made him, the pito tree. It is called *tz'ajte'l* in Tz'utujil. Do you know this tree? It has a small flower and some vines. It is a big tree.

So he answered that he needed a marimba, a song. But what song? So a marimba was brought, but he was not happy with the music of the marimba. So he danced and danced in a particular way so that finally, with his own ideas, just as when you want to make up a song from an idea in your mind, he made up music.

"So this song is what I want. This song, that song," said the doll. So he showed them: "Do it this way, do it that way," and finally the music came out. Maximón created it by dancing.

So the elders said they would send for the gourd marimba and the best player among the old men who played and sang songs well. He sang in Tz'utujil, inventing in his mind the words and the music that came from his mouth. So the doll was in agreement, and he said: "The first, the second, and each *son* is different."

So the figure appeared and stood up at last. When the gourd marimba showed up he was finally ready. The association of Mam with music is referred to in the songs as well:

Xpe' MaPla's Reanta	Francisco Reanda came
xuya' jtoch' mchat tzra ala'	he gave a machete blow to the boy
xpr mix palejtz acha.	but the man did not stand up.
Bar xpalejwa'?	Where did he stand up?
Chuxhe' k'ojom, acha	Together with the music, the man
chuxhe' k'ojom, acha.	together with the music, the man.

Old Mam. Illustration by
Peter Rothe.

Gaspar continues:

So they cut it and got a big piece and they started to make the figure by means of
words. They knew how many words they had to use in order to make the figure
come out perfectly, to realize their work. What did it matter to them if a figure with
a pretty face came out, or with an ugly face, or with nice feet, or with pretty arms?
To them this was not important. The thing was to make the figure according to
the *words*, according to the *words*, the prayers that they said. So they made it, blow
by blow, and the words kept on. And when they finished a figure emerged that was
rough and not so well shaped. Then they spoke to it. They stood the figure up and
they leaned it against the trunk of the tree.

Then they began to talk: "What name shall we give it? First of all we have to give
it a name in order to talk to it and see if it accepts." So they started to discuss what
name to choose. Finally the name came out. "We are going to call it 'Mam.'" And

Mam they call it. Maximón is a modern name. It's only fifteen to twenty years ago that the name Maximón appeared.

So when they had agreed on the name "Mam" they began to talk to him. "Mam, do you want to do this work, be like a policeman, take care of the women so they don't have that kind of contact with the men, to protect the women?" As they tell it, that piece of wood began to stir and twitch until its throat began to move—and, how would I know? This is what they say. So they said, "It is good, it accepts. It was going to speak to us, but we are not so perfect [we did not know how to carve it perfectly] and this is the best we could do. The thing is that it has to *do something*."

At this point I asked Gaspar, "What did it mean when they said, 'This is the best we could do'? That they hadn't made it very well?"

GASPAR: That they couldn't make him equal to themselves.
LINDA: So it was their fault that he couldn't talk, because they didn't know how to carve the throat well?
GASPAR: No, it doesn't mean that. I think maybe it means the power.

Juan, who was personally and politically concerned with the conflict between traditional beliefs and Catholic teachings, tells this part differently:

So they raised up figure of Judas. . . . To make a figure they had to arrive at an agreement. But [they wanted] a figure who would work for the Tz'utujils through their prayers and their powers. So they made a figure of Judas. It is Judas Iscariot that he represents, that they play with in Holy Week.[8]

He had to show what he was by moving and speaking. They did a strange thing. They wanted to make a figure, but they wanted it to speak. But it couldn't speak because it was made of wood. Another one of them said, "He has to speak." . . . At last the figure moved. But it is a doll, because it is not made like a Catholic statue; it is only a piece of wood in the head, the mask, and another piece is here in the arms, and another here in the legs. So they made a figure that is tied up with strings. They worked with all the materials, speaking, talking, tell him and explaining to him what he must do, how he must appear. They were working, but through prayers, this one talking, that one talking, everyone helping and crying that he must be formed into a statue, well-made and formal, that would be Christian and help us here on the earth.

So the doll appeared, but it was a doll with a lie, because he was tied together with string. So another one said, "This cannot be. We will dress him." They were embarrassed because he could not talk. Something was done then, secretly in some way, and they put clothes on him, and finally he spoke.

So they left him closed up in a room so no one would know, because it was a historic thing, a secret thing. He had to do a miracle.

Gaspar continues:

So they brought it. They put it in one of their houses and left it there. But what did this man do when he was all fixed up? They left him in the house while they went to do business in Pank'an, in Antigua. That's how they tell it. Well, when he found any woman who was talking with some man, they say he just scared her; and if a woman did nothing more than look behind her, she stayed that way, looking backwards with her head twisted backwards. That is, the back of her head was in front, and the front in back. That is what Mam did. According to what they say, he walked around, but not by day; only by night. But in the day, only in spirit. And he not only did things to the women. This was the worst thing, the worst fault of this Mam, no? If he found a female animal mating with a male animal, he grabbed its neck and did the same as to the women. So when they came back here to Santiago from the journey to Antigua, they say, they got very angry. "Well, what happened to this man," they said, "What happened? This was not the work of that we gave this man. Oh, no! This we will not permit. We are not going to allow it. We are going to do something to him."

They spoke again to the figure: "Why have you done such a thing?" The figure didn't answer. "Very well, if you won't answer we are going to cut off your head, your neck. We're going to cut off your arms, and we are going to cut off your legs."

And so they cut off his legs, they cut off his arms, they cut off his head. They turned his head around, just as he had done. They gave the figure the same punishment.

This was done by the same men who made Mam. So they said to him "You are not to do the same things as before. We want you only to take care of the women. Frighten them, nothing more, so they will not continue to have contact with the men."

"Very well," he replied. Since then all the kinds of crimes that Mam did before stopped. What he did, I heard about ten years ago, that his good work still went on. In actuality, I believe that not as much any more. Because what he did to a woman who talked, only talked, with another man was only to make her crazy. The woman went crazy and that was all. The sign that she talked with another man and Mam talked to her. This is how Mam was.

This is more or less all about the origin of Mam. If you want, we can go on to how this Maximón appeared, the other one. According to the story told by my great grandfather's father, he saw some of this. He saw some of this. The old Maximón was a small, rough-hewn statue made with an axe; but he was already altogether worn away, almost sawdust. If one should go up and touch him, he was ready to turn into dust.

So my great grandfather went to work. All the land around Chicacao used to belong to Santiago, and also the land by San Lucas. So they went to work, and were there for a while, and when they came back there was no more statue. They found—my grandfather worked as an *ajcun*, we could say. . . . My grandfather told me they found something very small, it was already powder, tied up in a cloth, a big cloth. That was the real, real Mam.

Now, since they weren't doing anything more with Mam, and he was disappearing, this don Chiviliu, and some other men he told me about, I think with this Diego Pacay, they constructed another figure in place of the real, real one. The one we have now is not the real, real one. The head they made was found here by the priest who came, and I believe he took it to France. That is the head that is now in France.[9] The head of Mam that they constructed.

LINDA: What happened to the real Mam?
GASPAR: My grandfather told me that his grandfather and also his father said that he was dust. And my grandfather saw this cloth with the handful of dust of Mam in it. The head, the legs, the arms didn't last. That's all. And instead of this they rebuilt another Mam, these men.
LINDA: And the cloth with the real Mam?
GASPAR: It disappeared. Where would it be? It disappeared. Who would have it? And they made another. Since they had left the first figure with legs and arms cut short, and with the head cut, too, they did the same, since they knew something about the real real Mam. They did the same thing with the other figure they made. That's why the Mam today doesn't have whole legs, whole arms, a whole head; everything is cut in pieces. When the fiesta comes they tie it up with string and it comes out well.
LINDA: Does that mean that because it's not the real figure, Maximón doesn't have much power?
GASPAR: I suppose so. Because as the old folks say, and even my grandfather told me, the figure from before could stand up, could do something. They even ridiculed those men who did what they did with the Mam that isn't the real one, the Maximón. But the real name is Mam. They made up the name Maximón about twenty or twenty-five years ago. If I ask an old man "Who is Maximón?" He won't understand. Ask him about Mam, and he will understand. I think the people who came here named him Maximón, the Spanish.
They say that Maximón represents the Judas figure that they make during Holy Week when they burn him. But they call Mam Judas also, and he really is not Judas. Formerly they didn't tie up Maximón [by the neck during Holy Week]. But by making him Judas who hanged himself because he betrayed his master and hanged himself from a tree, they started to do the same to Mam, but before they didn't do that to him.

The story is clearly not a historical account in linear time, but an account that occurs in the context of the ever-recurring events in the cycle of time. Although it takes place "in the beginning," the storytellers say the Nawals wanted to make something that would be "a Christian." The leader of those first Nawals, APla's Sojuel, is said to have lived in Atitlán within the lifetime of Juan's mother, and to have died not more than sixty years before. The house in which he is said to have lived still stood when these stories were told, and was used during the rituals of Old Mam during Holy Week. His return is expected at any moment—or he is always here—it is only a matter of recognizing him.

Today the figure of Old Mam is not a solid wooden carving, but rather a jointed puppetlike construction about three feet high, whose short arms and legs are said to be joined to his body with twine and rings. Mam is elaborately dressed in the purple and white striped embroidered pants and tie-dyed shirt of a Tz'utujil man, but also wears a suit jacket, many silk scarves, a big stetson hat, and very shiny oxford-style shoes or cowboy boots. His head, which may contain a gourd covered with cloth, is backwards, and is partly hidden by an imposing carved wooden mask that faces forward with the face of a man smoking a cigar. The mask and body are said to be made from the pito tree, the tz'ajte'l of the origin story, which stands just to the east of town. This tree had a large cavity in its side as if it had been struck by lightning, but out of which the original image was said to be hewn.[10] The tree is often the site of prayer rituals, evidenced by flat stones arranged like an altar before it that are always covered with candle drippings.

At the time of this research the four-foot figure of Mam was kept in the rafters of the *cofradía* Santa Cruz.[11] During Holy Week, near the time of the vernal equinox, the mannequin is disassembled and Mam's special priest, the *telinel* or "bearer," must know how to reconstruct it by using knowledge he has personally received from the Nawals in his dreams. His ability to do this is a test and a proof of his fitness to serve as *telinel* for a year. He carries out his task while the marimba and the guitar play the "Recibos of Mam," just as at the beginning of the present creation. If the *telinel* has not been faithful to the requirement of celibacy, it is said that Old Mam will become so heavy that he will not be able to lift or carry him. Mam's first creators gave him the power to stand up and to speak, and so he is made to stand up in the *cofradía* on the night of Tuesday of Holy Week, the Tuesday before Easter.

The "Songs of Mam" ("*B'ix rxin Mam*")

The *cofradía* where Mam is kept is often visited by prayer-makers who come with their clients to pray for a cure. Many stories tell of Mam's guardianship of women, and how he disguises himself as an animal or a young woman in an attempt to catch transgressors. He frightens a woman by making noises, shaking the bed or the house, or by suddenly appearing wearing his big hat and smoking a cigar. Songmen Gaspar Yataz Ramirez and José Sosof Coo' described the character of Old Mam in their songs. Gaspar's song recalls the original creation story but also the contemporary figure of Old Mam, who, dressed in his showy clothes, makes things move in the night; enjoys traveling to faraway places; takes the shapes of animals, insects, and garbage ("one hundred percent of the forms"); and does all of this while overseeing everything.

"B'ix rxin Mam"
Gaspar Yataz Ramirez, songman

"Song of Mam"

li lali lali lali lali la
li lali lali lali la
Ay cabeza ala', cabeza acha
ay ajbotin, ay ajchalec, ay
    ajchalin
ay ajtob'aya acha.

li lali lali lali lali la
li lali lali lali la
Oh smart boy, smart man
oh boots man, oh jacket man, oh fringed
    silk scarf man
oh towel man.

Nktz'itz', nkb'i'b'a' chwach

chwach nawal nik'a'
chwach nawal rkan.
lila lila lila li
Nktz'itz',
    nkb'i'b'a'
mil legua,
    cien legua, acha
nca'ya pr mujal jun aj'il
    jun ajma'c.

He makes scary noises at night, he makes
    things shake in the day
with his ancient hands
with his ancient feet.
lila lila lila li
He makes scary noises at night, he makes
    things move in the day
a thousand leagues away
    a hundred leagues away, the man
he can see in the shadows the criminal
    and the sinner.

li lali lali lali lali
li lali lali lali lali
Ay cabeza ala', cabeza acha
ay real ala', ay real acha.
Aregoya ruk'a', aregoya
    rkan
ay ral che', ay ral c'am.

li lali lali lali lali
li lali lali lali lali
Oh smart boy, smart man
oh royal boy, oh royal man.
Metal rings are his hands, metal rings are
    his feet
oh son of the tree, oh son of string.

li lali lali lali lali
Xwinkira, xtz'ijcara, ala',
    acha, "C'ojol Xe Ak'om" ala'

li lali lali lali lali
He was engendered, he sprouted, the boy,
    the man, in "the Medicine Place" the boy

Ay ajrojyu', ay ajrotk'aj

ay ral mutzmul, ay ral sajbach
majo'n nk'iwa ruk'a'
    majo'n nk'iwa rkan, ala', acha,
    ali.

li lali lali lali lali
li lali lali lali lali
Ay ala' acha ali ali ali
ay ral u'k, ay ral po't,
    ral sel, ay ral morado.

Nktz'itz'a
    nkb'i'b'a'
    chwach ruk'a', chwach rkan
ay ral ak'a', ay ral k'ejku'm
ay nc'astana, ay nmeyjana
ay ajguarda, ay ajront
    ay comisario, ay caporal
    ay mayordomo.
Nk'ach ej, nk'awchij
    nawal eskina
    nawal Palb'al
    nawal Chacalb'al
cxin kadta', cxin kate'
xin Diego, xin Juan Martín, Diego
    Martín
    Canon Martín, Coban Martín
    Chajul Martín.
Ay sel Martín, ay sel ali
ay ral YaMri'y Quemo'
ay ral YaMri'y Ch'ejquem
ay ral YaMri'y Tzitzu'
ay ral YaMri'y Q'uir
ay ral YaMri'y Skaj
ay ral YaMr'iy Canon, YaXwan
    Canon
ay ala', ay acha
ay ral Diego, ay ral Juan

Oh man of the mountain, man of the
    plain
oh son of drizzle, oh son of hail
no one has hands like his
    no one has feet like his, the boy, the man,
    dear.[12]

li lali lali lali lali
li lali lali lali lali
Oh boy man mama mama mama
oh son of the skirt, oh son of the blouse
    oh son of silk, oh son of purple stripes.[13]

He makes scary noises at night
    he makes things shake in the day
    with his hands, with his feet
oh son of the night, oh son of darkness
oh he enjoys himself, oh he has fun
oh he is the guardian, he is the watchman
    oh the comissary, oh the foreman
    oh the steward.
He blesses the house, he crosses to the
    ancient four corners[14]
    the ancient Resting Place [of Ángeles][15]
    the ancient Alighting Place [of Ángeles]
of our fathers, of our mothers
of Diego, of Juan Martín, of Diego
    Martín
    Canon Martín, Coban Martín
    Chajul Martín.
Oh silk Martín, oh silk girl
oh son of María Thread-Beater
oh son of María Warp-Beam
oh son of María Small Thread-Beater
oh son of María Small Heddles
oh son of María Large Heddles
oh son of María Canon, Juana
    Canon
oh boy, oh man
oh son of Diego, oh son of Juan

ay rcayibal, ay rtzub'al	oh image, oh figure made by
MaPla's Sojuel	Francisco Sojuel
ay rcayib'al, ay rtzub'al	oh image, oh figure made by
MaWtor Pablo	Salvador Pablo
ay rcayib'al, ay rtzub'al	oh image, oh figure made by
Andres Pacay, Salvador Pacay	Andres Pacay, Salvador Pacay
Juan Polin, Diego Polin	Juan Polin, Diego Polin
ay rcayib'al, ay rtzub'al	oh image, oh figure made by
Marcos Rujuch', Diego Rujuch'	Marcos Rujuch', Diego Rujuch'
ay rcayib'al, ay rtzub'al	oh image, oh figure made by
Max Cop Coo'	Tomás Cop Coo'
ay cabeza ala', ay cabeza acha	oh smart boy, oh smart man
real ala', real acha	royal boy, royal man
ay nktz'itz'a, nkb'ib'a'	oh he makes noise, he makes things shake
ay chwach ak'a', ay chwach k'ejk'um	oh with his hands, oh in the darkness
jn ji'k'a, jn po'la	he is out of breath, he is panting
chwach ik', chwach	in the north wind, in the winds from the
xlajyu'.	mountains.
Noca jo'k	He makes himself an ass wipe[16]
noca k'ayis	he makes himself garbage
joca tz'e'	he makes himself a dog
noca chcop	he makes himself an animal
noca jan	he makes himself a fly
noca snic	he makes himself an ant
ciento por ciento rjelba.	one hundred percent of the shapes.
Nc'astana, nmeyjana Honduras	He enjoys himself, he has fun in Honduras
Nicaragua, Mexico, Costa Rica	Nicaragua, Mexico, Costa Rica
nc'astana, nmeyjana	he enjoys himself, he has fun
nc'astana Francia	he enjoys himself in France
nc'astana, nmeyjana Estados Unidos	he enjoys himself, he has fun in the United States
Guatemala	Guatemala
nb'e k'ejlo'na, nb'echanb'ena	he greets them, he talks to them
ay nawal ala', nawal acha	oh ancient boy, ancient man
ay cabeza acha, biana acha.	oh smart man, short man.[17]
[7.72.28, item 169]	

José Sosof Coo's "Song of Mam" begins with the acknowledgment that Old Mam is present with us in the place where José is singing the old songs. He also thinks that the spirits of the dead might be present, so he addresses a woman who may be his mother or his wife, as "dear, my mother, mama," terms that are used for both. The second to eighth lines may be paraphrased: "I ask you, dear, why did you go and die? But at least I do have a brother who is still alive. Now we are singing the old songs." In the next lines he wonders if his mother or wife is here, dancing as the dead dance because they are here, having been called by the song. He decides instead to sing about Old Mam, whom he calls "ALucha," a name for Mam derived from "Pedro," for which "Perucho" is a nickname, shortened to "Lucha"[18] and preceded by "A," the title for "Mister." It is interesting that Gaspar sang about how Mam makes things move, but José reminds Mam that the songs he is singing *make Mam move*.

Interpretations have been added to help in the understanding of the text, in brackets.

"B'ix rxin Mam"   "Song of Mam"
José Sosof Coo', songman

                                                     [*Mam is nearby*:]
Ay ay ALuch   Ay, ay ALuch

                                                     [*José addresses his deceased mother or wife*:]
Quinbi c'ara chawa aleyana   I say to you, dear
quinbi 'ca chawa, nute'   I say to you, mama
quinbij c'a chawa aleyan   I say to you, dear

                                                     [*Why did you die and leave us*?]
Na ximban c'a nute'?   What did you do, my mother?

                                                     [*I at least still have a brother*:]
Pr c'o jun nuchak', yan   But there is my brother, dear
pr c'o jun nuchak' nute'.   there is my brother, mama.

                                                     [*We are singing the old songs*:]
An caw nkaban yan.   This is what we do, dear.

                                                     [*The spirits have come because they heard
                                                         the song*]
Mix nat cwina nat xjowa, yan   Maybe you will dance, dear
mix nat cwina nat xjowa, nute'   maybe you will dance, my mother
pr xec'o chic cnam ki'a.   because the dead are here now.
Cxin antiguo jawra.   This is one of the old songs.
Majo'n nksobsaj, yan   Now there's no way to dance, dear
majon nksobsaj, nute'   now there's no way to dance, my mother.

<table>
<tr><td></td><td>[*José decides to sing about Old Mam:*]</td></tr>
<tr><td>jo' c'a ruq'uin ALucha</td><td>Let's go with ALucha</td></tr>
<tr><td>jo'c'a ruq'uin nidta'.</td><td>let's go with my papa.</td></tr>
<tr><td>Pina pina ala', pina pina achi</td><td>Fine fine boy, fine fine man</td></tr>
</table>

[*He imitates the sounds of the guitar for Mam,
the Lord of Music:*]

Tina tina acha, rina rina acha	Strum strum man, thrum thrum man
tina tina ala', tuna tuna ala'	plink plink boy, plunk plunk boy
yana yana ala', yana yana acha	handsome handsome boy, handsome handsome man
tzana tzana ala', tzana tzana acha	strum strum boy, strum strum man
cpota acha, nwal acha	dressed in guard's uniform, the ancient man
tzebena acha, turina acha	the laughing man, the spellcasting man
bonit scaw pa'lwa acha	beautiful pants wears the standing-up man
tzin acha, tzin acha.	the scary man, scary man.

[*The song makes Old Mam move:*]

Wawe' nkasliwa'.	Here we make you move.
[7.72.86, item 401]	

The First and Second "Songs of the Road"

Examples of the "First Song of the Road" in my collection are few, and are exclusively guitar solos. Tz'utujil songmen say that the "Songs of the Road" are for "opening the road" by clearing it of obstacles and dangers to the traveler. The first song is called "the short one of the road, to walk around in town, with your mother or your friends, for example." The "Second Song of the Road" is similar to the first in that it accompanies walking, but it is for a considerably longer trip. Diego Cua Simaj explains:

> The "Second Song of the Road" is of the big road. It's for going outside the town, for example when one goes to the coast for work or for business. It asks for protection from misfortunes that could happen on the road. When you go to work on the coast, the song says "In the name of Dio's, may everything go well and may we come back again." Or also, when one goes to business, that is the "Second Song of the Road."

When this research was being done it was not unusual to see a young man walking in the street carrying a guitar, sometimes with others, one or two of whom carried guitars. At one time songmen accompanied travelers on longer journeys, perhaps to the coast, just as they do during Holy Week rituals. As time passed it would have become more and more unnecessary to walk, as travel by bus, truck, and car gradually became more possible. Songmen often told me the songs were "from before," meaning both that they were old and that they were disappearing.

On one occasion, Sacristan Juan Ajchomajay Set explained that a person undertaking a journey could ask for a "Song of the Road" (which he called a "*son*") in the *cofradía*, with an *ajcun*'s prayer and offerings of candles to protect him from something unfortunate that might happen on the road and to open the road for him, "as they say."

> LINDA [referring to a "Song of the Road" he just played]: Is this the one for gathering fruit on the coast?
>
> JUAN [understanding I mean a merchant's journey]: Yes, it's the same one. . . . For example, if you want to have a ritual with an *ajcun*, you go with your candle so he can do a prayer for you. This "*son*" is played when the prayer is for opening the road, and for protection from anything that might happen to you on the road. It can open the road, as they say.

The "Third Song of the Road": Songs of Courtship and Fertility

The songs called "Third Song of the Road" are songs of sexuality and fertility of both humans and the world of nature. This group includes many more titles than the first and second "Songs of the Road." These songs are both descriptive and prescriptive of customary behavior, verbal exchanges, attitudes, and reactions, imparting the mindset of the Nawals to young men and women in the process of courting and marrying, separating, reconciling, or lamenting that one has passed through the marriageable years without finding a mate.

One context of the "Third Song of the Road" is the streets of town where courting activities begin. Parallel to this personal level of the journey of courting and marrying, the metaphor of the road points to the arduous ritual journey that young men who have contracted marriage will make to the ancestral lands on the Pacific coast as part of the re-creation and fertility rites of Holy Week. They will take the same three-day journey as the first ancestors did, leaving on the Wednesday before Palm Sunday, to gather and bring back the sacrificial fruit.

"Songs of the Young Man" ("*B'ix rxin C'jol*")

Until perhaps the mid-1950s it was customary for a young man who wanted to find a girl to marry, or who wanted a certain girl, to wait for her in the road close to the place on the lake shore where girls went to fill their water jars (*tinajas*). Mendelson (1957) describes these customs before 1956, and both his informants and mine in 1966–1975 referred to them as "from old times." A young man would go there with his guitar and some of his friends to attract a girl or declare his desire for her to become his wife by singing her a "Song of the Young Man" for courting, usually referred to simply as "*B'ix rxin C'jol*" ("Song of the Young Man"). The guitar and the song were for "opening the road": the road to her heart equally as much as the road of their destiny.

The young man would grab hold of the cloth of the blouse or shawl of the chosen girl and keep her from walking away by holding on to it, and she would begin to yell at him, insulting and belittling him, and demanding that he let her go. Mendelson describes this

> particularly abrupt form of courtship practiced in Atitlán: the quasi-volcanic eruption of shouting taking place as soon as a boy seizes a girl's zute fringe on some street corner or some spot on the lake where she has come to fetch water. (1957, 50)

Mendelson also tells the following about courting customs:

> In the old days, according to Cristobal, the young man waited with a mangash [a kind of woolen coat] over his head, caught the girl at the door of her house and spoke with her for half an hour. After a few such encounters the girl usually managed to see the boy's face. No special voice was used by the boy and there was no special costumbre about the water pot, except that after several refusals, a boy might sometimes strike the jar down in a rage, in which case the affair was at an end. This was still done when he was young, some forty years ago.
>
> If the girl is held too forcefully she runs away, letting the water pot fall and break. Her mother goes to the boy's house to get the pot's price and the incident is closed. Sebastian agreed with Cristobal that this was not customary, at any rate as a deliberate sena (symbolic act) as the boy would not agree to pay the price. I heard of no case of a pot breaking during my stay. (ibid., 392, footnote 6)

A different explanation was given to me for the breaking of the water jar. If the girl is interested and wants to move the process of courting forward, she allows her *tinaja* to fall in feigned anger so that the young man will go to her mother to pay for it. That provides the mother an opportunity to tell him to stop courting her daughter, or to let him know that he is acceptable and may continue courting her if she will have him. The breaking of the water jar is also reminiscent of the ancient Maya goddess Ix Chel, who is depicted in the Dresden Codex pouring water from a gourd onto the earth. Again it connects with the broken water jar of the grandmother of the Hero Twins in the *Popol Vuh*. The broken water jar pouring out its contents is a metaphor for fertility, signifying the end of the grandmother's order and the new order in which the girl becomes a woman. In the same account, the broken water jar recalls the saliva that falls from the gourd/head of One Hunahpu into the hand of the maiden called Lady Blood, causing her to conceive the Hero Twins.

Another context for courting was the road just outside the compound in which the girl lived. The young man would go in the same way with friends, playing and singing to her and asking her to come out as he declared his desire for her in his song.

In the following "Song of the Young Man" Diego sings in the words of a young man to the girl he is courting. His argument is that she must be his wife in spite of his poverty, which accounts for the shabbiness of his clothing, about which he expects she will gossip with her friends. His desire is stronger than any criticism or objection, implying that he is able and determined and thus desirable for a husband. They are, after all, the same: their bodies are made of the same corn dough, of the same water, and of the same earth, and she is the daughter of the ancestral Marías, the wives of the original twelve Nawals. In the song Diego describes in detail the duties of a wife who follows the Old Ways. He told me about the song with a suggestion of its power over the girl: "This one is for the young man who wants to talk with a girl, and with this song he can get her to marry him. It is very old." In it Diego refers to the custom of breaking the water jar.

"Song of the Young Man"[19] ("*B'ix rxin C'jol*")
Diego Cua Simaj, songman

You are going to be my wife and my woman
I want you very much, and am very glad to see you
I want you with my soul and my heart
I am poor, I am young, and that is why you don't want me
I have no possessions.
You are a young woman, a pretty girl and
I am waiting in the street for you to come
and I want you.

I wait for you all night
and you have to come to my house
tomorrow or the day after.

Even though you don't want me
I am waiting for you in your street.
When you break your water jar
I will pay for it.

Even if your mother says, "don't go out"
I am always waiting for you.
Even though you stay shut up in the house
you have to come, my love, to my house and to my home
to prepare my food and my tortillas.
Don't stay shut up in the house.
Keep coming to the shore of the lake
and I will always wait for you.
You will come, my girl
and you will meet my parents.
You will come, my girl!
Oh, your door! Oh, the corner of the street!
You are a young woman, of blood and body
covered with a blouse and skirt. I desire you with love.
Look at me; see that I am poor, that I am dirty
without a good hat, without a good shirt
without good sandals.
You will talk about me with your friends
but, my love, you have to come to my house
because you are the daughter of sin
because we have the same blood and the same body.
You are a young woman
we are made of the same corn dough and the same water
we are of the same earth.
You are the daughter of María Chote, María Coca,
María Talena, María Colorado,
María Santa Elena, María Pojpol.
Since I have the pleasure of courting you, young woman,
you have to give me the pleasure tomorrow or the day after.
You have to come to my house.
Even if you say "I don't want to," yes,
you have to want me.

Even if your papa insults me
even if he has sticks and stones to beat me
I'm not afraid of him.
You have to take care of my house
you have to bring me water
you have to wash my clothes
and give me water to wash my feet and hands.
You have to work in my house.
[11.66.V, item 8]

In another song, Diego began with two lines that are also found in other "Songs of the Young Man." These are some of the stock phrases that occur in "Songs of the Road" that a songman can use to provide structure and rhythm, and to allow himself time to mentally construct his improvised lines. These particular opening couplets, so common in ritual speech, seem to be survivals from the times when the Tz'utujils were traveling merchants who complained to the Nawals that they are poor, lost, and fallen in the dust of the road. As well as "orphan," the word *meba'* can mean "slave" or "vagabond," both of which complain of loss of luck and of a good road in life.

Anen en powr, anen enmeba' I am poor, I am a wandering orphan
anen entzaknak, anen enpoknak I am lost, I am fallen in the dust of the road

These lines are also an example of the pedagogical function of the "*B'ix rxin Nawal.*" The song puts words of the Nawals into the young man's mouth, words that he will come to understand more fully when he participates in the initiation rites of Holy Week. When he is young and still looking for a wife, the apparent meaning is both a complaint and a profession of his limited means. Later the deeper meaning of these words will emerge, as he suffers and sacrifices during initiation rites, sweating with hurting feet on the steep road, carrying heavy baskets of fruit in his backrack, and so assuming the burden of the Old Ways that are always in danger of being disregarded, orphaned, and fallen in the dust. The songs he will hear on this journey tell him that without them the continuation of the divine economy between men and Nawals would disintegrate.

A common theme found in many courting songs is that the young man gives items of clothing to the girl, and she to him. The style and colors of traditional Tz'utujil dress have special significance and identify the wearer as an Atiteco, and the gift of clothing also signifies the bond between a man and a woman, each of whom weaves the more intimate garment (pants and skirt) for the other. Traditionally, men's pants and women's blouses are woven and embroidered by women, using cotton thread to form purple and white striped cloth and embroidering the colorful bird motifs and other old symbolic designs with silk thread on both garments. The purple color is an Atiteco identity marker, stemming from the proximity to coastal lands that gave access to the indigo dye obtained from certain molluscs, once a valuable trade commodity.[20] In the past the dye was an indicator of affluence. In one song the young woman says to the young man courting her: "Your pants have big red stripes [red dye is easier to obtain]. It's because you're so lazy."[21] The traditional red and black striped shirt and the woman's red and black corte, both with complex designs in traditional tie-dyed patterns, are woven on a large foot loom operated by men and provided by the husband.

It is usually the girl who tells her mother that she has been given a necklace, comb, or ring, or the more personal skirt, shawl, blouse, or multicolored headband that married women wear wrapped around their heads. The headband, decorated with the colors that recall the rainbow-serpent headband of Ix Chebel Yax depicted in the Dresden Codex as the ancient Maya goddess of women's arts, is an especially significant marker of a girl's arrival into full womanhood.[22] When she tells her mother she actually has used the comb or the shawl, or worn the blouse, the headband, or skirt, it means she has already become his woman.

Later in the rituals of Holy Week, clothing will play a significant role. The young wives-to-be place a small woman's shawl on the shoulders of their young men before their journey to the coast. Leaving dressed as boys who are still under their mother's shawl of protection, the young men will return (like Parsifal) from this journey as men, independent of their mothers, and use the shawl to help carry their burden.

Expressing another common theme, the singer teaches the young man that he should expect to receive harsh insults and ridicule from the girl. He says, "You see me as if I were a stinking dead horse, or like a dead chicken that reeks in the road." He personally experiences the insults that are part of the testing he will undergo as he becomes a full member of Tz'utujil society as a married man, and will remember when he hears these insults again in the fertility songs of the initiation rites, the "Song of the Flowers" and "Song of the Fruit." Songman Juan Petzey Takaxoy explains the metaphor:

> This is a song for cutting fruit on the coast, for the road. It is not exactly a song about the fruit of Holy Week. It is a song that has insults by a young woman and the young man who sings it repeats what the woman has said about him in her insults. Later the young man goes on the long trip on the road, saying what the woman had said to him earlier.

In most songs he describes the insults he expects from her or that she has already delivered. Songmen told me that if the girl doesn't insult him, it means she is not interested in him at all. Here he responds saying that, like her, he was in the womb for twelve months—"twelve stars"—referring to the twelve lunar months of twenty days that make up a year of the Maya lunar calendar. During Holy Week the old year dies, and the new year comes to birth through the rituals in which he will later take part. In the following song by Diego Cua Simaj, the young man assures the girl that he wants a peaceful life together without fights, using "wise words" that he will receive as counsel in the fertility rituals later on. This idea of "no fights" comes up often when, in their prayers, prayer-makers assure the Nawals that the petitioners have not been fighting, and so not fighting must be taken as part of the wisdom of the Nawals. He promises that he will not lead her by a bad road to live and work on a *finca* or coastal plantation.[23] Then he describes the daily routine of a married woman, which she will follow when he comes to his house to live with him.[24] In the following song, the young man declares his desire for her, and he promises to buy her clothing.

"B'ix rxin C'jol Triste"
Diego Cua Simaj, songman
AUDIO FILE 4

"Sad Song of the Young Man"

Anen enpowr, anen enmeba'
anen entzaknak, anen enpoknak.

I am poor, I am a wandering orphan
I am lost, I am fallen in the dust of the road.[25]

Catnwajo' k'poj, catnwajo' pb'ey
catnwajo' yan, catnwajo' nute'.

I want you girl, I want you in the street
I want you dear, I want you mama.

Dolors achi' yan,
   Dolors achi' nute'
Dolors achi' nxeñora, mlay,
   abakil
   axumlil.
Catnwajo' yana
catnwajo' nute', catnwajo' nk'poj

You have the face of the Virgin Dolores dear
   the face of Dolores mama
the face of Dolores lady,[26] I long for
   your bones,
   your body.
I want you dear
I want you mama, I want you my girl

catnwajo' nxeñora.
Mlay ixok u'k, mlay ixok po't,

mlay axk'ab, mlay ach'ejquem.

I want you my lady.
I long for your woman's skirt, I long for your
   woman's blouse,
I long for your headband, I long for the warp
   beams of your loom.

Catnwajo' yana, catnwajo' nute'	I want you dear, I want you mama
pr mpjul mpsiwan ta catruwc'aj wa'	I won't lead you on a bad road
mptak pinc mptak asient ta	I won't take you to the fincas
catnwajo' yan.	I want you dear.
Con tranquilamente	In peace
skach'ac ta kaway awq'in	we will earn our living together
con tranquilamente	in peace
mlay xkabanta buen awq'in'.	I want us to live well together.
Kes mquita jmej xtkaban ch'oj	I want us never to fight with each other
awq'in	
yana yana	dear dear
kes mquita jmej xtkaban ch'oj	I want us never to have problems
awq'in	
nute'	mama
kes mquita jmej xtkaban ayewal	I want there never to be hatred
pkochoch.	in our house.
Nkocanoja con tranquilament.	We will be peaceful.
Quimewajota nen yan, mlay lk'oj,	I want to buy dear, I long to buy your
tziak, kbestida.	clothes, your dress.
Kas atet k'poj	But you girl
na chquila cnatzu' pb'eya?	how do you see me in the road?
Kas atet xtan, k'najni' nchuwlaj	You lady, see me as if I were a stinking dead
quiej	horse
cnatzu' nchuwlaj ac' cnatzu'	or a dead chicken that reeks
pb'ey.	in the road.
Pr mtaban ta cara', yan	But don't think that way, dear
pr anen en ala'.	because I am a boy.
En q'uitsin en	They took me out of the womb to grow as a
c'walan	child
chcbeljuj iq', y ceblejuj ch'umil.	for twelve moons, and for twelve stars.
Cuest yaril, poknal enrq'itsin nute'.	It is hard to need, it is hard that they made
	me to be born of my mother.
Chatet chanen yana.	It is the same for you and for me dear.
Mjunam ta ruq'in jun chcop	It's not the same as for an animal
xc'je'b jun sman, qui'e' sman	that spends a week, two weeks
prusoc	in its nest

pre xq'uitsixa jun sman,
   qui'e' sman
   pruchoch
prusoc, pruc'alibal.
Pr anen yan, cbeljuj iq'
cblejuj ch'umil xinralaj,
   xinrc'walaj nute'.

they make it stay a week, two weeks

   in its home
in its nest, in its place.
But I dear, twelve moons
twelve stars I waited to be born, for them
   to make me the child of my mother.

Mlay ach'ejquem
mlay asakaj
mlay aq'uir, mlay
   awejkabal
mlay apop, quinwajo' c'anen yan.
Mlay a metz', mlay nk'.
   awach.

I long for the warp beams of your loom
I long for your large heddles
I long for your small heddles, I long for your
   beaters
I long for your mat, I long for them all dear.
I long for your eyebrows, I long for your
   eyes.

Mlay awxquin, mlay rkan awey
mlay abestid, mlay awuk

I long for your ears, I long for your teeth
I long for your dress, I long for your skirt

mlay apo't, mlay axk'ap.
   axk'ap.
Pr catn nyarij yan, ncatb'ey c'a
ncatc'astanana chwach b'ey
chwach klo'.

I long for your blouse, I long for your
   headband.
For I want you dear, when you walk
I can even feel when you go by in the road
where your steps are taking you.

Jara' quinwajo yana
prc xin powr, prc xen meba'
prc xen tzaknak, prc xen poknak.

That is what I want dear
for I am poor, I am an orphan
for I am lost, I am fallen in the dust of
   the road.

Prc Dio's, bar xtuc'amwa' ndta',
   nute'?
Prc xe powr ek tet
pc xe powr ek mama'

But Dio's, where will my mother and father
   get their tortillas?
For our grandmothers are poor
for our grandfathers are poor

e'ulew, e' poklaj chic
prc anen yan, en quiy en
   que mam.

they are earth, they are already dust
and I dear, came from my
   grandparents.

Nb'ixan cbeljuj iq', em b'ixan
   cbeljuj ch'umil

I have sung under twelve moons, I have sung
   under twelve stars

chwach chak'a', chwach
    k'ejkum.

in the face of the darkness, in the face of the
    night.

Anen yan
nak tzra c'a nute' mtcnawajo?
Ktzij k'ara'? enchuwlaj pi'k?

Me dear,
why then do you not want me?
It is true, dear? Do you see me now as if I were
    a corn husk, an ass wipe?

Enchuwlaj pamaj cnatzucana
    camic?

Or like excrement now?

Catnwajo' yan, catnwajo'
    nute'
Mlay xktekajta p wochoch, nac'ol
    nulak
ac'ol nbas.

I want you dear, I want you
    mama
I long for you to come to my house, gather
    my dishes
pick up my cups.

Nctel lajpono rxin ak'a, nach'ej
    achi'
xtch'ajtaja achi
    nacoj acpe'.

You will rise early and wash your
    mouth
after washing your mouth
    you will roast your coffee.

Xcojtoja' acpe', nawc'aj atz'o p
    mulines
xtimloj ta atz'o p mulines natzak,
    yan.

When the coffee is roasted, you take your
    corn to the mill
and when you return you will make tortillas,
    dear.

Xt c'chojcama a k'or, xt tzaktaj
    cana' away
n catba, nac'ol cana aca ncatba',
    yana.
Namos cana pk awuchoch
nac'ol cana alak, abas

When the tortillas are done, you put away
    your grinding stone
and you go, and then you go,
    dear.
You sweep your house
gather your dishes, your cups

c'despues yan, ncatba chiya'
wnac'ma' camej uxmej aya'.
Cx cat mlay ta ncatba pcaib'ala

then dear, you go to the lake
and you bring water two or three times.
When you return you want to go to the
    market

xtabna'ta alok'oj yan, xtabna ta
    alok'oj nute'.

to buy your things dear, to buy your things
    mama.

Ktzij yan, nya in chuwlaj quiej?	Is it true dear, that I am like a dead horse?
Ktizj nute', nya in chuwlaj aq'?	Is it true mama, that I am like a dead chicken?
Ktzij Dolors, n ya in chuwlaj?	Is it true Dolores, that you can't stand how I smell?
Ktzij yan, ktziju nute'?	Is it true dear, is it true mama?
Nmt saktaja nchwil	Very bad is my odor
nmt saktaja nc'yil.	very bad is my filth.
Catnwajo' yan a	I want you dear
catnwajo' nute'.	I want you mama.
Mlay yan, mlay nute'	I long for you dear, I long for you mama
prc nbakil, nxumlil	with my bones, with my veins
ncuerp, nsangr	with my body, with my blood
quic' nyarina awin yana	it is the blood that wants you dear
quic' nyarina awxin nute'.	it is the blood that wants you mama.
[8.71.10, item 78]	

"Songs of the Young Girl" ("*B'ix rxin K'poj*")

Young girls are instructed by the words of the songs in the appropriate responses to the experience of being courted by a boy. In some of the "Songs of the Young Girl" she addresses her mother or her parents and tells them what the young man has said to her. The following joyful expression of her pleasure in having received and accepted the gift of necklaces, one for her neck and one for her fingers, was among the many songs sung by José Sosof Coo'. The beads for her neck are a personal ornament, and the beads for her fingers remind her that she is now on the road of the ancestral Marías: some statues of the Santos in the church and the *cofradías* have strings of rosary beads hanging from their fingers. The Tz'utujil vision of the world is once again like a double exposure, in which the girl's gesture to receive the beads on her fingers is superimposed upon the profile of the Santos holding their beads, the Marías, who established the women's customs and who from the beginning have guided them by means of the teachings and counsels contained in the songs.

The nonlexical lines "*chana chana ni, chana chana na*" evoke the help of Old Mam, who is the lord of music and of fertility, whose attention is drawn by the simulation of the sound of strumming the guitar.

"B'ix rxin K'pok"

"Song of the Young Girl Who Says
Goodbye to Her Mother" [27]

José Sosof Coo', songman
AUDIO FILE 5

Chula, chula yan, quinbij c'a chawa	Pretty, pretty mama, I tell you
chana chana ni chana chana na	*chana chana ni chana chana na*
Quinbij c'a chawa	I tell you
yana yan ayana ya yayan	*yana yan ayana ya yayan*
La li lalali la li lalali la li lalali la li lalala	*La li lalali la li lalali la li lalali la li lalala*
Lalali ludidu dududu di dididi dai	*Lalali ludidu dududu di dididi dai*
Ale, quinbij, quinbij *chana na*	Mama, I tell you, I tell you *chana na*
"Quinya' c'a jun chlaj ak'o'p chakul	"I give you a necklace for your neck
quinya' c'a jun chlaj ak'o'p chawa ak'a."	I give you a necklace for your hand."
ayana ya yan ayana ya yan	*ayana ya yan ayana ya yan*
a ya ya yan a ya yan yana	*a ya ya yan a ya yan yana*
di dadada dai	*di dadada dai*
[7.72.82, item 387]	

Like this song and the following song, most versions of "Song of the Young Girl Who Says Goodbye to Her Mother" begin with the words "*Quimbij c'a chawa*" "I tell you"), "*Camic c'a nute'*" ("Now, then, mama"), or the more scolding words "*Xinbij c'a chawa*" ("I told you so"). Songman Gaspar Petzey Mendoza introduced his "Song of a Young Girl Who Says Goodbye to Her Mother" with an explanation that I am calling an extended title. This introduction shows how each song has a small story on which the songman bases his text. This song was recorded in the early period of my research, and I did not ask for the Tz'utujil to be written down. My translators at the time provided the following:

Now I will play this song, the song of a girl who found her husband. The husband gave the girl a shawl, and the girl wore it to the market. She bought her greens and took them home in the shawl. "The man I met," she says, "gave me a ring, and I put it on. He gave it to me and I wore it in the road. The husband I met gave me money, and with this money I made my blouse, and I put it on. Don't be angry with me, mama. The husband I met just gave me a skirt, and I put it on and went into the road." That is what she says. "I found a husband and he gave me my headband, and I fixed my hair with it, and he gave me a comb and with it I combed my hair."

That is what she says. "Don't be angry with me, mama."

Listening to the example in audio file 6, it is clear that much has been added by the translators to Gaspar's brief comments before he sang. This is interesting because it shows that the the story of the "Song of the Young Girl Who Says Goodbye to Her Mother" was known to these young men who were working as translators for Father Carlin, who were not songmen or traditionalists but members of Catholic Action. Drawn from their own work by the music to the desk where I was playing it on my tape recorder, they translated it with enthusiasm, vying with one another to add details to complete the explanation. This and similar comments suggest that most people at that time were familiar with specific songs and what the songs taught.

Because the girl says she has received clothing from the young man and has already used it, it is understood that she has already been intimate with him, which is why she is afraid to tell her mother but even more afraid not to tell her. At the same time she is concerned about the sadness her mother will feel because her daughter is leaving.

In some of the "Songs of the Young Girl," the songman sings in falsetto, which seems to be an imitation of the girl's voice. Mendelson's informant described an attempt on the boy's part to hide his identity, which may have included the use of falsetto:

> Boys used to cover their faces with the mangash[28] and spoke in childish voices: this was a special technique which not everyone could master. The girl was not supposed to know who he was. (1956, 392, footnote 6)

It is not clear why a young man courting a girl would want to hide his identity unless, like Cyrano de Bergerac, the songman might not always have been the suitor. This would happen when a young man who could not sing or play brought a songman along to do it his place. In any case, it seems likely in the following song by Gaspar Petzey Mendoza that the songman uses falsetto to imitate the girl's voice.[29] The first recording was unclear and the words could not be understood. So I asked Gaspar to sing it again, which he did without accompanying himself on the guitar. This second version of the text is printed below. The first recording, with guitar but unclear text, can be heard on audio file 6.

"B'ix rxin K'pok"	"Song of the Young Girl Who Says Goodbye to Her Mother"
Gaspar Petzey Mendoza, songman	
Camic c'a nute', ximbij c'a chawa	Now then mama, I tell you
camic c'a nute', ximwil jun acha'	now then mama, I found a man
camic c'a nute', ximwil jun acha'.	now then mama, I found a man.
Ximbuchij, nute'. Camic xbij chawa:	I am in love, mama. Just now he said to me:

"Quinlok', quinlok' c'a jun awuk"
    canbij chawa.
Pr xuya c'a chawa, nute'
    aleyan.
"Camic c'a nuyan, ncatba c'a
    aleyan."
Camic c'a nute,' ximwil c'a wichyil.
Nuya' npak rxin nupo't
xuya c'a nute', quincsaj c'a chnukul.
Camic c'a nute', xulok c'a
    nixk'ap
camic c'a nute', xulok' jun njchab.
Xinjic nwa' tzra camic.
C'ja c'ara xincsaj c'a nxk'ap.
Xpeta wichjil xuya c'a nusu't
ximwc'aj c'a pq'ebel camic, nute'
xinlok' c'a wichay xinya' pc'a
    chutzam.
Camic c'a nute' xnu'l c'a p wuchoch
camic mtpet c'a, awyewal chwij,
    nute'.
Xinwil c'a jun acha xttz'ubaj c'a
    nuchi'
xk k'etz'ej c'a ki' ruquin, nute'
camic c'a, nute'.
Meltiox, xinwil wichjil,
    nute'.
Pr camic c'a nute'
barl c'a xcatba wa' nute', camic
    aleyan?
Camic nute,' pr mcatba tc'a abar
pr okc'o c'a nute'
    xtatba c'a ko'q'uin.
Camic c'a nute' nkaya' c'a away
camic c'a nute', meltiox, xwenkira'
    wichjil.

[*Xcar nbij jawra b'ix*]
[*11.66.V, item 12*]

"I will buy, I will buy you a skirt"
    this is what he said to me.
But he has already given it to me, my mother
    mama dear.
"Now dear, you will leave me dear."[30]

Now my mama, I have found my husband.
He will give me money for my blouse
he gave it to me mama, and I will wear it.
Now my mama, he has bought me my
    headband
now my mama, he has bought me my comb.
I combed my hair with it already.
Since then I have used the headband.
My husband came and he gave me my shawl
I wore it to the market today, mama
I bought my greens and I brought them in
    the shawl.
Now my mama I have come home
now I came, so don't be mad at me,
    my mama.
I found a man and he kissed my
    mouth
we already embraced each other, my mama
already, my mama.
I am thankful that I have found my husband,
    my mama.
But now my mama
where will you go now, mama
    dear?
Now mama, don't go anywhere else
because we are here mama
    you will come with us.
Now mama we will give you your tortillas
now mama, thank you, for I have found my
    husband.

[*That is what the song says*]

Some songs are cautionary for parents, expressing the feelings of sorrow and anger a young girl will have toward them if they repeatedly refuse consent for her to marry. In some "Songs of the Young Girl," the girl complains to her mother about her distress over the mother's decision. The following song also shows that shame is a powerful mechanism of social control in this community. The girl will bring shame on her parents by eloping with a man, as if she is "undressing" them in front of the neighbors. House compounds in Atitlán are very close to each other and afford limited privacy from others. These same neighbors already voiced harsh criticism of the young couple, calling him a slacker and saying she is too lazy and foolish to make a good wife. The girl feels bitterness that her parents have forced her to do things this way. This song was sung by Gaspar Yataz Ramirez.

"B'ix rxin K'poj"

Gaspar Yataz Ramirez, songman
AUDIO FILE 7

Ay ximbij c'a chawa
ay nute' ale
camic quinc'ule' c'a ruq'uin a
    jun ala'.
Ay ximbij c'a chawa
nute' aley, *lale lalale*
lale lalale lale lalale

Ay jun ala'
ay xulok' jun nipk'a'
ay xocoj cho nuk'a'.
le lale lala le

lale lala li lale lala li
lale lala li lale lala li

Aya jun ala'
ay ajni'la quinrajo'
ay camic xinrajo' c'a ala'
ay nute' aley.

Ay ximbij c'a chawa
quinc'ule' ruq'uin jun ala'
ay ximbij chawa
quinc'am ala' jawa'.

"Song of the Young Girl Who Says Goodbye to Her Mother"

Oh I told you so
oh mama dear
now I am going to marry
    a young man.
Oh I told you so
my mama dear, *lale lalale*
lale lalale lale lalale

Oh a boy
oh he bought me a ring
oh he put it on my finger.
le lale lala le

lale lala li lale lala li
lale lala li lale lala li

Oh a boy
oh how I want him
oh now I wanted the boy
oh my mama dear.

Oh I told you so
I am going to marry a boy
oh I told you
I am going to take that boy.

Ximbij mquita ximbij chawa, nute'?
lale lala le
lale lala le lale lala le

Ay quinya'nc'a ayaj aq'uix
    nute'
ay quincoln c'a awu'k
quincoln c'a apo't, nute'.

lale lala li lale lala li
lale lala li lale lala li

Quinya'nc'a ruyaj
ruq'uix nidta'
mruyaj mruq'uix jun rij
rujay quinya', nute'.

Ruyaj ruq'uix nidta', nute'
quinya' nc'a nen, ale.
lale lala li
lale lala li

lale lala li lale lala li
lale lala li lale lala li

li lale lala li
lale lala li
li lale lala li
lale lala li

Ay quintzejox c'a pjun b'ey
quintzejoxna pjun clo',
    nute'.
"Ay ch'ujlaj xtan!"
xtbi'xn c'a chwa, nute'.

Majun nubanra', nute'
xintz'u'j n c'a awq'uin
ay nute' aley.
chani' chanani'

Did I tell you or didn't I, my mama?
lale lala le
lale lala le lale lala le

Oh I'm marrying the boy
    my mama
oh I'm going to take off your skirt
I'm going to take off your blouse, mama.

lale lala li, lale lala li
lale lala li lale lala li

I won't shame the neighbors
but it's a shame on my papa
it's no shame on my neighbors
but on my parents that I give, my mama.

A shame on my father, my mother
that I'm giving then, dear mama.
lale lala li
lale lala li

lale lala li lale lala li
lale lala li lale lala li

li lale lala li
lale lala li
li lale lala li
lale lala li

Oh even if they criticize me in the street
even if they criticize where my footsteps go,
    my mama.
"Oh foolish girl!"
they will say to you then, my mama.

It makes no difference to me, my mama
that people criticize me
oh mama dear.
strum strum

Ay jun ala'
xulok' jun nuxk'ap
ay xubic c'a nwa'
tzra nute'.

Ja' c'a quinwajo' c'a nen, nute'
ja' xinwajo' tzra ala'.
Pores checha, nute'
xinya' c'a gan ruq'uin ala'.

"Ay ch'ujlaj xtan," jawa'.
Xtuya' nc'a ruyaj ruq'uix rute'.
Ay xto'k' xtbison nc'a

xtruk'ej n'ca ala'.

lale lala li
lale lala li
lale lala li
lale lala li

"Jiy ch'ujlaj xtan!" nuya'.
ruyaj ruq'uix nute'.
lale lala li
lale lala li

Li lale lala li
lale lala li
"Ay xtan" jawa',
"yjargant. Nbi'xa."

Xtqueca'y nc'a wnak', "Mixt
wektajtc'a jun ala' mal?"
lale lala li
lale lala li

"Ay ch'ujlaj xtan
xtribej jun ala'."
Ay ajni'la xutzu'
jun ala'.

Oh a boy
bought a headband for me
oh I then put it on my head
my mama.

This is the one I want, mama
this is the boy I want.
That's why, mama
I have desire for him.

"Oh foolish girl," they say.
They embarrassed my parents.
Oh even if I should be sad
    with him
I don't care what people say.

lale lala li
lale lala li
lale lala li
lale lala li

"Oh foolish girl!" they say.
I am going to shame you mama.
lale lala li
lale lala li

Li lale lala li
lale lala li
"Oh that girl" they say,
"is lazy. She doesn't work."

People say about me, "Can that girl
work and take care of the boy?"
lale lala li
lale lala li

"Oh foolish girl
she ran off with a boy."
Oh who knows what they think
of the boy.

"Xuya'c'a njel rgan ruq'uin, jun ala'"
lale lala li
"jun ala' xuc'an, c'a."
"Xjargant," nbi'xa.

Nchik tak jargant pka, ale
xulok' jun nuwu'k.
Ay xincojc'a, nute'.

lale lala le

Jun ala'
xulok' jun nupo't
xincoj chnukol
nute' ale.

Ay xulok' jun nusu't
xin jecquejc'a, nute'
li lali lala li
lali lalali

lali lala li
lali lala li
lali lala li
lali lala li

Ay quinctzebej nc'a wnak
wja' wumja'ta xtimban nute'.
Ay majun ruk'a', rkan
jun wnak chwa nen aley.

Ay njelal wanma xinc'ulbej c'a,
    ruq'uin jun ala'.
lale lala le
Ximbij mquita ximbij chawa, nute'?
Quinc'ule' ruq'uin jun ala'.

Ay atet mit cati'yowc'a wxin
pr camic quimbac'a, nen
ay pruchoch jun ala'.
lale lala li

"A boy wants to marry her, then"
lale lala li
"A boy wants her, then."
"He's a slacker" they say.

The boy is not a slacker, pretty one
he bought me this skirt.
Oh I put on the clothes he bought me,
    my mama.

lale lala le

A boy
bought me a blouse
and I wore it
mama dear.

Oh he bought me a shawl
and I wore it in the street, mama
li lali lala li
lali lalali

lali lala li
lali lala li
lali lala li
lali lala li

Oh the people are laughing at me
but it's alright mama.
Oh the hands and the feet of those people[31]
don't matter to me, dear.

Oh with all my heart then, I want to marry
    this boy.
lale lala le
Did I tell you or didn't I, mama?
I want to marry the boy.

Oh you didn't let me go out with him
but now I am with him, I am
oh in the boy's house.
lale lala li

lali lala li	*lali lala li*
lali lala li	*lali lala li*
lali lala li	*lali lala li*
lali lala li	*lali lala li*
"Ay ch'ujlaj xtan	"Oh that crazy girl
xtribej jun ala'."	went nuts for the boy."
Ay canbi'x chwa nen	Oh that's what people are saying about me
pr jun ala' xinc'am xtan.	but this girl is going to marry that boy.
Metzel b'ey, metzel achnakta	It's not a bad road, it's not a bad one I am
ximban, nute'.	taking, mama.
lali lala le	*lali lala le*
lale lala le	*lale lala le*
lale lala le	*lale lala le*
[8.71.13, item 84/121]	

In some "Songs of the Young Girl," the songman teaches the girl how to deal with the conflict she will feel as she anticipates leaving her mother to go and live with her new husband. He takes her role and gives her the words and attitudes for the situation. She has always wondered if she would find a good husband, and now she loves a young man. To relieve her sadness about leaving her parents and her anxiety when she anticipates the unknown life she faces with a man, she wants to dance. The drinking that will accompany her dancing will help her to pour out her feelings in a catharsis, and her dancing feet will make the Santo Mundo stir and move to her rhythm, and open a good road of her destiny with the young man. In the rituals of Holy Week she will remember that the dancing feet of the young man will cause the Santo Mundo to open a good road for them as a fertile couple, just as his dancing will also move the womb of the Santo Mundo to give birth to a new year.

The first lines of this song are nearly identical to the previous "Song of the Young Girl." The following lines are the ending of the song. This version was also sung by Gaspar Yataz Ramirez.

"B'ix rxin K'poj"	"Song of the Young Girl Who Says Goodbye to Her Mother"
Gaspar Yataz Ramirez, songman	
Pr njelal wanma	But with all my soul
njelal nuc'u'x	with all my heart
inc'ulbej ruq'uin ala' nen, nute'.	I thought about the boy, mama.
lale lalale	*lale lalale*

Ay wiq'uil	Oh ever since my months in the womb
ay nich'milal	oh ever since I was a stinky baby
lale lalale	*lale lalale*
ximbij	I said to myself
xintzejoj nen, nute'	I wondered, mama
wixtinela wen	if it would come out well for me
wumixtinelta wen ruq'uin jun ala'.	or not come out well with a man.
Pr camic quinc'aya	But now I look at him
quintzu'na nen, nute'.	I see him, mama.
Quilaj ala'.	He is a sweet boy.
lale lalai lale lalale	*lale lalai lale lalale*
Camic quiwok'ej	Now I am going to cry
quimbisoj nc'a ala' nen, ale.	I will be sad about him, dear.
lale lalale	*lale lalale*
Ay malay jun quitar	Oh I want a guitar
malay jun k'ojom	oh I want a marimba[32]
quintej nc'a nen, ale.	so I can dance, dear.
lale lalale	*lale lalale*
Ay malay bis	Oh I want the sadness
ay malay ok'ej.	oh I want to cry.
Ay pr chi'bey	Oh on the corner of the street
ay pnic'aj rujay.	oh in the middle of the house.
lale lalale lale lalale	*lale lalale lale lalale*
[8.71.13, item 85/122]	

"AtPal": A Song of Courting

Among the songmen I recorded, only Antonio Quieju Culan sang songs that tell a story that consists almost entirely of conversation among family members. It is unfortunate that so few of this type of song were collected because they suggest the existence of anecdotal and biographical sung tales about real people whose actions entered the repertoire of texts. Antonio initially gave this song the title "Nicolás and Francisca," which is confusing because there is no mention of Nicolás in the song. Afterwards he told me, "Francisca told AtPal (Cristóbal) that he is worthless to her," which may mean that she insulted him when he attempted to talk with her. Then he said, "This one is called 'AtPal.'"

The conversation between Francisca and her parents reveals that Cristóbal has been courting her by the lakeside, but she is worried because his family has not sent the customary matchmaker as emissary to her parents to ask for her, which is the way to initiate the months-long process of meetings and agreements between the two families that precedes marriage. Francisca is the last of their children still at home, and her parents are anxious for her to find a husband before they die. Her father thinks she has not found one because he did not pay the diviners enough money when he engaged them to locate a good husband for her. The father also thinks that Cristóbal will not have the means to provide for her, but Francisca assures her father that she doesn't care what work he does, she still wants him.

AtPal	Cristóbal
Antonio Quieju Culan, songman	

[YaPas:]	[Francisca:]
Nute', ala	Mama, a man
c'o jun wixkayil	is with a wife
. . . .	. . . .
Xinba c'a chya a las seis	I went to the lakeside at six
xinba cha las dos	I went again at two
xinba c'a chya' a las cinc	I went to the lakeside at five
xinba c'a chya'a las cuatro.	I went to the lakeside at four.
Kas ja' AtPal.	Cristóbal was always there.
Kas ani'la ranm chwij.	He loves me very much.
Con xinwajo'!	How he wants me!
que chwach mjun ndta'	and I don't have a man[33]
. . . .	. . . .
[Papa:]	[Father:]
Kas tkal cha wij yan	He likes you very much dear
kas tkal chawij nute'.	he likes you very much my girl.
Ec'lan chic axibal	Your brothers are married
ec'lan chic awch'alal	your relatives are married
y c'oc' jun awejcham	and you have a brother-in-law
kas utz.	who is very good.
Xinkocama ajoj, okrija'	We will die some day, we are old already
com xawtkij cana asamaj	and you have learned your work
YaPas ca', ali.	Francisca, dear girl.
[YaPas:]	[Francisca:]
Kas miltiox chawa, wli'	I thank you very much, mama
xaya nch'ej quem.	you gave me my loom.

Meltiox chawa wli	Thank you very much, mama
xaya' ncmo'.	you gave me my threadbeater.
Meltiox chawa wli'	Thank you very much, mama
. . . .	. . . .
Meltiox chawa wli'	Thank you very much, mama
xinach'ey tzrij nsamaj	you beat me over my work[34]
chana chani chana	*chana chani chana*
chana chani chana	*chana chani chana*
chana chani chana	*chana chani chana*
chana chani chana	*chana chani chana*

[Te':]	[Mother:]
Ay YaPasca', ale	Oh Francisca, my girl
ay YaPasca', ale	oh Francisca, dear
ay YaPasca', ale	oh Francisca, dear
. . . .	. . . .
bi'x tzra ma'c rute'	your mother told you
"Tic' ma' cana asamaj, yan	"Take up your work, dear
tic'ma' cana asamaj, nute'."	take up your work, my girl."
Xcmic chic kij joj, ali	Death comes near to us, dear
axok rxin chic nixti' joj.	we already belong to the cemetery.

[Ajb'ix:]	[Songman:]
Xpet chic rdta' tzra:	Then the father came and said:

[Papa:]	[Father:]
Kas quix c'le' cana, nme'al.	Get married, my daughter.
Atch'ijp tet. Mt cach'ey ta cjola',	You are the youngest. I didn't pay the boys much,
aj'itza'	the diviners
condenados.	the damn [diviners].
Nak xchpow awxin c'a?	Who has chosen you?

[YaPas:]	[Francisca:]
Ax AtPal chipyona wxinwal	Cristóbal has chosen me
wal wala ala'.	pa papa papa.

[Papa:]	[Father:]
Jax, AtPa'l chok ruq'uin.	Yes, you are already with Cristóbal.
Nac' nbij ala' chawa, nme'al?	What did the boy say to you, daughter?

[YaPas:]
"Can nc'utuj."

[Papa:]
Ncatba p c'olbic, yan
ncatba p c'olbic.
Nc'lun chic rxin anmal
p jay.
Majo'n rbayal nqueban jaxela'
dembal.
Jat! Jat! Jat!
Ximbij, "Majo'n njo'n rxin
    nme'al."

[Ajbij:]
Xc'a xax chwa ma'c rute':

[Te':]
Pr nak xaban c'a, YaPas c'a?
Achnak xaba?

[YaPas:]
Majo'n chic, wli'
majo'n chic quincha'pta nen.

[Te':]
Xach'aj prwa' k'alaj
quinbijna abi' tzra awal.

[Ajb'ix:]
Xu'l chic rtat ala'.

[Papa:]
Nctri' chic chi' ya',
    nme'al.
Ctpe' c'a ruq'uin.

Jax mjun nme'al
xten sa k'pita, ali
Majo'n nmeal

[Francisca:]
"I will ask for you."

[Father:]
You will go [to live] where they tell you, dear
you will go where they tell you.
I already arranged things for your sister.
She and her husband will live with us.[35]
The things sons-in-law do
are no good.
Go! Go! Go!
I thought, "Nobody wants my daughter."

[Songman:]
Her mother asked her:

[Mother:]
Well what did you do then, Francisca?
Who has come?[36]

[Francisca:]
Nobody, mama
nobody actually came to get me yet.

[Mother:]
Maybe you scolded too much
I told your papa.

[Songman:]
The boy's father came.

[Father:]
He will meet you again at the lakeside,
    daughter.
Stay with him.

I didn't have a daughter
that I allowed, dear
I don't have a daughter

nen xterbnata rch'ojlal.
Quinya' tzra jun c'jol
quinya' tzra, ali'.
Quinya' tzra jun c'jol
kas c'ota . . .
kas c'ota rsquerment.
Ja che chanani

[YaPas:]
Mscna' xc'yil si'
mscna'x ch'roy chaj
mscx kloy much'
mscx kloy echaj
Mscx pk'oy skil
mscx y k'ul wajqex
bnoy ch'it ruya'l chit mukil . . .
mscx chpoy tap
mscx s luy akok
mscx chpoy ch'u'.

Mne' byom, ali'
mne' byom, mama
mne' byom, achi
mne' byom, acha

[Papa:]
Trukijela nme'al
. . . .
Npet na jun awxin
npena jun awxin.
Trukij canalaja a Cristowl.
Ec'ol na mas extni'
ec'ol na mas c'jola'
. . . .

[YaPas:]
Quinba.
Majun nkujo'na.
Tpet naCristowl, mama, MatPal.
China china ani, china chinana
[9.76.97, item 430]

to let her go and joke with the boys in the street.
I will give you to a young man
I will give you, dear.
I will give you to a young man
who has . . .
who has a good spirit.[37]
Ja che chanani

[Francisca:]
Even if he is a firewood-seller
even if he cuts heart-of-pine
even if he cuts *chipilín*[38]
even if he cuts *yerbita mora*
even if he sells pumpkin seeds with chile
even if he keeps cattle
even if he sells *matatito* . . .
even if he is a crab fisherman
even if he butchers chickens
even if he is a fisherman.

I don't want a rich man, dear
I don't want a rich man, mama
I don't want a rich man, boy
I don't want a rich man, man.

[Father:]
Throw him out daughter
. . . .
Someone will come for you
yours will come.
Throw out this Cristóbal.
There are other boys
There are other boys.
. . . .

[Francisca:]
I'm going.
Nobody else wants me.
Let Cristóbal come, mama, Mr. Cristóbal.
China china ani, china chinana

"Songs of the Young Men and Young Girls, of Insults and Ridicule"
("*B'ix rxin C'jola K'poja Xyo'k'a Xtz'u'ja*")

Songman Antonio Quieju Culan sang several songs in the form of a dialogue among the girl, the boy, and one or both of their parents. In the following dialogue between the boy and the girl, insults are exchanged both ways. Although they are a customary part of courtship, the insults sting nonetheless. The young girl is conflicted; she wants the process to end quickly, saying "Hurry up, boys!" (that is, "I want to get married soon!"), and at the same time she is glad to have suitors who insult her.

> So much pain felt my heart
> so much pain felt my soul!
> I went, happily
> I go.

The young man in the song sings of his own dilemma: no girl wants him because his clothes are dirty, but because he is an orphan he has no woman to wash them for him. The song is not about personal misfortune, however, as much as it is about norms and values during courting. These words are put into a young man's mouth by the song, and these attitudes are those formed by the Old Ways. A young man can plead his case to the Nawals this way, telling them, "I, your child, have nothing, I have no one." One bears up under these insults, hoping that the period in which they are exchanged does not last very long. An insight into the function of the insults is revealed in the song: that they explain the complementarity of the roles of the couple that bring a man and woman together. The young man will hear these insults again in the fertility rites of Semana Santa, when the sacred fruit speaks, complaining of the same things in the same words. When she points out that his clothes are dirty, the girl affirms his need for a woman to wash them and provides him the opportunity to make an equivalent response.

In this song, the couple's courting ends without success. A recurring theme in songs of "lost luck" like the "Sad Songs" or "*Tristes*" is the desire to relieve emotional pain by dancing to the marimba or the guitar in the *cofradía*, when one can drink until the tears flow and the feelings are released. In this way, the "*Tristes*" could be called the "Tz'utujil Blues." We see here again the double significance of the act of dancing: one moves one's feet to music, the Santo Mundo feels it and the Nawals hear it, and the road opens and becomes favorable.

During a *costumbre* during the annual celebration of the feast of Santiago, July 25, YaLen Botrán, a *tixel* (female official) of the *cofradía* San Juan, told me the following about the ritual use of alcohol:

It's a touchy thing when we take drinks. Since it's a custom in the *cofradía*, the drinks are passed around by the headman of the *cofradía*. Now we will drink some *guaro*, because it comes from our fathers, our mothers. And the headman and his wife, the *xo'*, are drunk. Here it is permitted, but in the streets it is dangerous to drink. In the *cofradía* no one ridicules you, because it is your service that you are doing.

"B'ix cxin C'jola' K'poj
Xyo'k'a Xtz'u'ja"
Antonio Quieju Culan, songman
AUDIO FILE 8

"Song of the Young Men and Young Girls, of Insults and Ridicule"

[K'poj:]
Chana na ni
Xatzu', mamá
quintz'u' nc'a ala'
quintz'u' nc'a acha.
chana na ala'
chana na ni
chana chana ni
chana chana ni

[Girl:]
Chana na ni
You saw him, mama
I saw the boy
I saw the man.
strum boy[39]
strum na ni
strum strum ni
strum strum ni

Ximba p b'ey nen
xintz'u'ja anen
xintz'u'ja acha
xintz'u'ja k'poj.
Tela' c'jol ala'
tela' c'jol achi
tela' c'jol ala'
tela' achi.
Kas pkan xuna' wanm,
kas pkan xuna' nuc'u'x!
Xenba chuna'
quimba *nani*

I went into the street
they insulted me
they insulted me man
they insulted me girl.
Hurry up young boy
hurry up young man[40]
hurry up young boy
hurry up man.
So much pain felt my heart
so much pain felt my soul!
I went, happily
I go *nani*

Xintej jun octaw ya'
ksech'il xinna'
ksech'il xinna'
ksech'il xinna'.
pona poni pona pona
tana ta ni tana ta ni

I drank a pint of *guaro*
I felt so bad
I felt so bad
I felt so bad.
plink plink plink plink
plunk plunk plunk plunk

[C'jol:]:
Xinchap jun k'poj
ya xin rutz'uj:
"Majo'n c'a awc'atzil!
Sak asca'w
sak acwton
sak apas, atnwkon."
[K'poj:]
"Quin che'xa" ala'
"quin che'xa" achi.
pona poni pona pona

[C'jol:]
Ja' c'a xa, YaSión
xinrutzu', ale.
Choni Choni Chona Choni
Choni Choni Chona Choni

Kas nswert anen
nmajo'n awq'uin
kas nswert anen.
nana na ni

Poccha' k'poja quintz'juwa
quintz'juw ptak b'ey
pocch k'poja'
y nmajo'n njo'n wxin.

Jnpak c'ola
nmajo'n njo'n wxin.
Kas etzel wa'!
Kas etzel nuna' wanm.

Px majo'n cha nute'
majo'n cha ndta'.
Pr majo'n chbnow nway
pr majo'n cha wajaw
majo'n cha, ala'
majo'n cha, achi
majo'n cha, ala'
majo'n cha, ala'

[Boy:]
I courted a girl
and she insulted me:
"You are good for nothing!
White are your pants
white is your shirt
white is your belt, your sash."[41]
[Girl:]
"I have dressed you" the boy says to me
"I have dressed you" says the man to me.
plink plink plank plank

[Boy:]
She saw me, Concepción
she saw me, mama.
Choni Choni Chona Choni[42]
Choni Choni Chona Choni

Truly my luck
is not with you
Truly my luck.
nana na ni

Lots of girls insult me
they ridicule me in the street
lots of girls
and there is not one that wants me.

I have money
and nobody wants me.
How bad!
How bad my soul feels.

Because I don't have my mother any more
I don't have my papa.
Because I have no one to make my tortillas
because I have no one to be in charge of me
no one, boy
no one, man
no one, boy
no one, boy

Quinwajo' quinc'le ruq'uin jun k'poj   I want to marry a girl
pr majo'n wxin   but nobody wants me
majuna a . . .   nobody . . .
. . . .

Camic c'a ala'   Now boy
camic c'a c'jol   now young man
camic c'a nen   now I
kas etzel nu'on.   I feel very bad.
Xinteja ya', xinteja . . .   I drank *guaro*, I drank . . .
ks ngan xeno'c p cantín   with pleasure I went to the bar
ks ngan, k'poj.   with pleasure, girl.
tana tani tana tana   *plink plink plink plink*
tana tani tana tana   *plink plink plink plink*

Nmajo'n xbin chwa nen.   No one told me to.
Njelal ngan xnetja't jun octaw   I myself chose to go and drink a pint of
   ya'   *guaro*
Xinmaj jun tzij, xpaxij bis   I started talking, and my sadness
                                             poured out[43]

wq'uin . . . anen.   of . . . me

"Majo'n asca'w   "You don't have pants
majo'n acuton   you don't have a shirt
njunoc njalja' ri' chacul,"   you don't have another to change into,"
quinche'xe anen.   they said to me.
nana na ni nana na na   *nana na ni nana na na*
pona pona pona poni   *plunk plunk plunk plunk*

[K'poj:]   [Girl:]
Nar c'atzil c'ala'?   What good are you, boy?
. . . .
Tz'il rij rcuton   Dirty is your shirt
ta'il rij rxca'w.   dirty your pants.

[C'jol:]   [Boy:]
Pero majo'n nich'jow wij   But there is no one
majo'n nich'jo nwach.   there is no one to wash my clothes.
nana na na nana na na   *nana na na nana na na*

Ay, YaSión   Oh, Concepción
kas njel xuban consej tzra   everybody gave you advice

kas xya' rbixic:
"Mtac'am c'a ta ala'.
Mtkalta chawij."
Nch'il xana'.
pona poni pona pona

they gave you their words of counsel:
"Don't lie with the boy.
He's not good for you."
I felt bad.
pona poni pona pona

Ja' YaCla'x,
jara' xyo'w tzij.
. . . .
pona poni pona pona
[9.72.92, item 416]

She, Nicolasa,
she gave her advice.[44]
. . . .
pona poni pona pona

"Songs of the Old Maid"

Songman Juan Petzey Takaxoy sang and played this "Song of the Old Maid," a
"*B'ix rxin B'ey Triste*" ("Sad Song of the Road") about a "*rilaj k'poj*," an older, unmarried woman whose luck is lost and whose road has disappeared because
she hasn't found a husband and is past the age of marrying. When this happens a woman may be left in later life without family or children to help provide for her, and possibly without a house to live in, and she consequently may
suffer seriously from poverty.[45]

But when one's path leads to a solitary life that implies a degree of celibacy;
it is often recognized as the concentration of special powers given by the Nawals and is taken as a sign that one has a calling to become a ritual specialist
like an *ajcun* or a rain priest, or if a woman, a midwife. Nicolás Chiviliu, with a
wise twinkle in his eye, used to call me "*rilaj k'poj*," the "old girl." He had examined the top of my head and found that I have three cowlicks, those spirals of
hair that rotate around an axis on the top of the head, which showed that I was
destined to be a midwife.

"B'ix rxin Rilaj K'poj"
Juan Petzey Takaxoy, songman
AUDIO FILE 9

"Song of the Old Maid"

Camic quimba anen, leyan
cnetja' jun traga ngust.

Now I am going, dear
to have a drink with pleasure.

Xach' nubey, leyan
pc majun bar quimbawa', leyan.

Lost is my road, dear
and I don't know where to go, dear.

[*"xin K'poj'" ja'wra*]

[*This one is "of the Girl"*]

Juan Petzey Takaxoy,
songman, 1971.

Majun acha quinjo'na, leyan
pr nisuert perdid una vez
leyan nuté.

Bar quintza'k, nute' leyan?
   pc camic . . .
majun xjo'n wxin, pc
xin rilaj k'poj nen, nute'.

Misc kas xtinq'isna wulew xin nidta
xin nute', leyan.
Con gust quntej jun traga mejor,
   porque

There is no man who wants me, dear
because my luck is gone for good
mama dear.

Where will I wander, mama dear?
   because now . . .
there is nobody who wants me because
I am an old maid, mama.

Even if I should sell all my papa's land
and my mama's, dear.
With pleasure will I have a drink,
   because

José Pop Ajuchan,
songman, 1971.

nak kas bey xtin wc'aj, bar kas
  bar kas xquimbawa' leyan?
Por nomber Dio's Pagr, nute' leyan
Bar kas ximbawa', Dio's?

C'o colew nidta', nute'.
Quintina jch'ap jun traga mejor.
Con gustamente quimban gastar.

[9.72.105, item 452]

what road should I take
  and where should I go, dear?
In the name of Dio's Padre, my mama dear.
Where will I go, Dio's?

There is my father's land, and my mother's.
I will take a little drink.
With pleasure I am going to spend some
  money.

Audio file 10 is a guitar solo of the same melody played by Diego Cua Simaj,
who calls it simply "Song of the Road."

As mentioned by the girl's father in the song "Cristóbal," the songs some-times tell of the role played by an *ajcun* who the parents and the couple con-sult to divine the good or bad fortune of a possible marriage, and who grants approval of the match or warn of an unhappy future. Another mention of this custom is found in the lines of a song by José Sosof Coo':

Xmajru' k'ij tc'ara'
   inawchjil
	There are only a few days left 'til I become
	   your wife

br c'o kpak yan	because we have some money, dear
c'o kpak nute'.	we have some money, mama.
Aprobad ka tiemp awq'uin, xiñora.	Our time together has been approved, lady.

Witchcraft and Shapeshifters in the Songs

The *ajcuns* in Atitlán, however, are not all specialists in benevolent work. Some of them, called *ajitz*, can be consulted to identify the person who has put some evil in your path or who has taken away your luck, and they can do harm to the one you believe has wronged you. The *ajitz* have strong power to harm oth-ers through witchcraft by using "bad prayers."[46] One of the songmen, Diego Cua Simaj, when emboldened by several drinks, boasted to me about his power as an *ajitz* and his ability to use it to get revenge against another *ajitz*. Diego boasted a lot that night, and some was exaggerated and hard to believe. Song-man Antonio Quieju Culan reveals in some of his songs how this dark side of the power of an *ajitz* can be invoked if one suffers too much rejection or de-ception in the process of courting. In the following lines, Antonio sings of a young man who has been rejected and is angry because his chosen girl, un-grateful for his many gifts, has received advice from her girlfriend against mar-rying him because he is a drinker and wears Ladino pants. The entire song has 176 lines. He talks with his friends:

[*C'jol:*] Majo'n ch quinrajo't YaChon pc xya' rconsej ch pam.	[*Young man:*] Concepción doesn't want me any more because they gave her heart some advice.
[*Wamig:*] Achnakc' xbin tza', 'a'?	[*Friends:*] Who told her, man?
[*C'jol:*] J'e'. YaTun bin tzra.	[*Young man:*] Yes. Antonia told her.

[*Wamig:*]
Kcamsaj, ali'
kcamsaj, acha.

. . . .

Mc'o cht jun
ajcun? Tekma'ta tzrij.
Kch'ilij pa k'ak'
kc'atsaj ruchoch.

. . . .

[*K'poj:*]
Ax! pandlon rcsan lja'.
Axscaw quinban anen.

. . . .

[*C'jol:*]
Natzrc'a jnswert?
Nak nisipan nswert?
Mxe c'ol aj'itza
ebanyon nswert.
Mxc'ol acha
mxc'ol banyon tzrij
mxc'ol nc'aj tak k'ij
mxc'ol rxin k'ejku'm.
Mxc'ol achi'
cpa ban mal pnub'ey.

. . . .

M'iltna'x c'ot jun acha xtinwil
k'naj'itz
quinya', quinya' jun ch'ut ch pam.
Luch, don Pegr Simón
Pagr Santa Cruz Divino
tanwaran ak'a, Luch
nwaran ak'a, achi
nta xca'y ic', ch'umil
[*9.72.96, item 428*]

[*Friends:*]
Let's kill her, mama
let's kill her, man.

. . . .

Isn't there an
ajcun? Let's look for her.
Let's burn her in the fire
let's burn her house.

. . . .

[*Young girl:*]
Ugh! he wears long pants.
I weave Tz'utujil pants.[47]

. . . .

[*Young man:*]
Why is my luck so bad?
Who can give me back my good luck?
Maybe some witch
has given me this [bad] luck.
Maybe some man
has done this to me
maybe in the light of day
maybe in the dark.
Maybe some men
put evil in my road.

. . . .

Maybe I can find some man
a real witch
to put, to put a thorn in his stomach.
Lucha, don Pedro Simon
Padre Santa Cruz Divino
I am waiting in the night, Lucha
I am waiting in the night, man
the moon and the stars saw me

"Songs of the Young Girl" ("*B'ix rxin K'poj*")

Things can go seriously wrong for a young man who discovers that the girl he has been courting has some serious defect. In this song the young man has had the bad luck to court a shapeshifter called a *characotel* or *isom*. The wound or split that he discovers in her hand is a sign that she is a transformer, a person who can change her physical shape. At the end of the song it emerges that her foot is also split open.

I learned from friends and other informants in Atitlán, both Ladinos and Tz'utujils, that a person is an *isom* from birth because it is their predetermined luck or destiny. Consequently they are not harshly judged but pitied, because they are not believed to be responsible for their nature or their actions as an *isom*. The transformation of an *isom* into a dog or a cat or other animal takes place at night, after which the shapeshifter returns to his or her own body. The *isom* are believed to emerge from the cross in the central plaza and often run in packs through the town, which is said to account for the fact that there are so many more dogs and cats at night than there are in the day. To protect oneself from *isom*, one should walk in the middle of the street at night, because they tend to hide in the shadows close to the walls. One should also carry a flashlight to shine in their eyes, which blinds them and keeps them at bay. *Isom* are dangerous because they can cause *susto* and do serious damage to one's soul by knocking out a part of it, resulting in emotional trauma. One can also carry a guitar for protection and be ready to play an appropriate *b'ix*, which will control them.[48] Remembering Lady Blood, the maiden in the *Popol Vuh* who conceives when she receives semen in the form of spittle in her hand,[49] the split-open hand may signify the vagina, also suggesting here that the girl in question is not a virgin.

Antonio Quieju Culan sings of a young man's experience with a shapeshifter:

"*B'ix rxin K'poj*" "Song of the Young Girl"
Antonio Quieju Culan, songman
AUDIO FILE 11

Nachina ali   *Nachina ali*
runa rina ru   *runa rina ru*
chini china na   *chini china na*
lala lala li   *lala lala li*

[ATico:]   [Diego:]
 Xanen ATico   I am Diego
nmbeyta ximban.   and this is not the road I took.

[Mama:]   [Mama:]
Naxaban c'a, 'a'?   What road did you take then, boy?

[ATico:]
Kas jun k'poj xhichpa cana camic
xpa'c rpam ruk'a'.

[Mama:]
Ajru' c'a iq' xatpe' ruq'uin?

[ATico:]
Oxi iq' ximpe' ruq'uin.
Xinya' ruchil
xinya' ruk'o'p
xinya' jun ruk'op
ksta'na rpam ak'a', yan
ksnjelal ngan tzrij.

Xinrbaj tzra, nute'.
Ali'a!
Ks jun k'poj xinchap nen pa'c
    rpam ruk'a'!

[Mama:]
Acuy! Narc'a'tz!
Xnuya' ruquic' pnway.

[ATico:]
Jap nute'. . .

[Mama:]
Mne' jlal, ta'!
Natzrc'a naban, mo's?
Ksatenter ala'
ks at MaDieg
ksnim atza'm.

Achnakc' wnak xachap?
Tya'c' chwa.

[ATico:]
Axje'w'wnak

[Diego:]
I went to court a girl just now
and the palm of her hand is split open.

[Mama:]
How many months did you court her in
    the road?

[Diego:]
Three months we courted in the road.
I gave her chewing gum
I gave her a necklace
I gave her one necklace
and I saw her hand, dear
I really wanted her.

I talked with her, my mama.
Oh mama!
I courted a girl who had a split in
    her hand!

[Mama:]
Oh, she is no good!
She will put her blood in my tortillas.

[Diego:]
But mama . . .

[Mama:]
I don't like her, not one bit, papa![50]
Why are you doing this, boss?[51]
You are a handsome boy
you are Mr. Diego
and your nose is really big.[52]

What kind of person did you court?
Tell me.

[Diego:]
She's one of those people

axk'isoma' rj'e'.
Kas etzel xuna' wanm.

shapeshifters they are.
I felt so bad inside.

[Mama:]
Narubi' ja' xtan ala'?

[Mama:]
What's that girl's name, boy?

[ATico:]
YaMri'y Sosof
ks YaMri'ya Sosof
mttela pn k'nwach.

[Diego:]
María Sosof
and still I can't get María Sosof
out of my head.

[Mama:]
Npa'c ruk'a, ala'
npa'c ruk'a, acha.

[Mama:]
But her hand is split, boy
her hand is split, man.

[ATico:]
Pa'c ruk'a', ali.
li lala li

[Diego:]
Her hand is split, dear.
li lala li

Ksquetn k'etej
k'etej njenam
anen, ala'.
lalalala

When I embrace her
I embrace her with all my heart
I do, boy.[53]
lalalala

Ks saklaj k'poj ptzij
pxruk'a' rbnon palt
sak ak'a', saklaj xtan
kas . . .

So white is her skin
but only her hand is wrong
her hand is white, the girl is white
so . . .

Kas ngan tzrij
ksxenok wajki' k'ij.
"Naximban c'a?"
xbi'x chwa ma'c nute'.

Still I want her so
that I could cry for six days.
"Well, what have you done?"
my mama said to me.

[Mama:]
Ala' natejc' rway
nuya' quic' chpam?
Cu'y! Xqnin xibej wi'nen.

[Mama:]
Young man, are you going to eat tortillas
that have blood in them?
Oh! It frightens me.

[ATico:]
Mne' c'ara', ali'

[Diego:]
I don't want to, dear

mne' c'ara, mc'ajol
kas anen enchapyon
xpeta rye wal, nc'ajol.

[YaMri'y:]
Nta xuchap chwixquin, ala'.
. . . .
Cas njun ak'awach . . .

[Mama:]
Je'e'a jual, jual.
Tbeba' jual tzra'.

[YaMri'y:]
Xlsaj quic' chwixquin, nc'ajol.

[Papa:]
Canbij chwa chik jun c'unc'un si' 'a'.

YaMri'y xmajcuna awq'uin
mes cxtuya' tzij
mesc xtuya' consej
mes xtuya'rbixic
mes xtuya' rnatxic.
tana tani tana tani

Tich pa' chic jun rub'ey!

[ATico:]
YaMri'y Tiney.
Kas xinchap k'poj
kas xinchap chna ruk'a

xinya' ju rupk'a'
rjelal vent cinc centaw.
Xin tz'a ruk'a.
Kas ch'it ven!

. . . .
"Kas ech'aj ch'oj wnak jara'."
Jlal minganta ruq'uin nen

I don't want to, my boy
but I have made love to her
and now she's angry, my boy.[54]

[Maria:]
He pulled me by the ear, that boy.[55]
. . . .
But an eye . . .

[Mama:]
It's alright, son, my son.
Let her have it.

[Maria:]
He drew blood from my ear, the boy.

[Papa:]
I say we add fuel to this fire.

María sinned with you
even though I told you in words
even though I gave you counsel
even though I gave you advice
even though I told you not to forget it.
tana tani tana tani

Take a different road!

[Diego:]
María Tiney.
When I took the girl
when I took her hand

I gave her a ring
worth twenty-five cents.
I saw her hand.
It was so pretty!

. . . .
"What clean-living folks," I thought.
But now I don't want her

itzeltak quintz'at nen
msak, xk'ak.

she seems bad to me
not white, but black.

[Mama:]
Pirkan chic ja', ala'
k'in rtron ri pa'c.

[Mama:]
And her foot, boy
is also split by the evil that she has.

[ATico:]
Xmajo'n nislobt wanma
nwar wq'uin.
Tra quinya' can chic jmej
at jun waming tbi'na chwa
"Pa'c majun nuban 'a'."
a chana chana a li

[Diego:]
My heart does not want to
sleep with her.
I am going to leave her soon once again
even if my friend tells me
"That split hand doesn't matter, boy."
a chana chana a li

Xnechpa' chic jmej
k'ninbi'n quic' pirkan.
. . . anen
Camic xinc'e c'a amolest
quinbiba' c'a prixquin
"Poc nmak pa'c pnawkan, tet."
"Nanuban nu pa'c;
na tz'ubaj" c'ha'.
Q'uix nuna' nuchi'.
Mne'jlal.
"Na xbi'n chwa?"
YaJuanita, ale.
chana chana ala' . . .

When I went to court her a second time
blood was running from her foot.
. . . I
Now I am angry
and I say in her ear
"The split in your foot is bigger, you."
"That split won't do anything;
you can just kiss it" she said.
It will prick my mouth.
I don't want to.
"Who told you?"[56]
Juanita, dear.
chana chana ala' . . .

Tax xpe ryewal chwij, ja',
xin chap jun tk'poj chwach.

And she got angry with me, she did,
when I courted another girl in front of her.

[YaMri'y:]
Tic'sa' ruq'uin, tic'sa' ruq'uin!

[Maria:]
Go with her, go with her!

[ATico:]
E ax itzel. Pa'c pnawkan tet.
Chi'it ruk'a' wen ptzij.

[Diego:]
She is from bad people. Split is her foot.
But her hand was pretty.

Xpe chic jun wixbil
AMquiel
y ja', AMquiel

A friend came
Miguel
and he, Miguel, said

"Tic' ma' xtan jala', poc nis maja."

"Take that girl, for she knows how
    to work."

Ke p kas pirkan; k'mtit bin chic
mal pa'c.
Ajru' c'a rjuna'?
Cbeljuj rjuna' ja' xtan, hombr
pr kas rupa'c
nbic' b'ix pirkan.
[9.72.95A, item 426A]

Yes, but her foot; now she can't walk
because it's so bad.
How old is she?
Twelve years old is the girl, man
but badly split open
is her foot.

The "Sad Songs" or "*Tristes*"

The songs often have the character of morality stories that teach behavior that
is consistent with the example left by the Nawals. "*Tristes*" or "Sad Songs" provide people in painful situations with acceptable attitudes and ways to deal
with problems and offer examples of possible resolutions. Among them are the
aforementioned songs associated with courting when there are insults or rejection, and the laments of a man or woman who has grown old without marrying, or of a parent mourning the death of a child or spouse.

"They Fought" ("*Xqueti' qui'*")

Many sad songs are about difficulties between couples. For example, Antonio Quieju Culan sings about reconciliation after a fight in the following song
called "They Fought" or "They Threw Out Nicolás Tz'ina' Because of Elena."
After the couple shares their complaints against each other, they reach a mutual understanding of their problems and feel the cooling of their anger. In
the dialogue of the song they consider the losses for each of them that separation would involve, and finally the affection they have for one another breaks
through. The song ends with the realization that they fought over trivialities
and offended egos, and they decide to forget it. The presence of the ubiquitous
Old Mam, the Lord of sexuality and music, is acknowledged in the lines that
replicate the sound of his guitar, "strum, strum, boy."

Xqueti' Qui'
Antonio Quieju Culan, songman

They Fought

[Nicolás:]
Kas ngan nk'a'xa ali'
kas ngan nk'a'xa achi
camban Mama ALu

[Nicolás:]
With pleasure I'll drown [my sorrow] girl
with pleasure I'll drown it man
I'll do it Mam Lucha

Ximba c'a ali'
ximba c'a achi
ximba c'a YaLen.

I'm leaving then girl
I'm leaving then man
I'm leaving then Elena.

[YaLen:]
Tpet c'a, ATz'ina'
jep ec'ola wlic'wal nen
eq'e wlic'wal nen.

[Elena:]
Come back, Tz'ina'
because I have the children
I have two children.

[Nicolás:]
Quinba nen, wixkayil.
Mxin c'u'lta, ali
mxin c'u'lta, achi
mxin c'u'lta, ali.
Xabij njite'
xcatajchij tz'e' chawij.

[Nicolás:]
I'm going, my woman.
I didn't marry you, girl
I didn't marry you, man
I didn't marry you, girl.
You told your mother
and they set the dogs after me.

[YaLen:]
Xeka'j c'a, wlicwal.
Quimba ruq'uin alcal
—namo ncat tzejon
ruq'uin ixok jalila?

[Elena:]
You came here, boy.
I'm going to the authorities
because—why are you talking
with that other woman?

[Nicolás:]
Mnuk'a't, chawa . . .
china china ala'

[Nicolás:]
It's not my fault, you . . .
china china ala'

Je', p ksara nen
kas njel ngan tzrij.
Xek'a, anen
njel nuc'u'x tzrij.

Yes, I really
want to come back.
Yes, I
want to with all my heart.

Xcanaja jun nk'anwach
pona poni
xcanaja wka.

My eyes stay with you
pona poni
my feet stay with you.

[YaLen:]
C'o kwaj cax, achi.
Kas pkan xenuna, ATz'ina'!
Majo'n nyuk'un nwajcax
nwajcax, achi.

[Elena:]
We have our bulls, man.
How sad I've been, Mr. Tz'ina'!
Nobody will take care of my bull
my bull, man.

Jax attjoy ya', amo's

You drink, handsome

jax attjoy ya', ametz

you drink, my dear face[57]

jax attjoy ya', ametz

you drink, my dear face

. . . .

. . . .

jax attjoy ya', achi

you drink, man

. . . .

. . . .

tona tona ala'

tona tona ala'

Ay nc'ajol, ala'!

Oh my young man, my boy!

Jun ATec Tz'ina'

That Diego Tz'ina'

nc'ani'la lomlaj acha.

is one great man.

Juna nme'al

My daughter

YaLor Tz'ina'

Dolores Tz'ina'

ay, nme'al, ala

oh, my children, man

bal xebachw camic?

where will they go now?

Atjun Dio's

I need Dio's

atjun Sant

I need a Santo

atjun prcipal

I need an elder

atjun rmament

I need right now

atjuna wuc'

I need my family

atjuna wch'alal

I need my brother

atjuna wamig

I need my friend

atjuna . . .

I need . . .

atjuna acha

I need a man

atjun . . .

I need . . .

Catibna c'a, a'

This is what you are doing, boy

. . . .

. . . .

[Nicolás:]

[Nicolás:]

Mne' chic jun ixok.

I don't want a woman any more.

. . . .

. . . .

kas xya', ale.

I want a drink, dear.

Xinwich c'aj myer nuban nway.

I dreamed [last night] she was making my tortillas.

Kas xya', ale!

What a drink, dear!

xka'j ncaj rmal.

I got down my money box for her.[58]

china china ala'

strum strum, boy

lala lala li

lala lala li

[YaLen:]

[Elena:]

Ja' AClax Tz'ina'

That Nicolás Tz'ina'

mjun nch'jow rij.
china china ala' lala li

chana chana ala' chana chana ala'
chana chana ala' chana chana ala'
chana chana ala' chana chana ala'
chana chana ali chana chana ala'
. . . .

MaClaxa Tz'ina'

[Nicolás:]
Kajach taki, yan
kajach ki', wixkayil.
Nktz'ubaj kachi'
numaja tzeb
kas nkatzu' chukan.
Catnema' ta, yan.
"Xjun tak jun ixok"
xbin chawa ali'.
. . . .
. . . .
. . . .
. . . .

[YaLen:]
Kas c'a nen ala', xnc'sel
atco ch'ap wawan anen kejyu'.

[Nicolás:]
C'ola nujal
penak xe' jyu.

Majuna yal, majuna
kas b'ix xinwc'aj.
Xin wc'axaj, YaLen
nc'le' ruq'uin jun acha.
Xin w c'axaj, YaLen
jun acha
njo'n rxin rta' nuya'.

hasn't washed his clothes.
strum strum boy lala li

strum strum, boy, strum strum, boy
strum strum, boy, strum strum, boy
strum strum, boy, strum strum, boy
strum strum, boy, strum strum, boy
. . . .

Nicolás Tz'ina'

[Nicolás:]
We separated, dear
we separated, my woman.
We kissed each others' mouth
and we laughed
when we looked at each other.
I will take you, dear.
"Only one woman"
my mother told me.
. . . .
. . . .
. . . .
. . . .

[Elena:]
But then, boy, my namesake[59]
you have a little cornfield by the piedmont.

[Nicolás:]
I have my corn
just close to the roots of the mountain.

I don't have a net, no
but what a sadness I have.
I heard, Elena
that you are going to marry a man.
I heard, Elena
a man
your papa is giving you to him.

"Xajun acha."   "Only one man."
Diez cantaw nuya'.   He's giving ten cents.
Majo'n, ala'   No, boy
majo'n, acha   no, man
majo'n, ala'   no, boy
majo'n! *lala lala*   no! *lala lala*
. . . .
Catjo' wq'uin, YaLen   Come with me, Elena
YaLen, nane'.   here, Elena.

[YaLen:]   [Elena:]
Catjo' wq'uin, achi.   Come with me, man.

Mxkaban ta, ala   Nothing ever happened, boy
mxkban ta, achi.   nothing ever happened, man.
[9.72.97, item 431]

"Sad Song of Our Fathers, Our Mothers"
("*B'ix rxin Kadta, rxin Kate' Bis*")

In another "*triste*," Juan Petzey Takaxoy's "Sad Song of Our Fathers, Our Mothers," a son struggles with regret over the harsh words addressed to him by his mother before she died. Comments from the translator suggest that the message here is actually one of gratitude combined with sadness for having lost a mother who correctly disciplined her son and thus benefited him.

"B'ix rxin Kadta, rxin Kate' Bis"   "Sad Song of Our Fathers,
                                             Our Mothers"

Juan Petzey Takaxoy, songman

Xabij c'a, nute' leyana *lale i a*   You talked to me, my mother dear *lale i a*
xabij c'a nute', xinatz'uj, nute'   you talked to me, you scolded me, mother
ay nidta', ay nute'.   oh father, oh mother.

Bis c'o wanma camic   My heart is sad now
p kan xaban chwa, nute'   for you hurt me so much, my mother
a lala lala le a lala lala li la   *a lala lala le a lala lala li la*

Kas anen nta xaban cordar nidta'   Now I remember my father and my
    nute'   mother

alaley

p kan xaban c chwa, nute' *lala lala*

k'an bis c'o wanma nen nute' *alala*

p kan xabancan chwa nen

nute' leyana *lilala*

p kan xaban ca chwa

nuyon xinya'cana, nute' *lalali*

Camic xatin p kornsay, nidta'

aley, aleyan

camic xatnuban acordar nidta'.

P kan xaban cchwa ojer, ndta'

Dio's Sucrist

bis c'a ok'ej c'a c'o wanma anen,
    aleyana

pr camic jun trago, aleyan.

[9.72.103, item 448]

alaley

for you hurt me so much, mother *lala lala*

my heart is very sad, my mother *alala*

for you hurt me so much

my mother dear *lilala*

for you hurt me so much

now you have left me alone, mother *lalali*

You left me poor, without a father

mama, mama dear

now you make me remember my father.

It hurts what you did before, father

Dio's Sucrist

so sadness and tears are in my heart,
    mama

and now I want a drink, mama.

"Songs of the Flowers and the Fruit" ("*B'ix rxin Cotz'ej, Sk'ul*")

Ethnographic studies, beginning with Mendelson's work in the 1950s (Mendelson 1956), and later O'Brien (1975), Carlsen (1997), Prechtel (1999), Christenson (2001), and Stanzione (2003), provide accounts of the ritual that provides the context of the "Song of the Flowers and the Fruit" in Santiago Atitlán. Stanzione has written extensively about this ritual in which he personally participated, and his work informs the following discussion (2003, 166*ff.*).

For a young man, the beginning of courting is a recognizable threshold of his evolution into manhood. Courting is a first step on the path to assuming responsibility as a member of the civil-religious society of the *cofradías*. His initiation into this society begins with a ritual in which he and other young men who have contracted marriage within the current year, undertake a long and very arduous walk to the coastal lands that once belonged to the Tz'utujil people, to gather and carry back flowers and fruits that will be used in the equinoctial rituals of Holy Week. This journey is laden with layers of symbolism that emerge as part of the complex relationship between human sexuality, fertility, and service to the community, and the fertility of the world of nature, including rain and the rebirth of Old Mam. The young men will learn through their ritual experience about the visible and invisible economy of the Santo Mundo. The songmen who accompany them on the journey sing and play the appropriate songs, the "Song of the Flowers" ("*B'ix rxin Cotz'ej*") and the "Song of the Fruit" ("*B'ix rxin Sk'ul*"), the first of which accompanies the gathering of the flowers of cacao and others that grow in the area that is called Suchitepequez (from Nahuatl meaning "Place of the Flowers"), which once belonged to the Tz'utujils. These and the fruits they bring were items of trade that recall their ancestors, the traveling merchants whose actions they repeat in these rituals. Among them, for example are the fragrant flowers of the corozo palm (*orbignya cohune*) that will fill the church with their heady fragrance when they are hung on a large screenlike structure of rope netting in front of the carved altarpiece of the church, specially constructed each year for the Holy Week rituals. The corozo is a useful item of trade: it is a tall tree with leaves up to 30 feet long and 6 feet wide used for roofs, fans for fire, and rain capes, and its veins can be made into brooms. The young shoots are eaten raw, toasted, or boiled, and can be made into a strong intoxicant when fermented. Its fruit is food for cattle, used for making oil, sweets, and soap. Its hard husk makes good buttons, and tobacco pipes are made from its seeds (McBryde 1947, 413; Orellana 1984, 165, citing Ocaña 1932–33, 302; and Betancour and Arboleda 1964, 105).[60]

The initiation journey of the young men, who are called *alguacils* (Spanish for "constables" or "elders' assistants"), takes place during the height of the hot, dry season, close to the time of the vernal equinox. At this time the five chaotic, unstable days that were called *wayeb* by the ancient Maya and come at the end of the Maya 360-day solar year are fast approaching. Sometime in the past, no doubt because of the imposition of the Church's Gregorian Calendar, the *wayeb* was transferred in Atitlán to Catholic Holy Week, the week preceding Easter beginning with Palm Sunday and ending with Holy Saturday, the day before Easter. The old year, embodied in the person of Old Mam, is now exhausted and dried up, and must be replaced by a new year of fertilizing rain and young corn.

One or two songmen accompany the *alguacils* with their music, together with the *matraca*, a large very loud wooden rasp, which is played all through the trip. The "Songs of the Fruit" belong to the return trip when the *alguacils* are carrying the fruits on their backs in racks. Women are not allowed to go on this walking journey down to the coast in which the songmen interpret the experience of the young men by playing and singing the "Song of the Flowers" and "Song of the Fruit." I was, however, able to record two of them in the homes of the songmen.

In these highly symbolic songs, the songman sings in the voice of the young man and in the voice of the fruit itself; the *xul* or cane flute and the drum also

speak, all of which are also the voice of the Santo Mundo. It is the voice of Old
Mam, too, who taught them and who put these words in their mouths at the beginning of the present creation. This is the road, the *real* road, the road of the
Nawals, the road that established the ancient calendar that initiates the cycles
of time in the Santo Mundo. It is the road of Our Father the Sun across the sky,
and the White Road of the Milky Way that is central to the creation story of the
ancient Maya.

The fruit makes the same complaints and suffers the same insults that are
familiar from the "Songs of the Young Man" and "Songs of the Young Girl,"
clearly identifying this as a courting ritual between men, led by Old Mam, and
the Santo Mundo.

The fruit's complaints, scoldings, and warnings are the direst reminders to
these young men of the disastrous consequences to the harmonious cosmic order of the Santo Mundo should these customs be treated lightly, neglected,
scorned, or abandoned. The fruit ridicules the *alguacils* for complaining or for
wanting relief from the arduous journey that is of such pivotal importance for
the survival of the world. The fruit calls them "thief" and "lazy," spurring them
on, telling them not to be temped to "steal" and eat the sacred fruit themselves or to be careless or fainthearted on their difficult journey. The young
man hears again the words of his courting song, now sung to him by the fruit:
"I am poor, I am a wandering orphan [slave, vagabond], I am lost, I am fallen
in the dust of the road." Now it is the fruit of the old year that is tired, fallen
in the dust, and at the same time, the new fruit whose seeds will fertilize the
Santo Mundo. The north wind, the whirlwind took it, the fruit complains, because the *alguacils* picked it off the tree and separated it from its mother, forc-
ing its coming of age. It is happy when the *alguacils* sing it a lullaby as they rock
it on their backs, "singing like its mother, the wife of Old Mam," my translator
explained. The fruit is happy when they sing or dance with it as they walk, because the music—and the plentiful *guaro* on this trip—relieve the sadness of
its heart so its tears can flow. The full baskets of fruit are like the full wombs of
the young men's wives, and the cacao their children, and the singing and the
dancing "make the road dance," make the Santo Mundo dance and move like
the belly of a woman in labor, as the song says:

> I sing, they say
> and I sing with power on the road, they say
> I will make the road dance, they say

And so the Midwife deity YaMri'y Iyom (Maria Midwife) brings the Santo
Mundo to give birth again to a new year and to Old Mam, the Lord of Maize
and Rain.

"B'ix rxin Sk'ul"
Juan Petzey Takaxoy, songman

"Song of the Fruit"

[Sk'ul:]
Xinco'sa nen, yan
xinco'sa nen, nute'
chujyu'
chutk'aj.

[Fruit:]
I am tired, dear
I am tired, my mother
on the mountains
on the plains.

Como atet at powr
anen enmeba'.
Majo'n wc'atzil, quinatz'at.

Just as you are poor
I am a wandering orphan.
This is how you see me, good for nothing.

[C'jol:]:
Ja c'ara' rxin xul
ja c'ara' rxin k'ojom
ja c'ara' xintzujtaja
ja c'ara' xinyok'taja

[Young man:]
This is the ritual of the flute
this is the ritual of the big drum
for this ritual I was insulted
for this ritual I was ridiculed

como atet atbiyona.
"At jo'k,
at k'ayi's!" quinatz'at.

just as you said.
"You are an ass-wipe
you are garbage!" you said to me.

Como atet cara' nabij c'a chwa:
"Majo'n awc'atzil
at jargant, elk'om."
Pr ja c'ara nbij k'ojom
ja c'ara' nbij xul, cha'
ja c'ara' nbij quitar,
    cha'.

That is what you said to me:
"You are good for nothing
you are lazy, a thief."
But that is what the marimba says
that is what the flute says, so they tell it
that is what the guitar says,
    so they tell it.

[Sk'ul:]
Ok powr
okmeba'.
Nocaya xoktzaknak, cha'
ja c'ara quiemb'ixaj p b'ey, cha'.
Xinco'sa c'anan, cha'
chujyu', chutk'aj, ch yan,
    cha'
rxin b'ey, rxin clo', cha'
como ja' nbij, quinb'ixana, cha'.

[Fruit:]
We are poor
we are wandering orphans.
They see us as lost, so they tell it
this is what I sing on the road, so they tell it.
I got tired on the hills, so they tell it
on the mountains, in the valleys, dear,
    so they tell it
on the road, with footsteps, so they tell it
as I was told, I sing, so they tell it.

[C'jol:]:
Quintorina tzrij tak b'ey, cha'
quinsobsaj b'ey, cha'.
Quimb'ixana chujyu', chutk'aj,
    cha'
qui' ruc'u'x wanma, cha'

vrac'ara, cha'.
Kas pkan xuna'
wanma xinatz'uj c'a!, cha'.
Y anen xinxle'a' chwach b'ey
xinjte'a', xink'e'a', cha'
"Jat ctojte'a'! Jat!"nabij chwa, cha'.
Utz c'a, cha'
ja c'ara xinatz'uj c'a, cha'
x'natz'ila', cha'
x'nayo'k' c'a, cha'.

Em powr, cha'
en meba', cha'
xinco'sa, c'a.
Xbij c'a chwa
ch yan, cha'
y anen, aley; y anen, yan
xabij c'a chwa.

Quinxle'na c'a chujyu'
chutk'aj, cha'
como anen xabij c'a chwa, cha'.
"Jat elk'om," cha'
"jat c'a rxin chujyu'," cha'.

Kas meltyox c'a chawa, yan
kas meltyox c'a chawa
xabij c'a chwa, nen.
Xinco'sa c'a chwach tk'aj
kas cara' nabij c'a chwa
kas njelal chwach wanma, cha'.
Kas xabij c'a chwa, nute'
xabij c'a chwa, yan

[Young man:]
I sing with power on the road, so they tell it
I make the road dance, so they tell it.
I sing on the mountains, on the plains,
    so they tell it
sweet is the heart of my soul, so they tell it

and it hurt me very much, so they tell it.
How it hurt my heart
that they ridiculed my soul!, so they tell it.
And I went down the road
I went up, I crossed the roads, so they tell it
"Go on! Go up!" you told me, so they tell it.
It is alright, then, so they tell it
that they ridiculed me like that, so they tell it
that they insulted me, so they tell it
that they criticized me, so they tell it.

I am poor, so they tell it
I am a wandering orphan, so they tell it
I am tired, then.
You talked to me
to me, little girl, so they tell it
to me, little girl, to me, dear
you talked to me.

I must go down on the hills
on the plains, so they tell it
just as you said to me, so they tell it.
"Go on, thief," so they tell it
"go on, go up the hills," so they tell it.

Thank you very much, little girl
I thank you very much
that you said this to me, dear.
I got tired on the hills
because you talked to me that way
because you said it to my heart, so they tell it.
You really said this to me, my mama
you said this to me, girl

"Majo'n awc'atzil" xabij chwa cha'
"Jat!" cha', "Jat ctojte'a!"
   cha'.
Utz c'a, xabij c'a chwa, cha'
kas pkan xuna' wanma
xabij c'a chwa cawra',
   cha'.
Xinjte'a c'a chujyu'
xenqu'a' chutk'aj, cha'.

[Sk'ul:]
Xneco'sa chwach jyu
xinco'sa chwach b'ey
xinco'sa chwach tk'aj, cha'.
xinba c'a, xinxle'a c'a.
xunjte'a', c'a
xinrc'aj k'ik'
xinrck'aj silcum c'a, cha'.
Xach'aj p nwa', cha'.

[C'jol:]
Utz c'a, cha', yan
utz c'a, nute', cha'
utz c'a, yan, cha'.
Meltyox chawa', yan
meltyox chawa', nute', cha'.
[8.71.5, item 43]

"You are worthless," you said to me
"Go!" you said, "Go on the hills!"
   so they tell it.
It is good, then, you told me, so they tell it
and it hurts my heart so much
that you talked to me that way,
   so they tell it.
So I went up the mountains
I went down on the plains, so they tell it.

[Fruit:]
I got tired on the mountains
I got tired on the road
I got tired on the plains, so they tell it.
I went up, I went down
I went up, then
the north wind took me
the whirlwind took me, so they tell it.
You scolded[61] me, so they tell it.

[Young Man:]
It is alright, so they tell it, dear
it is alright, my mama, so they tell it
it is alright, girl, so they tell it.
Thank you, dear
I thank you, my mama, so they tell it.

The similarity of the following text of the "Song of the Fruit" that was sung on a different occasion by Nicolás Coche Sapalu is interesting and may show the extent to which the stylized language of this sacred and highly important ritual song may be less open to improvisation than the more individualized songs of the courting customs. This is indicated as well by the constant reference in both songs to their origin in the words of the Nawals in the word *cha'*, "so they tell it" or "as they say." The second version ends with the striking series, "thank you dear, thank you my mama, thank you, Midwife," addressing the ancestral Midwife Nawal YaMri'y Iyom who delivers Old Mam, the Lord of the reborn corn, and who will also be present when the *alguacil*'s wife gives birth to their own children, who may have good or bad luck in the Santo Mundo because of this ritual.

"B'ix rxin Sk'ul"   "Song of the Fruit"
Nicolás Coche Sapalu (voice) and Juan Petzey Takaxoy (guitar)
AUDIO FILE 12

Xin co'sa nen, yan	I got tired, dear
xin co'sa nen, nute'	I got tired, my mama
chojyu'	on the mountains
cho tk'aj.	on the plains.
Como atet majun wc'atzil quinatz'at.	The way you see me I am good for nothing.
Ja'c'ara xin xul	This is the ritual is of the fruit
ja' c'ara' xin k'ojom, cha'	this is the ritual of the big drum, they say
ja'c'ara xin tz'ujtaja	for this ritual I was insulted
ja'c'ara xin yok'taja, cha'.	for this ritual I was ridiculed, they say.
Como atet c'a	Just as you said
"At jo'k, quinatz'at," cha'	"You are an ass-wipe as I see you," they say
"at k'ayis."	"you are garbage."
Quinatz'at, cha'.	This is how you see me, they say.
Como ate c'a	And you
"Majo'n nabi c'a chwa," cha'	"Don't talk to me," as they say
"majo'n awc'atzil," cha'	"you are worth nothing to me," as they say
"at jargant," cha'	"you are lazy," they say
"at ilk'om," cha'.	"you are a thief," they say.
Ja' cara' xbij k'ojom	This is what the big drum said
ja' c'ara' xbij b'ix	thus is what the song said
ja'c'ara' xbij quitar, cha'.	this is what the guitar said, they say.
Ok powr, ok meba'	We are poor, we are wandering orphans
nko c'aya ok tzunak	we have seen this custom
ok tzunak.	we have seen it.
Ja'c'ara' quimb'ixaj tak quinjte'ta, cha'.	This is what I sing when I go up, they say.
Xin co's, c'anen	I got tired, then
cho jyu'	on the mountain
cho tk'aj, yan	on the plain, little girl
xin b'ey, xin clo', cha'	on the road, on the walk, they say
com ja' nute', cha'.	as my mother said, they say.
Quimb'ixana, cha'	I sing, they say
quintorij pb'ey, cha'	and I sing with power on the road, they say
quinsobsaj pb'ey, cha'	I will make the road dance, they say

quimb'ixana cho jyu', tk'aj, cha', cha'.

Kas qui' nuc'u'x wanma, cha' cac'ara', cha' jar nbij.

Kas p kan xuna' wanma xnatz'uj!

y anen xin xle' pjun b'ey xin xle', xin jte', cha'.

"Jat! Catjte'!" nabij chwa, cha'.

Utz c'a, cha'.

Ja'c'ara' xina tz'uj c'a, cha', chnabij c'a chwa, cha' quinayok'c'a, cha'

E impowr inmeba', cha'.

"Xin cos's c'a," xabij c'a chwa, xinyo'r

que anen, nute'
que anen, yan

xabi c'a chwa, cha'.

Xin xle'c'a cho jyu', cho tk'aj, cha'

com anen xabij c'a chwa, cha'.

"Jat, ilk'om!" cha'
"jat xin chojyu'," cha'.

Mas meltiox c'a chwa, yan kas meltiox, c'a

xabij c'a chwa nen cho jyu', cho tk'aj, cha' kas nabij c'a chwa.

Kas njelal q'uin wanma, cha', kas xabij c'a chwa, yan kas xabij c'a chwa nute', cha'.

"Majo'n awc'atzij, xabij chwa," cha'
"Jat!" cha', "Jat, ctojte!" cha'.

Utz c'a xabij chwa, cha'.

Kas pkan xuna' wanma xabij cara', cha'

Quinjte' c'a cho jyu'
quinjte'c'a cho tkaj, cha'

I will sing on the mountain, on the plain they say.

So sweet is the heart of my soul, they say like this, they say this it what it says.

What pain my heart felt when you insulted me!

and I went up a road
I went down, I went up, they say.

"Go on! Go up!" she said to me, they say.

It's alright, then, they say.

This is the ritual, they say that you say this to me, they say you ridicule me, they say.

I am poor, I am a wandering orphan, they say.

"I got tired," you said to me, lady

to me, mama
to me, girl

you said to me, they say.

I went down the mountain on the plain, they say because you said this to me, they say.

"Go, thief!" they say
"go to the mountain," they say.

Thank you very much, dear thank you very much, then

for saying this to me on the mountain, on the plain, they say that you say this to me.

With all my heart, they say everything you said to me, dear everything you said to me, my mama, they say.

"You are worthless, you said to me," they say
"Go on!" so they say, "Go on, go up!" they say.

It is good that you said this to me, they say.

Such pain my heart felt because you said this to me, they say

I will go up the mountain, then
I will go up the plain, then, they say

Xneco's chwach jyu'	I got tired on the mountain
xinco'sa chwach b'ey	I got tired on the road
xinco'sa chwach tk'aj, cha'	I got tired on the plain, they say
xinba c'a, xin xle c'a, xin jte', cha'	I went, I went up, I went down, they say
xin rc'aj i'k	the north wind took me
xinrc'aj salcum, cha'	the whirlwind took me, they say
xach'ej pinwa', cha'.	you scolded me, they say.
Utz c'a yan	It is good, dear
utz c'a, nute', cha',	it is good, my mama, they say
utz c'a, Iyom, cha'.	it is good, Midwife, they say.
Xuban.	It is done.
Meltiox chawa, yan	Thank you, dear
meltiox chawa, nute'	thank you, my mama
meltiox, Iyom.	thank you, Midwife.
[8.71.3, item 38F]	

The rituals of this power-laden period of the year renew the re-creation of the Santo Mundo and of Old Mam as the Lord of Corn and Rain. To accomplish this, Old Mam assumes the role of the old, spent year that will be sacrificed in the symbolic action of the dismemberment of his almost lifesize doll-like figure. In anticipation of Old Mam's journey to the underworld with his wife, YaMri'y CastilYan, the *alguacils* are gathered by the *cofradía* elders on the Thursdays of Lent to be prepared for their own journey on the ancient road down to the coast where they will collect the fruit that will be the couple's food.

At the same time that the fruit is the food of Old Mam, it also represents seed-bearing phalluses, just as their women are represented by the breast-shaped cacaos. In the beginning, Old Mam was assigned by the Nawals as their guardian and protector, so now Old Mam returns in the form of his newly re-constructed figure, reborn as the new year and as the lord and bringer of the rains:

> [Old Mam] is "the Man" par excellence, the shaman whose power enables him to cross on the roads to the four corners, to ascend to "the ancient chairs, the ancient tables" of the gods on the mountain tops. He can fly to the sky to draw down the blessings of the spirits of nature, especially the sun, upon men. He is the pre-eminent Lord over all aspects of fertility that are activated by the agency of man: the bearing and implanting of seeds. Thus, he is the guardian of human sexuality represented by the phallic seed-bearing fruits of Holy Week. This guardianship he exercises in his role of "policeman, warden, watchman." These fruits are harvested when he has drawn the sun to its fullest heat in the center of the sky at the time of the vernal equinox. (O'Brien 1975, 249–250)

The *alguacils* present the boxes of fruit.

The *alguacils* fast and are sexually abstinent for a period of time before their journey, during which time they will endure fatigue, hunger, and thirst, coming back to town with sore feet, exhausted from the weight of their *cacaxtles* or backracks in which they carry the phallic-shaped plantains, huge elongated *melocotones* that they call "sweet-smelling swollen male members," and two kinds of cacao. The fruit refers unmistakably to the sexual energy active in them as they return to their new wives after this time of sexual abstinence, and at the same time it points to the fertility of the natural world. Reminding us here of the oft-depicted ancient Maya theme of the sacrifice of captives brought back by their warriors, most notably expressed in highland Guatemala in the dance-drama *Rabinal Achí*, the fruits are also the captives brought back by the young warriors to be sacrificed for Old Mam. The *alguacils'* self-control will be transformed into rains that inseminate the world. These young men who left on this road as boys still attached to their mothers, return proven by suffering and, like Parsifal, newly independent from their mothers, as rain-men. As Stanzione puts it, "Human sexual order and wet acts of fertility will bring about cosmic sexual order and divine rains of sustenance" (2003, 13).[62]

As they return on Saturday morning, they come up the hill into town still dancing to the "Song of the Fruit" with their boxes on their backs, full of fruit and covered with purple orchids, as they are welcomed with ritual speeches by

A young woman censes
the fruit boxes, Semana
Santa, 1972.

the *cofradía* officials dressed in their finest ritual clothes and by their new wives
who wave censers that bellow fragrant incense around them. The fruit is carried amid the clouds of incense to the sound of the flute and big drum, the marimbas, and the guitars playing the "Recibos of Old Mam," as all go together in
procession to the house of the *Primer Mayor* or First Elder. Until Wednesday of
Holy Week the fruit will ripen, surrounded by the powerful influences of music, dancing, and the drinking of the sacred semenlike *atol* made of corn gruel
and *guaro,* just as the Nawals were taught at the first festival in which Mam was
created. From there the fruit will be taken to the center of town to meet the
newly reborn figure of Old Mam, who is enthroned amid it as the lord of the
fruit.

    At the time of this research the figure of Rilaj Mam was kept on the rafters
of the *cofradía* Santa Cruz.[63] Each year a new priest or *telinel* is chosen to carry
him for the rituals of Holy Week.

The secret rituals of the telinel [priest of Rilaj Mam] and his helper, the third cofrade, take place there and are hidden from outsiders. Some time before Monday
of Holy Week, Mam is undressed and taken apart. His clothes are put away in a special trunk containing clothes he has worn from years before, and other articles
which have been given to him. A new set of clothes is selected: twelve shirts, twelve
sashes, twelve typical Tzutuhil-style pants of purple and white knee-length cotton
with fine embroidery of birds from knee to thigh. These washable items are put in
a bag of knotted twine which is brought down and placed on the table in the cofradia. To this the mask of Mam wearing the hats is tied, and a large lighted cigar is
put in his mouth. Those present may offer him gifts of guaro, cigars, or clothes by
presenting them to the telinel.

Near midnight on Monday the new clothes are taken by the telinel and the third
cofrade accompanied by others of the cofradia to a spot on the Lake shore south of
town, which is described as "the real center of the earth." The clothes are washed
by three men cofrades upon three flat rocks which are kept from year to year for
this purpose. These are set in the shallow water in a straight row from east to west.

The telinel directs this process and as each article of washed clothing is returned to him he packs it in the rope bag until all are finished. The bag of clothes,
heavy with water, is carried by the telinel to the house where they will be put out to
dry. (O'Brien 1975, 187–189)

The "others of the *cofradía*" mentioned above include young women who wish
to conceive and who bring vessels to collect the water that runs from Mam's
clothes so they can drink it to obtain its powers of fertility. All of this takes
place at the lakeside in the amazing soundscape of the loud chorus of the
croaking frogs of Lake Atitlán. The clothes are dried in the house of the *telinel* and put away in a wooden trunklike chest for future use. New clothes have
been donated for this night of renewed creation.

On Tuesday night the *telinel* and third *cofrade* ascend the ladder that leads
from the single room of the *cofradía* to the rafters above. Mam's body is assembled there in secret. The *telinel* is required to know without instruction the
proper way to do this, so that all the pieces are properly used and the finally
assembled figure will stand erect without support. The body of Mam is said to
contain the following secret: "Twelve screws, twelve stars, twelve locks, twelve
keys, twelve strings."[64] The *telinel* and third *cofrade* take the finished body down
the ladder into the midst of the gathered *cofrades*. They descend the ladder hidden behind straw mats, which are held up by *cofrades* surrounding them. Behind these mats, on the floor, the body is dressed in the new clothes. When this
is finished, the mats are dropped, and all can see the figure of Mam, dressed
in fine clothes, his imposing mask, and a big cigar (O'Brien 1975, 189–190).

In 1972 I was there among the *tixels*, having been given the special long
huipil, a shawl, and a candle, and the invitation to be the third *tixel* for the rit-

uals of this period. The experience of this night was profoundly moving. The small room, packed with *cofrades* and *tixels* whose sculptured faces were gently lit by the flickering candlelight, was hot and full of the smells of bodies, of liquor, tobacco, pine needles, incense, and flowers, and the sound of the "Song of Mam" coming from the soft strumming of a songman's guitar. As I watched and tried hard to understand I suddenly had a flash of insight: although the active roles in these rituals were played by men, this was clearly a birthing, and I knew it must have a female presence. I could sense it and feel it, and thought I had identified the female element. I leaned over to the *tixel* sitting next to me on the mat and whispered, "Tonight the *telinel* is Mam's woman, isn't he?" She brightened and with some emotion looked at me and whispered, "Yes!"

The *telinel*'s role on this night is complex, as he is also the agent of the Midwife goddess YaXper, who brings Mam to birth, as well as being Mam's carrier or bearer. At first we could see that the reconstructed figure of Old Mam was limp like a newborn, and then was later propped up for us to see him in his new and glorious regalia. At this point Old Mam was lifted onto the shoulder of the *telinel* who danced him to the music of the Recibos, just as he was made to "stand up" by the music and dancing at the first festival. Later that night, though, Old Mam rested like a helpless newborn, lying on a mat on the floor of the *cofradía*.

On Wednesday Old Mam was carried to the center of town to meet the ripened fruit. At one time Mam used to be carried into the church amid the fruit and flowers, and hung among them on a screen erected behind the altar, but because this was no longer permitted by the Catholic priests he was taken to a small chapel close to the church where, dressed in all his finery of flowered silk scarves, big shiny shoes, and Stetson hats, he was hung from a branch of a leafy dahlia tree that had been cut for the purpose. From Wednesday to Good Friday he stayed there, finally to be taken by the *telinel* to join the long procession of people coming out of the church after the Mass of Good Friday in which JesuKrista, now taken down from the large cross in the church, was carried in a glass casket complete with decorations of tinsel, flowers, and colored lights in a long procession around the town on the usual ritual route to the four directions. The procession would return near midnight, very beautiful and glowing with hundreds of candles snaking along in the dark like a moving Milky Way on its path back to the church. In the days of Rilaj Mam's hanging on the tree, Stanzione sees his journey to the underworld, perhaps as one of the newly resurrected wonder-workers, the Hero Twins of the Popol Vuh, who—during their dancing—were able to bring themselves back to life to foil the gods of the underworld:

> Some people say he is asleep. Some people say he is dead. Some people say he is
> like fruit hanging from a tree waiting to be picked. Some people say he is like a

Old Mam comes into town, Semana Santa, 1972.

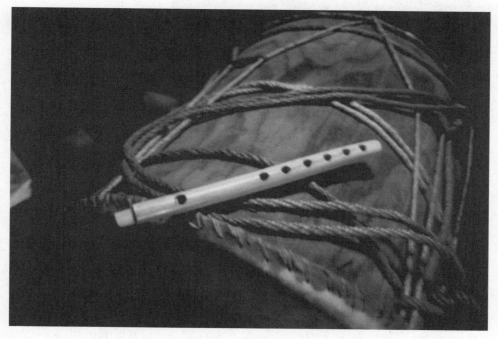

The flute and drum, Semana Santa, 1972.

Dancing with the Primer
Mayor, Semana Santa,
1972.

K'ichean hero twin who has been sacrificed, a being who will resurrect through the
sacrificial death of his hero twin brother MaNawal de Jesus. (2003, 274)

Other remarkable and obvious parallels exist between these Tz'utujil rituals
and the creation myth of the ancient Maya as told in classic period iconography
on ceramics and inscribed texts at sites such as Quirigua and Palenque, and as
told in the *Popol Vuh*. The accounts, which vary in details, tell of the day of creation when the male and female Creator Gods, among them "*Tz'aqol, B'itol;
Alom, K'ajolom*" ("Framer, Shaper; She Who Has Borne Children, He Who Has
Begotten Sons")[65] "made things appear," the same language used for Mam's
standing up. Then First Father, the Maize God, caused three stones—the
hearth stones in the center of a Maya house—to be set up to form the hearth
or center of the sky for the first fire of creation. These three stones of creation

can be seen in the stars in the constellation Orion, a constellation that represents a turtle carapace in the ancient story. This part of the story is reenacted in Atitlán when the three stones are placed in the water of Lake Atitlán during the night of Monday of Holy Week for the washing of Old Mam's clothes.

Across the sky stretched the *sak b'ey*, the white road of the Milky Way. On this road the Maize God was then brought in a canoe by the Paddler gods to the site of the turtle carapace. There, with the help of rain-men, the Maize God emerged newly reborn from the cracked carapace of the turtle where the three stones lay. When he stood up, young women helped him to dress, assisted by priests. The Maize God, now standing up, raised the sky out of the primordial sea by means of a tree, thus forming the *axis mundi* and starting the motion of the stars, which marked the beginning of time. The surface of the earth then was able to emerge like a table, slightly unsteady and sometimes wobbly, reminding us of the movements of the Santo Mundo in Tz'utujil prayers and songs. In some depictions, the Maize God carries with him a bag of seeds to plant on the earth.

CHAPTER FOUR

The Poetics of Tz'utujil Songs and Their Relationship to K'iche'an Literature

READERS FAMILIAR WITH THE COSMIC PARADIGM of the Maya of the highlands of Chiapas and Guatemala will recognize many common concepts, stories, and elements of myth in the Santo Mundo described by Tz'utujil songs and prayers. The content of the song texts that relates to specific modes of behavior in liminal life situations may also be found to be consistent with ethnographic data of social behavior in highland Maya communities. But questions arise about the origin, poetic structure, and design of the song texts. What kind of poetry is this and where did it come from? How is it composed? Is there a similar tradition to which the songs can be compared? What is the influence of the melodies on the text, and vice versa?

About fifty-two of the songs I recorded have significantly long poetic texts.[1] To my knowledge, no other extensive documentation of similar traditional songs of the highland Maya has been made. Fortunately, a long Maya poetic work written down in colonial times escaped the flames in which Christian missionaries burned most Maya manuscripts. That work is the *Popol Vuh*, or *Book of the Council* (or *Book of the Mat* [*on which the leader sat*], or *Book of the Community [gathered around the leader on the mat]*), of the K'iche' Maya, close relatives of the Tz'utujil.

The *Popol Vuh* is a largely poetic text of an epic poem that probably was composed in its present form at Santa Cruz del Quiché and was copied in the K'iche' language using the Spanish alphabet in the town of Santo Tomás, Chichicastenango, northwest of Santiago Atitlán, between 1554 and 1558. Scholars increasingly agree that it is a translation of a manuscript that was written in Maya glyphs before the Spanish invasion. Allen Christenson describes its provenance:

Of the numerous hieroglyphic bark-paper books which once existed in the Maya lowlands, all that escaped the Spanish purges of the sixteenth century are four incomplete codices. Of those written in the highlands of Guatemala, not a single Precolumbian codex is known to have survived.

But these tragic acts of destruction did not mean that Maya literacy ended with the arrival of the Europeans. Soon after the Spanish conquest, literate members of the highland Maya nobility made a number of transcriptions of their Precolumbian books utilizing a modified Latin script in an effort to preserve what they could of their recorded history and culture before they could be destroyed or lost. By far the most important extant example of such a transcription is the *Popol Vuh*, a lengthy document composed by anonymous members of the Quiché-Maya aristocracy in Guatemala soon after the fall of their capital city to the Spanish conquerors. (2007b, 25)

The K'iche' version was again copied and translated into a new Spanish version by the Dominican friar Francisco Ximénez around 1701. In 1861 this was recopied and published by a French priest, Charles-Étienne Brasseur de Bourbourg, together with a French translation.[2]

The *Popol Vuh* was chosen for comparison to Tz'utujil songs because of its predominantly poetic character and its length, and because they share common themes and characteristics. It tells of the creation of the world, of humans and animals by the gods, the adventures of the heroic ancestors, and the journey of the K'iche'an peoples to their present home in the Guatemalan highlands. According to the account, thirteen tribes originated in the east together with the K'iche'. The Tz'utujils, who speak a language closely related to K'iche', were among them.

With Munro Edmonson's publication in 1971 of the *Popol Vuh* as poetry arranged in couplets with a side-by-side translation into English (1971a), it became apparent to me that a common tradition was shared in the texts of the songs I was collecting among the Tz'utujils and the poetic passages of the *Popol Vuh* (O'Brien 1975, 34, footnote 1). Since K'iche' and Tz'utujil languages are very similar, I could easily identify common words, phrases, symbols, and concepts. I could see a resemblance to the parallel verse that Tz'utujil songmen created, and that there were other common stylistic and mythological elements, like lists of gods and animals, lines ending with *cha'* ("so they tell it"), an endless number of common ideas and themes (gourds, dolls of wood, colors, cords or rope, roads), even the name "Face of the Earth," which songmen gave as the general title of the *b'ix* ("Songs of the Face of the Earth"). In comparing Tz'utujil songs to the *Popol Vuh* I am fortunate to be able to rely on the extensive scholarship of Denis Tedlock and Allen Christenson, whose deep understanding of the work has made the comparison possible.

The consensus among scholars is that, in spite of Spanish efforts to destroy indigenous Maya culture, it in fact persisted thanks to the Maya's "capacity to transform their models of the cosmos without destroying the basic structures of the models themselves" (Freidel et al. 1993, 38). The *Popol Vuh* is itself evidence that Maya authors continued to record their traditions in writing even under Spanish prohibitions against any traditional arts that would preserve the "memory of a world that had no Spaniards and no church in it" (Tedlock 2010, 299).

Unlike the *Popol Vuh*, the songs of the Tz'utujils have remained an unwritten oral tradition that survived the upheavals of history into the twentieth century, and analysis can only suggest that they are from much earlier times. Song-men and prayer-makers assure us that they stem from a written tradition that is "from the root" of time. The writer of the *Popol Vuh* refers to a lost book:

> We shall bring it forth because there is no longer the means whereby the [Book of the Council] Popol Vuh may be seen, . . . The original book exists that was written anciently, but its witnesses and those who ponder it hide their faces. (Christenson 2003b, 4)

In a similar way in his prayer, Tz'utujil *ajcun* Cruz Tiney Takaxoy expressed the desire to find the books of the ancestral Fathers and Mothers, to be able to see and study the words in the books stretched out before the Nawals, where the songs also are found:

> *Meltiox, ndta Dio's. Stewilt na jlibr cxin Kad'ta, jlibr cxin Kate', Dio's JesuKrista; jtzojbal jcnoc'bal, Dio's. Clojden, cpajken, ajnipa Dio's tz'ubala, natala, Dio's nechpan, narpan, xe'rek'a, xe'wkan bar c'owa b'ix, cha', bar natalwa, cha'.*

> Thank you, my father Dio's. May the books of our Fathers be found, the books of our Mothers, Dio's JesuKrista, the words, to be able to review them, Dio's. You carry them in your arms like a baby, you carry them in your hands carefully like a basin of water, where you are seated, you are remembered, Dio's. You have hold of them, you have them open in your hands, under your feet, where the singing is, so they tell it, where the songs are, so they tell it.

The Poetics of the *Popol Vuh*

Maya script before the Spanish invasion was arranged in columns of pairs of glyphs, and this pairing was continued by the writer of the alphabetic text of the *Popol Vuh* by using parallel verse. In the *Popol Vuh* a few consecutive lines of verse tend to be identical or "parallel" except for small variations: a synonym, a contrasting word, or an elaboration, for example. These may form groups of two lines (couplets), three (triplets), or four (quatrains) or longer. These groups are often preceded or followed by a single line that is in some way different and provides a contrast or a completion of the meaning, and often an interesting variation in the rhythm.

Rhyme exists in the parallel verse of the *Popol Vuh*, but not the end rhyme familiar to us from its use in European poetry, but rather internal rhyme that is within a line or that links parallel lines. Within a line, words having the same initial sound may be repeated, a poetic device called *alliteration* (for example, **bl**ue **b**ells), and vowel sounds inside words may be repeated, which is called *assonance* (for example, br**a**ve, v**a**in). These devices, while belonging to the formal poetic structure, also tend to draw attention to the *meaning* of the words that have been repeated or emphasized by the assonance or alliteration. Referring to the continuity between Mayan literature before and after Spanish contact and its difference from Western poetry, Tedlock points out:

> One of the features that unites texts in the Mayan script with those that Mayas wrote in the alphabet is that many passages take the form of parallel verse, in which recurrent patterns of sound reflect recurrent patterns of meaning rather than operating at a level below that of meaning, as they do in metrical verse. (2010, 2)

Several songs are mentioned in the *Popol Vuh*, and two short song texts are quite similar, one of which follows:

Akarok xojsachik!	Alas we were lost!
Chi Tulan xojpaxin wi qib'.	At Tulan we split ourselves apart.
Xeqakanaj chik qatz,	We left behind our older brothers
Qa chaq'.	and our younger brothers.
Awi mi xkil wi q'ij?	Where did they see the sun?
Awi on e k'o wi ta mi xsaqirik?	Where were they when it dawned?
(Christenson 2007b, 6212–6217)	

The parallelism of the lines can be seen in the repeated words, phrases, and sounds in both the K'iche' text and in the English translation:

xojsachik	we were lost
xojpaxin	we split ourselves
chik	our older brothers
chaq'	our younger brothers

| Awi mi xkil | Where did they see |
| Awi on k'o | Where were they |

In the K'iche' text, the parallels are created by repeating initial sounds (*x, ch, A*), by repeating meanings ("we were lost"/"We split ourselves [up]"), by forming contrasting meanings ("our older brothers"/"our younger brothers"), and by offering small variations in meaning ("Where did they"/"where were they").[3] In the K'iche' we can pick out rhyming vowels inside the words: *Alarok* and *xoj*, *sachchik* and *paxin*, and a whole line of internal rhyme on the sound "i": *Awi, mi, xkil, wi, and a'ij*.

Other poetic devices used in the *Popol Vuh* can best be pointed out in comparison to the songs of the Tz'utujils.

The Poetics of Tz'utujil Song Texts

Parallelism

In the following transcriptions I have arranged the lines in a way that reveals the poetic structure, following when possible the singers' pauses and the musical phrases. The poetic norms of the oral tradition are flexible and style varies from songman to songman, and parts or all of some song texts do not display the poetic features of those here described.

In the "*B'ix rxin Nawal*," songmen construct parallel lines, most often couplets, as they sing. As in the *Popol Vuh*, couplets, triplets, or quatrains are often preceded or followed by a single line that is different. In the "Song of the Spirit-Lord of the World" sung by Diego Cua Simaj (page 26), a couplet and a triplet united by the repetition of words are followed by a final line that is different.

Naya' rabendicion,	You give us your blessing,
naya' rainstrumentos	you give us your instruments
con bona santa voluntad Dio's.	with good and holy will Dio's.

Naya' kicxilway,	You give us our tortillas,
naya' kichaj	you give us our herbs
naya' kimunil,	you give us our fruit,
ay'on kic'aslemal.	you give us our life.

In the "Song of the Young Men and Young Girls, of Insults and Ridicule," Antonio Quieju Culan (page 120) constructs a triplet that has a final line that completes the thought in a similar way:

⎧ Camic c'a ala'   ⎧ Now boy
⎨ camic c'a c'jol   ⎨ now young man
⎩ camic c'a nen   ⎩ now I
     kas etzel nu'on.   I feel very bad.

Later he constructs a triplet that is preceded by a single line that introduces it. In the final line he drops a word and substitutes a synonym, "your sash," creating a parallel meaning and a variation in the rhythm:

   "Majo'n c'a awc'atzil!   "You are good for nothing!
⎧ Sak asca'w   ⎧ White are your pants
⎨ sak acwton   ⎨ white is your shirt
⎩ sak apas,   ⎩ white is your belt,
     atnwkon."   your sash."

Similar verse structures are found in the *Popol Vuh*, in which a couplet or triplet is followed by a phrase in which a word is dropped, calling a halt to the rhythm, as in:

   ca catzininoc,   it still ripples,
   ca cachamamoc,   it still murmurs,
     catzinonic   ripples
   (Tedlock 1983, 222)

Quatrains are common in both the *Popol Vuh* and in Tz'utujil songs. A "Song of the Young Man" by Diego Cua Simaj has an example of a quatrain, again with a completing fifth line at the end:

⎧ Pr quinwaj c'a jun nsantaw,   ⎧ Because I want to have a penny of my
⎪   nute'   ⎪   own, my mama
⎨ pr quinsmaj c'a, nute'   ⎨ because I work, my mama
⎪ pr quinsmaj c'a, nidta'   ⎪ because I work, my papa
⎩ pr quinsmaj c'a, in'ay'on canc'a   ⎩ because I work, but you have left me alone
     chwach mund, Ruch'lew, nute'.   in the world, the Face of the Earth, my
                       mama.

Although not common in the *Popol Vuh*, Tz'utujil songs contain frequent examples of five and more parallel lines. The following example is from Antonio Quieju Culan's "Song of the Young Girl," which also has the name "Cristobal" (page 115):

Mscna' xc'yil si'	Even if he is a firewood-seller
mscna'x ch'roy chaj	even if he cuts heart-of-pine
mscx kloy much'	even if he cuts *chipilín*[4]
mscx kloy echaj	even if he cuts *yerbita mora*
mscx pk'oy skil	even if he sells pumpkin seeds with chile
mscx y k'ul wajqex	even if he keeps cattle
bnoy ch'it ruya'l chit mukil . . .	even if he sells *matatito* . . .
mscx chpoy tap	even if he is a crab fisherman
mscx s luy akok	even if he butchers chickens
mscx chpoy ch'u'.	even if he is a fisherman.

Another example comes from his song about a couple, "They Fought" (page 133):

Atjun Dio's	I need Dio's
atjun Sant	I need a Santo
atjun prcipal	I need an elder
atjun rmament	I need right now
atjun awuc'	I need my family
atjuna wch'alal	I need my brother
atjuna wamig	I need my friend
atjuna . . .	I need . . .
atjuna acha	I need a man

Meter

Tedlock notes Edmonson's observation that

> there is no meter—in the strict sense of recurrent quantifications of stresses, vowel lengths, or syllables . . . in the indigenous verbal arts of the New World. (Edmonson 1971b, 99, in Tedlock 1983, 218)

Tedlock adds:

> Even in songs whose texts consist entirely of vocables rather than words, where tight metrical patterns would be easy to achieve if they were desired, there are seldom more than two or three successive lines that even have the same number of syllables. (1983, 218)[5]

This same unevenness in the metrical patterns of the parallel lines is found in many Tz'utujil songs. The following lines of Diego Cua Simaj's "Song of the

Spirit-Lord of the World," used above as examples of couplets and triplets, are examples of unevenness of the number of syllables in successive parallel lines. Accented syllables in the lines of parallel verse are in capitals:

NaYA' raBENdiCION,	6 syllables
naYA' raINstruMENtos,	7 syllables
con bona santa voluntad, riDio's	
NaYA' kicxilWAY,	5 syllables
naYA' kiCHAJ,	4 syllables
naYA' kimuNIL,	5 syllables
ay'on kic'aslemal.	

But in contrast to what these authors have found to be true of the verbal arts of the New World ("seldom more than two or three successive lines that even have the same number of syllables"), Tz'utujil songmen often create several successive lines in an even metrical pattern, using words or nonlexical syllables or both. The following lines, for example, begin with an initial line of four syllables followed by six lines of five syllables:

Ximba p b'ey nen	I went into the street
xintz'u'ja⸜anen[6]	they insulted me
xintz'u'ja⸜acha	they insulted me, man
xintz'u'ja⸜k'poj.	they insulted me, girl.
Tela' c'jol ala'	Hurry up, young boy
tela' c'jol achi	hurry up, young man
tela' c'jol ala'	hurry up, young boy

The following, from a "Song of Mam," is another of many examples of several lines of nonlexical vocables in regular five-syllable rhythm:

yana yana li
yana yana la
nana nana na
nana nana nu
nana nana ni
nana nana nu
nana nana na
nana nana nu
nana nana na
nana nana nu

Onomatopoeia

The use of nonlexical syllables that imitate the sounds they refer to, or ono-matopoeia, is a characteristic of K'iche' poetry. Tz'utujil songmen also often imitate the sound of a musical instrument, for example, *china china* imitating the sound of strumming the guitar, or *tana tana* and *tuna tuna* for the sound of the drum. The following seventeen lines, from a "Song of Mam," maintain a steady five-syllable rhythm. The nonlexical lines in italics are not devoid of meaning, but rather they imitate the sound of the drum and the guitar.

china china acha	*ching ching man*
china china ala'	*ching ching boy*
Xawxin c'a ala'	Yours then boy
xawxin c'a guitar	yours is the guitar
xawxin c'a ventur	yours is the bandurria[7]
xawxin c'a scarment	yours is the instrument
xawxin c'a k'ojom	yours is the big drum
xawxin c'a a'a	yours it is boy
xawxin c'a papa	yours it is papa
ak'ojom, ALu	your drum, Lucha
tuna tuna na	*tuna tuna na*
tuna tuna na	*tuna tuna na*
Anen c'a, anen	I then, I
anen c'a mamá	I then mama
ak'ojom, a'a	your drum, boy
tana tana ni	*tana tana ni*
tana tana na	*tana tana na*
Tatjic' wq'uin a'a	Come with me boy
tatjic' wq'uin acha	come with me man
awxin ventur	yours is the bandurria
quink'ojomana.	I play it.

Some songs contain successive lines of onomatopoeic syllables that each end with a single final word:

tana tana ala'	*tana, tana boy*
tana tana alí	*tana tana handsome*
tuna tuna ALu	*tuna tuna Lucha*
tuna tuna ala'	*tuna tuna boy*
tuna tuna ALu	*tuna tuna Lucha*

Lists

The *Popol Vuh* contains various lists of deities, animals, plants, names, titles and so on. Here is a list of the names of the gods:

Juraqan,	Hurricane,
Ch'i'pi Kaqulja,	Youngest Thunderbolt,
Raxa Kaqulja,	Sudden Thunderbolt,
Tepew Q'ukumatz,	Sovereign Queztal Serpent,
Alom,	She Who Has Borne Children,
K'ajolom,	He Who Has Begotten Sons,
Xpiyakok,	Xpiyakok,
Xmuqane,	Xmucane,
Tz'aqol,	Framer,
B'itol	Shaper

(Christenson 2007b, 5102–5112)

Tz'utujil songmen also often create lists in their songs. A song in which a young woman appeals to the female ancestral deities to send her a husband who wears expensive clothes, a hat made of *vicuña* wool, and sandals, lists their names:

Natzirc'awa', Dio's?	Why, Dio's?
Natzirc'awa', Mund?	Why, Mundo?
Natzirc'awa', Ruch'lew?	Why, Face of the Earth?
Natzirc'awa', Mriy?	Why, María?
Nute' Mriy Perdon	My mother María Perdón
nute' Mriy Dolors	my mother María Dolores
nute' Mriy Santuaria	my mother María Santuaria
nute' Mriy Santa Ana	my mother María Santa Ana
nute' Mriy Dolors	my mother María Dolores
nute' Mriy Saragost	my mother María Saragosa
nute' Mriy Dolors	my mother María Dolores
nute' Mriy Saragost	my mother María Saragosa
tia' jun ala' chwa	give me a boy
tia' jun ajcuñ chwa	give me one who wears a vicuña hat
tia' jun ajscaw chwa	give me one who wears sandals[8]

In another example from the *Popol Vuh* the animals made by the gods are named:

Maja b'i'oq	There is not yet
Jun winaq,	One person,
Jun chikop,	One animal,
Tz'ikin,	Bird,
Kar,	Fish,
Tap,	Crab,
Che',	Tree,
Ab'aj	Rock,
Jul,	Hollow,
Siwan,	Canyon,
K'im,	Meadow, or
K'eche'laj.	Forest.

(Christenson 2007b, 107–117)

Similarly, Diego Cua Simaj lists the animals in his "Song of the Spirit-Lord of the World." Here an introductory line is followed by a list in which the parallelism of couplets is varied with a triplet and an explanatory line:

prk Dio's JesuKrista	because Dio's JesuKrista
msc mejor quej,	even the best deer,
msc mejor wacax	even the best bull
chi jun jan,	a fly, or
chi jun snic	an ant
chi jun chkop	or an animal
c'ola pmontaña Ndta'	on the mountain my Father
chi jun tz'e',	or a dog,
chi jun syaw	or a cat
atrpalben Mund	is always standing on you World
atrpalben Ruch'lew.	is always standing on you Face of the Earth.

A similar construction occurs in the same song when the the words "my Father," which introduce the passage, are replaced with "honey," "tortilla dough," and so on for a quatrain, followed by a summarizing line, and then another couplet:

awxin, Ndta' . . .	yours, my Father . . .
awxin cab, awxin cxilway	yours is the honey, yours the maize dough
awxin lok', awxin canel	yours the produce, yours the cinnamon
awxin rexwach, awxin tuja'	yours the black corn, yours the yellow corn
awxin pujuy . . .	yours the mottled corn . . .
Selwir pnak'a xlaxa' pujuy.	In your hands the mottled corn was born.

{ Awxin much', awxin chaj
  awxin. . . , awxin xcoy.

{ Yours is the *chipilín*, yours the resinous pine
  yours. . . , yours the tomato.

Assonance and Alliteration

Another characteristic common to both sources is the use of assonance and alliteration. Note the assonance in the succession of "ā" sounds (*rmaj, car, maj, quinya', c'a, chawa,* and so on), and the alliteration in the repetition of initial "k" sounds in this song (*car, quinya, camic, Qui',* and so on), in which a young man promises to hire marimba players for a young woman to dance "one *son,* two *sones*":

[C'jol:]
Jun rmaj, car maj
quinya' c'a chawa.
Tantzej bijc'a camic
camic c'a nkoba chjay.
Qui' c'a nuc'u'x.

[Young Man:]
One *son,* two *sones*
I'll give you then.
Now I say to you
let's go home now.
I am happy.

Composition of the Texts and the Influence of Musical Rhythm

Songmen identify a song by its extended title, which is a short summary of the story it tells or of the situation for which it is sung.[9] In part they improvise their own lines of text and in part rely on stock phrases that are used for that story or occasion, like "I tell you, mama" for the "Song of the Young Girl." Some stock phrases can be used in any song, like *Lucha Lucha acha* and nonlexical lines like *chana chana li.* Songmen Diego Cua Simaj and Antonio Quieju Culan sang many lines of text using very few stock phrases, and may have memorized parts of their texts.[10] Other songmen used stock phrases to different extents, some exclusively with no improvisation of their own.

The melodies of the songs are often in triple meter, or in duple meter with occasional hemiola, which will be discussed further in Chapter 5. The songs are not always metrical in a strict sense, though; an extra beat or an extra measure is sometimes added, whether sung or instrumental. This rhythmic flexibility creates occasional asymmetry in the rhythm that is not confined to songs, but is found also in Tz'utujil instrumental music. In the songs this flexibility in the length of the musical phrase allows the songman to stretch the melody if he needs to accommodate a longer line of text that he has improvised, or to provide a moment for thought about the line he will improvise next. However, regular rhythm is more common.

It is clear that comparing the rhythmic patterns of the sung lines of Tz'utujil songs to the written lines of the *Popol Vuh* is in some ways like comparing apples and oranges. This is because the poetic scansion of a song text—counting the number of accented and unaccented syllables in a line—cannot provide complete information about the regularity of its rhythm when it is sung. Unlike written or recited texts, in songs the rhythms of the melody and the instrumental accompaniment, plus the unique interpretation of the individual singer, can bestow a regular pulse on a text that, counting only its syllables and accents, is irregular in rhythm. That is to say that in a text sung to a metrical melody, the regularity of the rhythm or lack of it does not always depend on the number of stressed and unstressed syllables, or on the number of poetic feet in a line, as is the case for poetry. This is because the rhythm of stressed and unstressed beats provided by the rhythmic pulse of the music may—and usually does—predominate over the rhythm of the words fitted to it. Subdivisions of the beat by the addition of unstressed notes are commonly found in songs in order to accommodate such extra syllables. Consequently, lines of verse may have an unequal number of syllables but the same number of musical beats.[11]

Therefore, if we were to consider the song texts without any reference to the music and the musical rhythm, sets of lines that are not parallel in patterns of sound or meaning, and that have uneven rhythm, could easily be taken for prose passages. For many years, the *Popol Vuh* seems to have been treated this way, because the manuscript was at some early point copied mainly as prose.

Although Tedlock found that written Mayan poetic literature seldom contains more than three successive lines having the same number of syllables, if these lines were originally sung, the rhythm of the music may have provided regular beats (1983, 218).[12] When this was indeed the case, the rhythm of the sung verse would have depended on the musical pulse, probably regular, of the music and not on the number of syllables. It should be added that the few lines cited above from the *Popol Vuh* that are identified as a song are not rhythmically regular, but they might well have been so when conformed to the regular pulse of a melody. Because the writer of the *Popol Vuh* tells us it was part of a performance, and because it contains many references to songs and dances, and given the abundance of documentation that highland Maya performances in colonial times included music and dance, it seems likely that parts of the *Popol Vuh* beyond the few short lines of songs we find identified there were sung. Tz'utujil songs and the pervasiveness of dance easily allow us to imagine this to be true.

Further, we observe that the *Popol Vuh* is a document that was produced and copied by persons of sufficient education to be literate in K'iche', whereas at least for certain periods of their history, Tz'utujil songs were passed down orally by persons who were not literate, as songmen certainly were not at the time I recorded the songs. Yet metrical symmetry and regularity, and the basic techniques of the art of versification appear to be more developed in Tz'utujil songs than in the *Popol Vuh*, in which a sense of metrical rhythm is less obvious. This could be partly explained if the K'iche' scribe of the *Popol Vuh* behaved as did my translator, who seldom wrote down more than two lines of a series of nonlexical lines of a song, probably because they are repetitious and he judged them to be insignificant or superfluous; nor did I insist, knowing I could add these later when I listened to the recording. The scarcity of successive lines of equal rhythm in the *Popol Vuh* could be explained if the scribe did not write down all the nonlexical lines, perhaps knowing that a singer could use as many nonlexical lines as convenient while he improvised a text from the given content. So while the occasional rhythmic irregularity of the Tz'utujil songs helps to place them squarely in the tradition of Mayan literature, it is also possible—and the song texts suggest—that the irregularity of Mayan verse is not really a universal feature of its poetic style, but a result of the fact that much of it was sung and thus acquired a regular rhythm not from the text but from the music.

CHAPTER FIVE

The Music of the "Songs of the Nawals"

UNLIKE THE SONG TEXTS, the musical form and style of several of the "*B'ix rxin Nawal*," and the playing technique and the construction of the guitar that songmen use, suggest roots in the guitar culture of Spain in the middle sixteenth to early seventeenth centuries. During this same period an intense Spanish presence in Atitlán was related to the trade in cacao produced on Tz'utujil coastal lands (MacLeod 1973, 235–243). The metrical melodies seem to be an expression of variation forms popular in Europe in the late sixteenth and early seventeenth centuries, the *chaconne* and the related *zarabanda*.[1] The nonmetrical melodies, however, are a hybrid form, stemming from liturgical chant psalmody fused with indigenous interpretation and style.

The excellent scholarly work of Frank and Joan Harrison (1968) on the relationship of the instruments and music of the Maya of Chiapas, Mexico, to European antecedents, and the comprehensive and insightful ethnomusicological study of the music of the Achi of Rabinal, Guatemala, by Sergio Navarrete Pellicer (1999, 2005a, 2005b) have laid an invaluable foundation for research into the origins and history of the music of the highland Maya. Their studies provide a strong basis for comparison to Tz'utujil musical forms that enable the identification of common elements and differences.[2]

Form and Style of the Songs

Most of the metrical songs consist of two or four units of two bars of a melody in simple $\frac{3}{4}$ time, but songs in $\frac{6}{8}$ are not uncommon. In both, the meter is interpreted with considerable flexibility and may in the same performance flow casually from one meter to another, as from $\frac{3}{4}$ to $\frac{2}{4}$ or $\frac{5}{4}$, by addition or subtraction of a beat or its suspension in a sustained fermata. Changes in the placement of the accent are common, as is the insertion of hemiola, in which the subdivision of the measure changes from two pulses (for example, two groups of three eighth notes) to three pulses (three groups of two eighth notes), commonly represented as 3:2, creating a rhythmic pattern, for example, of 1–2–3, 1–2–3, 1–2, 1–2. In most songs a rhythmic pattern and melodic contour are repeated through many variations.

The harmonic vocabulary of song melodies is limited to major chords I, V, and IV, and sometimes II. These are provided by *rasgueado* or strummed chords on the guitar, or are implied in vocal solos.

Songs or part of songs may depart from metric regularity altogether to an interpretation in nonmetrical rhythm that strongly resembles formulaic plainsong melodies used for singing the psalms in Catholic liturgy, from which some songs probably derive. Guitar-accompanied songs may have an ending formula or cadence consisting of a series of *rasgueado* chords unrelated to the chords and rhythm of the melody, that ends on the dominant chord. Sometimes the cadence involves a change of key, and often a change in meter, and is usually played *molto ritardando*. In their 1968 study of a similar style in Chiapas, Harrison and Harrison describe this feature as a "short coda with a descending scale," but they include no further analysis or musical transcription (12).

The songman has a clearly defined musical style and a finite number of melodies from which to choose when he sings or plays. As is common in other oral traditions and apparent in the song texts, variation on a theme is the prevailing stylistic feature. What Christenson observed about the poetry of the *Popol Vuh* could well be a statement describing this feature of the songs:

> The Quiché poet is much like the composer of classical music who begins with a
> simple tune and then weaves into it both complementary and contrasting harmonies to give it interest and depth. Thus endless variations on a given theme are possible. (2007a, 42)

Songmen seemed completely comfortable improvising a variety of iterations of a melody, and took pleasure in playing their own unique variations on the guitar when they possessed this facility. They interpreted the songs they sang with their own choice of vocal interpretation, making comments and adding spoken dialogue.

The songs are a soloistic form in which each songman performs by himself, whether the song is sung or only played on the guitar. This allows for the improvisation that characterizes this musical style. Sometimes, however, one or two people in the *cofradía* might join in the singing of familiar stock phrases like "*chana chana la*" in the "Song of Mam," for example, which has a very familiar melody. In the context of the *cofradía*, sometimes the songman plays while another person sings a lament, as on one occasion in the *cofradía* San Juan when I witnessed a widow who was mourning the death of her husband begin to dance and eventually to sing her tearful lament, a "Sad Song of Women" ("*B'ix rxin Ixok Bis*") while the songman continued to play and accompany her on his guitar.

The melody that is associated with the content of a song is actually a simple melodic contour and a harmonic sequence on which to improvise the song and its variations. The characteristic flexibility of the meter allows the songman to use extra beats to extend the melodic and rhythmic patterns, sometimes out of the need to accommodate the text he is improvising, but songmen also use this flexibility in the rhythm when they play the songs as guitar solos. A songman may sing the melody simply, or may improvise on it while playing a rhythmic chordal accompaniment on the guitar. Some play technically challenging *punteado* guitar variations that are plucked on a single string with the first and second fingers, as solos or interludes between sung parts. Unaccompanied singing is not very common.

The "Recibos of Old Mam": The Vessel of Tz'utujil Culture

Old Mam, the Spirit-Lord of music, at that first celebration gave his people the "Recibos" or "Reception Songs," six pieces he taught them to play for dancing at his grand reception at the beginning of what is regarded as the present creation. These Recibos are of the same genre and style as the songs called *b'ix*; both are also called *sones*. The Recibos are somewhat longer and more formal musical compositions than the songs. When played by a marimba, the formality is necessary because several men need to play together in ensemble. At the time of the recordings of these pieces that are specific to the rituals of the town of Atitlán, marimba players from another town where the Recibos were not known had to learn them by rote from a local marimba by memorizing their specific version, and thus contributing to the standardization of an improvisation performed by one specific marimba. The marimbas from out of town did not possess the freedom to improvise that comes from real familiarity that is born of frequent exposure to the melodies. When played by local songmen on the guitar, the Recibos involve more improvisation, as is apparent in the recordings. Songmen who had proficiency on the guitar usually wanted to play one or more of the "Recibos" so I could record them (audio files 13–16 on the website).

From the melodic motives and variations of these six Recibos the melodies of the songs called the *"B'ix rxin Nawal"* apparently all flow. The titles and performance contexts of the Recibos suggest that the belief system and the cultural codes of the Nawals are expressed in the songs that also originally flow from the Recibos. At that first celebration the Nawals were taught the Old Ways of living and behaving in the Santo Mundo, that is, the fundamental content of their culture. Inasmuch as the songs are the vehicles for the transmission of their teachings, the Recibos are the vessel that contains them all. We could say that they function as the "Great Book of the Old Ways," not subject to destruction by flames or decay—the Old Ways that will last as long as the "Recibos" are remembered, played, sung, and danced with Old Mam. The loss of a local marimba to play them, and the consequent standardization of this musical form impresses this writer as representative of a serious process of erosion of the Old Ways.

The Recibos are sometimes said to have been taught by Old Mam, but others say they were composed by the Nawals. The following are some of the titles used for the six Recibos:

1. "First Recibo of Mam"
2. "Second Recibo of Mam"
3. "Third Recibo of Mam"
4. "First Recibo of Santiago," also "Fourth Recibo of Mam," "*Son* of the Deer [Dance]," "*Son* for the Women to Dance," "Triste," or "Song of the Flowers"
5. "Second Recibo of Santiago," also "Fifth Recibo of Mam," "Song of the Fruit," or "For Dancing Santiago"
6. "Third Recibo of Santiago," also "Sixth Recibo of Mam," "Sad Song of the Women," "Of the *Tixels*," or "*Son* of San Juan"

In the 1960s and 1970s the Recibos were played on a marimba inside the *cofradía* house whenever it hosted a calendric celebration, and in the central plaza of town by a *conjunto* or band that included a marimba, a saxophone or two, and snare and bass drums. On major days of celebration the music would go on all day and into the night. The outdoor marimba band would also play pieces of popular music like cumbias and rancheras. Anyone living in town for more than a few weeks would become familiar with this repertoire because of the inescapable highly amplified sound. The soundscape at these festivals was an amazing and highly entertaining cacophony created by the marimba band, the flute and large drum ensemble, the tinkling of little bells on the ice-cream vendor's cart, the occasional pealing of the church bells from the tower, all playing together and frequently punctuated by the loudly exploding "*bombas*" of homemade fireworks.[3]

Because the Recibos and the songs are clearly related in style but not identical, and the Recibos are of great ritual importance in public rituals but lack texts, I puzzled for a long time over the relationship between them. It was only after listening many times that I realized that the song melodies are derived from the Recibos. Because songmen improvise on abbreviated snippets of the Recibos melodies that form the motives of the songs, it was not immediately apparent that the song melodies are borrowed from the Recibos.

The "Songs of Mam"

This study has focused on *b'ix* that were sung with texts because of their cultural content and the poetic quality and elevated language of the texts. Unless a songman could play *punteado* melodies, he played only simple chords and rhythms that did not reveal the melody if he chose not to sing. In a ritual context the songs are more commonly played this way in the background without actually being sung.

The melody of the "Song of Mam" or "Song of Old Mam" is often added to many other songs and is the most commonly heard and recognized. To insert a few bars of a "Song of Mam" or words that imitate the guitar or drum into any song is to acknowledge his presence and invoke his assistance. In 2011 I found that the "Song of Mam" has survived in the songmen's repertoire while most other melodies have disappeared. The song appears both in a metrical form and nonmetrical form. The following transcriptions illustrate some variations of its metrical melody (see Example One).[4] Its characteristic shape or contour is defined by the descending and ascending pattern of the quarter notes E–B–D–A, corresponding to tones v, ii, iv, and i of the major scale, in measures 2, 3, 4, and 5 of the first (and most common) variation. Large Roman numerals below the staff indicate chords; small ones above the staff, as in Example Three, indicate pitches like *do, re, mi*, and so forth.

"Sad Song of the Young Man"

In the case of the "Tristes," the emotional content of the song may affect the songman's choice of the style, and even the melody. "Tristes" are sometimes metrically free, as in the "Sad Song of the Young Man" in which Diego Cua Simaj expressed the sadness of the text by singing a nonmetrical version of the "Song of Old Mam" without guitar accompaniment, using the tones of its melodic contour to create variations as he goes. The following is a loosely descriptive representation of the first four variations of the melody. The whole text is on page 101.

Transposition of the first five measures of this example to A Major allows a

EXAMPLE 1. "Song of Old Mam"

1. A - nen en - powr, anen in- me ba', anen en-tzak - nak, anen enpok - nak.

2. Catnwajo' k' - poj, catnwajo' p - b'ey, catnwa - jo' yan, cat-tn-wa-jo' nu - te'.

3. Dolors achi' yan, Dolors achi' nu - te', Dolors achi' nxe- ñor - a, mlay abakil, axum - lil.

4. Catnwajo' ya - na, catn-wa-jo' nu - te', catn - wa - jo' nk'a poj.

EXAMPLE 2. "Sad Song of the Young Man"

Diego Cua Simaj

[8.71.14, item 91]

EXAMPLE 3. Comparison of Examples One and Two

comparison to the first metrical version of the "Song of Old Mam" in Example One, revealing the common melodic contour on tones v, ii, iv, and i. The repeated eighth notes in the metrical version have become extended reciting notes in the nonmetrical version.

For the "Sad Song of the Young Man," Diego Cua Simaj transforms the melody of the "Song of Mam" by using a nonmetrical melodic formula that resembles a Gregorian chant formula used for singing the psalms. Antonio Quieju Culan, in his "Song of Martín" (on page 61; audio file 2) that is partly in Latin, used a melodic formula that is recognizably part of that chant repertoire. As mentioned, these survivals are likely traceable to the musical legacy left by the Franciscans of the monastery that flourished in Atitlán in the late sixteenth and seventeenth centuries. The daily chanting of psalms is part of the Divine Office, a central component of the common prayer of monastics. As I wrote in 1975, it is unlikely that after 1650 "the difficult and time-consuming task of teaching psalm-singing to the Tzutuhils would have been undertaken by the secular clerics who were as a rule alone, and singly responsible for the administration of the religious needs of several villages" (259).[5]

"Song of the Young Girl Who Says Goodbye to Her Mother"

Most songs entitled "Song of the Young Girl Who Says Goodbye to Her Mother," in which a girl tells her mother that she has found a husband and will soon be leaving her, are associated with the melody in Example Four, extending from the first measure to the first quarter note of measure five. Only songman José Sosof Coo' sang the additional melodic extension that follows, from measure five to the first quarter note of measure nine. He sang three verses in his relaxed and playful style. The text is on page 106 and can be heard on audio file 5.

Gaspar Petzey Mendoza sang the "Song of the Young Girl Who Says Good-bye to Her Mother" in an almost wordless falsetto in which only an occasional phrase of text is intelligible and used a melody which is unique in the collection. He introduces the song on his guitar in triple meter, but as the song progresses there are passages in duple meter, to which the rhythm gradually migrates in the solo parts on the guitar. Some rhythmic motives and the ending formula are shown in Example Five. The text is on page 107 and can be heard on audio file 6.

Songman Gaspar Yataz Ramirez sang the "Song of the Young Girl Who Says

EXAMPLE 4. "Song of the Young Girl Who Says Goodbye to Her Mother"

José Sosof Coo'
[7.72.82, item 387]

EXAMPLE 5. "Song of the Young Girl Who Says Goodbye to Her Mother"
Gaspar Petzey Mendoza
[11.66.V, item 12]

Goodbye to Her Mother" to still another melody, which extends from measure 1 to the first beat of measure 9 of Example Six.[6] After each verse he added a refrain made of mostly nonlexical syllables like "*lale lala le*," to the tune of the "Song of Old Mam." The first of these begins with *"Nute' aley"* ("My dear mama"). The song is audio file 6, and the text is on page 107.

Notable in this performance is the sense, at least for western ears, of being out of tune. It is worth commenting here that accurate tuning or singing to the exact pitches of the western scale was not a primary value in the musical aesthetics of traditional Tz'utujil musicians. The reason may be that

> the influence of indigenous style is responsible for the modification of the underlying rules of Western style which governed the use of pitch, harmony and rhythm in the original Spanish models." (O'Brien 1975, 38)

The loose correspondence to the rules of western music is widespread in the music of the Guatemalan countryside, as could be heard in the 1960s and

1970s on the very popular daily radio broadcasts from TGW, a station in Hue-huetenango.[7] This freedom was manifest especially in popular vocal and in-strumental music, even in fixed-pitch instruments such as marimbas. This proclivity may not be accountable to ignorance or to the lack of exposure to western standards of pitch or metrical accuracy, but to an underlying hierarchy of aesthetic values that were particular to the indigenous tradition. In my ex-perience, the highest value for them was the singer's ability to create a rich and fluent text, and to play guitar variations of some complexity. The same fluency and ability to create variations was appreciated in traditional marimba ensem-bles. Accurate tuning was important to some, however, as songman Juan Petzey Takaxoy expressed in the following conversation.

While we were at his house listening to him play and sing we heard outside the sounds of a visitor who was from San Pedro saying goodbye to Juan's wife and leaving the *sitio*. Juan then picked up his guitar and, finding it had gone out of tune, said to me:

The Pedrano who just left ruined it! The guy who just left fucked it up so we can't play. I am ready to play, but what for? You have to know how it is tuned. See, I told you a while ago about him. I don't know how to tune it, so it's pure shit now. The Pedrano who just left did something bad to my guitar.

Then his wife said to him, "It's your fault because you let just anybody in here! You wouldn't even say anything if he lay down on your bed! You just say, 'Wait, wait.' You should have sent him away."

Then Juan said, "But Dio's is one, only one Father Dio's. . . . He wanted me to take him to San Pedro in the canoe. What am I going to say, 'Go away, go away?' . . .

EXAMPLE 6. "Song of the Young Girl Who Says Goodbye to Her Mother"
Gaspar Yataz Ramirez
[8.71.13, item 84]

your friends may love you but they fuck you over." When we asked why, he said, "Because he was jealous."

I wondered if it was because I was there recording him. (O'Brien 1972b)

Vocal styles vary from singer to singer, but in general the quality is relaxed and often very expressive. In Antonio Quieju Culán's "Song of the Young Men and Young Girls, of Insults and Ridicule" (text on page 120 and audio file 8) and "Song of the Young Girl" (text on page 128 and audio file 11), Antonio interprets the melody of the song of Old Mam with a fervor and an emotion in his voice that infuse it with feeling and with a tuning of his guitar that is far from the standard for western ears. He plays an accented *rasgueado* rhythm during guitar solo parts, which is common in the accompaniment of the songs.

"Song of the Old Maid" or "Song of the Road"

The "Song of the Old Maid" by Juan Petzey Takaxoy on page 123 is certainly a "*triste*," judging from the theme of lost luck, and from the nonmetrical style of the vocal part, although the guitar part is metrical (audio file 9). Juan sings it to the formula in Example Eight. Between the reciting tones, he articulates some pitches of the scale or glides down to the next tone. He also speaks parts of it, expressing the emotion of the words. This treatment offers an interesting example of the fusion of a Spanish liturgical style (the nonmetrical vocal part) and a rhythmic dance form (the metrical guitar part), which serves here in the cultural context (the textual content) as a lament for the loss of a woman's path on life's road.

A metrical version of the same melody was played as a guitar solo by Diego Cua Simaj, who called it simply "Song of the Road," the beginning of which is transcribed in Example Nine (audio file 10). In spite of the irregularity of the meter, its lilting rhythm suggests a dance form in which the turns of the melody cue the moves of the dance.

"Song of the Fruit"

The first of two examples of the "Song of the Fruit" was played by Juan Petzey Takaxoy, while Nicolás Coche Sapalú spoke the text. Juan did not like to sing and so this arrangement seemed agreeable. This melody has a repeating rhythmic pattern and a chordal sequence in which the melody itself ends on the dominant. The ending formula is again in an unrelated meter and also ends on the dominant. The text of this song is on page 144 and is audio file 12. Example Ten is a representative excerpt of the melody with the ending formula.

EXAMPLE 7. Rasgueado rhythm

Antonio Quieju Culan

EXAMPLE 8. Formula of "Song of the Old Maid"

Juan Petzey Takaxoy
[9/72/105 item 452]

EXAMPLE 9. "Song of the Old Maid" or "Song of the Road"

Diego Cua Simaj
[11.66.V, item 2]

EXAMPLE 10. "Song of the Fruit"

Juan Petzey Takaxoy and Nicolas Coche Sapalu Damian
[8.71.5, item 43]

The Tz'utujil Guitar

The guitars songmen use were built for six strings from which the lowest or sixth string was removed. They are simply constructed classic style acoustic guitars, made with available, inexpensive materials for affordable sale to the rural peasants. When asked where one could be purchased, songmen responded that they were sold at the Terminal Market in Guatemala City.[8]

These guitars are comparable in their dimensions to modern acoustic guitars now in popular use, with the exception of the difference in the body depth and the width of the bouts, which are smaller than the average. One that I own measures 38″ in total length, 10″ at the upper bout, and 13.5″ at the lower bout, about one inch smaller than the average acoustic guitar. The body depth is uniform (instead of tapering from the heel) and is 3.5″ deep, approximately 0.5″ smaller than the average acoustic guitar. The scale length is 25″, consistent with the average. The body is made of medium-density solid wood of the mahogany family, with a top of a single piece about 1/16″ thick. It is unadorned, without perfiling at the joints between the top and sides or around the soundhole. The neck is thick and heavy, and the headstock has holes for six wooden friction pegs. It has eighteen frets, twelve between the nut and the neck/body joint. The last four frets are shorter, extending as far as the fifth, fourth, third, and second strings respectively. It has five metal strings, of which the fifth is of the same caliber as the third, and one peg hole is left empty. No identification is visible through the sound hole. The whole is finished with spray lacquer, except the neck is painted black.

Even songmen who could afford them did not prefer the larger, improved modern guitars with metal tuning machines, although outside the traditional context of the *cofradía*, six-string guitars were played for popular music by both Tz'utujils and Ladinos. On one occasion Antonio Sosof Coo' told me he would like to sing for me, but his guitar was broken. I said I would bring him one, and he agreed, and said to my translator:

> ANTONIO: OK then, tomorrow, with pleasure. Before when we used to go in the street, Diego, there were lots of guitars, but now the guitars are all the new kind. The boys are now only listening to the radio. They go in the streets, but just with radios.
>
> LINDA: Do you want one *trchiad* [bass string]?
>
> ANTONIO: Yes, one.

The tuning is re-entrant, and can be represented as in Example Eleven. Actual pitches vary, however, because songmen tune without reference to a standard pitch. It is not uncommon that the intervals also are approximated rather loosely, with the result that the pitches may be outside the limitations of standard western notation. This tuning is called *jun trchiad* by songmen, who translate it as *un bajo* ("one bass"). Gaspar Reanda Ramirez told me, "The strings are different [from the six-string guitar], because there is one bass, and a first, a second, a third, and a fifth." The fourth string, which he doesn't number, is the lowest, the *trchiad*. I asked Sacristán Juan Ajchomajay Set about this.

> JUAN: This guitar doesn't have three *trchiads*. We only play old *sones* on this guitar.
>
> LINDA: And this guitar, how many *trchiads* does it have?
>
> JUAN: Only one.
>
> LINDA: Is it a bass?
>
> JUAN: Yes. It is called "*trchiad*."
>
> LINDA: And your guitar has only one?
>
> JUAN: Yes, only one. It is the old guitar, and that is why we only play old *sones* on it. It is not like the guitar for *canciones* [popular songs]. Those guitars have three *trchiad*.

Songmen play the guitar using two techniques. *Rasgueado* strumming, in which the fingers or fingernails and sometimes the thumb are drawn across

EXAMPLE 11. The tuning of the Tz'utujil guitar

the strings to play a chordal rhythm, is used by all. Some songmen also use the more difficult *punteado* technique, in which the nail of the first and sometimes the second fingers are used to pluck a melody on the E or first string.

Historical Origins of the Tz'utujil Guitar

Evidence for the introduction of the Tz'utujil guitar from Spain during the late sixteenth or early seventeenth centuries is strong and can be gathered from tuning, playing style, repertoire, and from the existence of conditions in Atitlán that were favorable for transmission and survival.

Tuning

The tuning of the Tz'utujil guitar provides the clearest evidence for its origin in the "*guitarra española*"[9] of late sixteenth to early seventeenth century Spain that gradually replaced earlier forms of the guitar, becoming the established instrument during the early seventeenth century.[10] The re-entrant tuning A–D–G–B–E appears first in compositions published in Miguel de Fuenllana's *Libro de Musica para Vihuela, intitulado Orphenica Lyra* in 1554 in Barcelona, and became the standard until the early eighteenth century.[11]

The Tz'utujil guitar no longer has double courses, but single strings, tuned as in Example Eleven. The double course fourth and fifth strings of the *guitarra española* were tuned in octaves, but the Tz'utujil guitar omits the upper octave of the fourth or D, and the lower octave of the fifth or A, leaving one bass string (D), or *jun trchiad*.

Unlike other highland towns in which instrument-making traditions that were established in colonial times continued into the twentieth century, Santiago Atitlán, a town of traveling merchants, seems not to have had local luthiers but instead had to purchase guitars from elsewhere. Access to double-course guitars would have disappeared in Guatemala with the further evolution of the guitar that led to its modern form of six strings in single courses. The six-string guitars were easily adapted by removing the sixth string and substituting a string of lighter gauge for the fifth, which is what songmen do today.

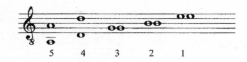

EXAMPLE 12. The tuning of the sixteenth-century five-course *guitarra española*

Francisco Coche Yaj, songman, 1972.

Playing Style and Technique

The *rasgueado* combined with *punteado* style of playing was characteristic of the five-course *guitarra española*. The first known method book with compositions, *Guitarra española y vandola de cinco órdenes y de quatro* by Juan Carlos Amat, was published in 1586 in Barcelona. This publication made the *rasgueado* style of playing, with its simple chordal accompaniments, easily accessible to students. The more challenging *punteado* style derived from lute technique was already part of the playing technique of the best guitar players, and with Amat's publication of mixed tablature that included both, it became readily accessible in a very simple, popular style. Amat's book contained instructions that enabled players to simply strum *rasgueado* chords in sequences of I, IV, and V, and provided a simple method for accompanying the voice. Its popularity caused the complaint by Covarrubias that "there is not a stable lad who is not a musician on the guitar" (Turnbull 1991, 41–42).

The *rasgueado/punteado* playing styles have continued to be used by songmen to the present day. Tz'utujil songmen Francisco Coche Yaj and José Pop Ajuchán played *rasgueado/punteado* melodies with assurance and clarity in "Song of the Widows" (audio file 17) and "Song of the Women" (audio file 18).

EXAMPLE 13. An early *zarabanda*

Repertoire

The published repertoire of the *guitarra española* attests to the popularity of variation forms based on a rhythmic chordal sequence, such as the *passacaglia*, the *sarabande* (or Spanish *zarabanda*) and the *chaconne* (*chacona*), for which a sequence of chords outlining an ending formula was also often provided. In view of the cadencial formulas that end on the dominant found in the songs, it is interesting that in 1694 Francisco de Guerau included in his *Poema Harmonico* fifteen *passacaglias* that end on an unresolved leading tone of the dominant chord, anticipating that a variation ending would be added by the player (Bellow 1970, 102). Ruiz de Ribayaz, in *Luz del Norte* (1677), included *zarabandas* using hemiola rhythms that are found in Tz'utujil songs as well (Harrison and Harrison 1968, 17).

The Tz'utujil songs, then, seem to fit the general style of the genres popular for the five-course *guitarra española*: solo guitar variation forms based on a simple sequence of chords, which may be used to accompany the voice, often having an ending formula with its final on the dominant chord, implying a final improvisation that is now absent or rudimentary in the Tz'utujil recorded examples. The melodies themselves may come from the repertoire that was popular at the time of transmission.

The occasional appearance of hemiola in the songs and the Recibos may point to their origin in the *zarabanda*. From about 1580 to 1610 the *zarabanda*, often described as wild and energetic, seems to have been the most popular of Spanish dances, finally superseded by the *chacona*, with which it is frequently mentioned. "The [*zarabanda*] dance was accompanied by the guitar, castanets and possibly other percussion instruments, and by a text with refrain" (Hudson 2001, 273). An early example of the *zarabanda* for the *guitarra española* is provided by Hudson in Example Thirteen.

The *zarabanda* as a musical form has also been found in more distant towns in the highland Maya area of Chiapas, which in colonial times was attached by governance to Guatemala. In their study of the music of the Tzotzil of Chamula and Zinacantán, Frank and Joan Harrison identified the *zarabanda* in Zinacantán, describing it as a short-unit variation dance form in ternary rhythm or $\frac{6}{8}$ with hemiola, and including singing, sometimes in falsetto (Harrison and Harrison, 1968).

> The constant factor was a musical design consisting of a number of divisions, each of four rhythmic units—transcribable as $\frac{3}{4}$ measures—with the same harmonic and rhythmic pattern in each unit. The total shape is a continuously unfolding one, open-ended in the sense of having no formal or even necessary ending. The divisions are grouped by twos, threes, and occasionally fours into sections; some of these are instrumental only and in others the players also sing, either in full voice with words or in wordless falsetto. The grouping of sections into sets according to such differences outlines the overall design. (Harrison and Harrison 1968, 12)

The example studied by the Harrisons is called "Canto de San Sebastián," which is played on a guitar in an ensemble with violin, harp, and voices. The Harrisons describe the re-entrant tuning of the guitar as the same as that in Luis Briceño's *"Metodo mui facilissimo para aprender a tañer la guitarra a lo Español"* (1626), which is a form of Amat's tuning, although an octave lower (1968, 9). As shown above, Amat's tuning is that of the Tz'utujil guitar, lacking the double courses. The Zinacantán guitar is locally made and preserves the sixteenth- and seventeenth-century style and shape of construction. It has five courses, the first triple and the rest double, leaving one peg unused. The playing technique the Harrisons found is exclusively *rasgueado* across all the strings.

In his insightful study of the *zarabanda* in Rabinal in the Province of Baja Verapaz, Guatemala, Navarrete Pellicer describes the genesis of the *zarabanda* in that town:

> The historical sources attribute two meanings to the term zarabanda: one being a social event where people drink and dance to the music of *sons* at cofradía fiestas, in funeral vigils for children, or in cantinas, and the other meaning being a private dance done by men and women during cofradía fiestas, and by inference, the music of this dance. The zarabandas were a form of popular religious expression considered pagan by the authorities. In Rabinal the word is used to refer to a social event with marimba *sons*, dancing, and alcohol. In the neighboring department of Alta Verapaz, there is today an instrumental group of harp, a *guitarilla* and a *rabel* that was identified by Sáenz-Poggio (1997: 81) in 1877 as a kind of orchestra called zarabanda (2005a, 140).[12]

In Navarrete Pellicer's recording of a *zarabanda* ensemble from Alta Verapaz, the melody and rhythmic and melodic motives of "Son San Juan" are found to be similar to "Song of the Young Girl Who Says Goodbye to Her Mother" in Example Four.

For comparison, "Song of the Young Girl Who Says Goodbye to Her Mother" is transcribed in Example Fifteen in the same key as "Son San Juan."

A very similar melody was recorded by Richard Alderson in Chamula, also in Chiapas between 1971 and 1974. The ending of this version leads to the final on the dominant. It can be heard on track 1 of a compact disc entitled "Batsi Son: The Music of the Highlands of Chiapas, Mexico" (Alderson 2004).

The *zarabanda* is best known today as a component of the baroque suite, but it has a complex early history. It appears in sixteenth-century Spanish and Mexican sources as a poetic form, as a dance, a dance-song, and a popular song. Its origins, whether in Spain or Mexico, remain theoretical. From its earliest mentions in the New World it is described as a lascivious dance characterized by erotic body movements, perhaps an amalgam of African, indigenous, and Spanish dances and rhythms (Navarrete Pellicer 2005b, 76). Because it was a wild dance form associated with drinking, the *zarabanda* was the subject of numerous prohibitions by civil authorities both in Spain and in the New World during the time when the Spanish presence was intense. The church frequently prohibited it as well. Aguirre mentions one prohibition imposed on a small town not far from Atitlán, San Pedro la Laguna, which was occasioned by the *zarabandas* that were being held in the church of that town (1972, 232)[13] In Atitlán, the name *zarabanda* is used to refer to music on records (or now CDs) played in the cantinas, and also to the *b'ix* when they are for simple enjoyment rather than ritual occasions. Juan Ajchomajay Set told me, "[This song] is just for enjoyment, so we can feel contented. Yes, it is a kind of zarabanda."[14]

Although Tz'utujil songs share common roots with the *zarabandas* in Alta Verapaz and Chiapas, they differ most greatly because of their character as solo guitar–accompanied songs. Unlike the larger and louder string or marimba ensembles, the songs do not produce the volume needed for public performance for large groups of people. If the forbidden *zarabandas* existed in Atitlán during the time of the Spanish presence, the need to hide them from the attention of the church would have found an easy solution in the privacy of the *cofradías*. The texts of some Tz'utujil songs that have a component of sadness mention dancing, drinking, and the catharsis these represent, which recalls the same behavior associated elsewhere with the *zarabanda*. Indeed, women drink, dance, and cry in the *cofradías*, lamenting the sadness they feel in their lives. In the "Song of the Young Girl," the songman sings for her:

Ay malay jun quitar	Oh I want a guitar
malay jun k'ojom	oh I want a marimba
quintej nc'a nen, ale.	so I can dance, dear.

EXAMPLE 14. "Son San Juan." *Q'eqchi' zarabanda* ensemble of gourd guitar, harp, violin, and percussion on harp box from Paapa Chamelco, Alta Verapaz

EXAMPLE 15. "Song of the Young Girl Who Says Goodbye to Her Mother"

EXAMPLE 16. "Navidad-Mitontik," for violin, guitar, harp, and bells

lale lalale	*lale lalale*
Ay malay bis	Oh, I want the sadness
ay malay ok'ej.	oh, I want to cry
Ay pr chi'	Oh on the corner of the
bey	street
ay pnic'aj	oh in the middle of the
rujay.	house.
lale lalale lale lalale	*lale lalale lale lalale*

How the Songs Survived: The Process of Assimilation and Transmission

Just as the *guitarra española* reached the height of its popularity in Spain, the coastal lands around Suchitipequez, which was then Tz'utujil territory, became an important focus of Spanish trade. During the decades of the late sixteenth and early seventeenth centuries, these Tz'utujil lands on the Pacific piedmont experienced heightened Spanish economic activity due to the rising demand of European markets for the cacao which was abundant there.[15] The years of this elevated Spanish presence in Atitlán are also known to have been a time of intense cultural transmission by the Franciscan missionaries. The friars who resided in Santiago Atitlán initiated the religious indoctrination of the people, and later they chose the site to build the church and their convent, novitiate, and house of studies, as well as a school for children to learn religion and to read and write. From this time until the mid-seventeenth century, the Tz'utujils were instructed in the Catholic liturgy and liturgical music by the friars. In 1585 Fray Pedro de Arboleda and Alonzo Betancor wrote of the success of their musical activities among the Tz'utujils, revealing the origins of the chant and psalmody that still survive there:

> The natives of this town are of good intelligence, docile, and well inclined to understand and learn all those things which they are taught, especially those who work in the Church, the cantors, who know how to write and sing. They have learned the chant and polyphony as well, and they are able to serve at Mass, Vespers and the other Divine Offices. The wind-instrumentalists know how to play the organ, trumpets, flutes, sackbuts and shawms and other instruments which are in the Church for the service and the enhancement of Divine Worship. There is a school where the children of the town come to learn Christian Doctrine in their mother tongue, and to learn to read and write, and of this the Father Guardian and the Religious have charge, who have chosen and appointed an Indian, an elder of the town, who is the teacher of the children and who is very apt for this, hav-

ing faculties from the *Real Audiencia*, and his salary is paid from the holdings of the community. . . .

The said Religious gave an order that in this town there should be a school for the children so that they should learn to read and write and sing and serve at Masses and Divine Offices with plainchant and polyphony, in which, at this time, they are docile. (Betancour and Arboleda 1964, 96–97)[16]

The guitar is not among the instruments mentioned by Betancour and Arboleda in their journal of 1585, nor is there any mention of instruction in secular music by the friars. It can be considered probable, however, that the transmission of the *guitarra española* and its popular repertoire also took place during this period, either by the friars themselves or perhaps by other resident Spaniards, though these were very few.

The Harrisons cite Franciscan Juan de Torquemada's description of the music of colonial Mexico published in 1615 in which the guitar is mentioned. After listing the instruments used in the churches, he says:

The other instruments, which are played to give pleasure to secular people of rank—the Indians make and play them all: small fiddles, guitars of two sizes, vihuelas, harps and keyboard instruments. . . . Further, only a few years after they learnt the arts of music they themselves began, on their own, to compose polyphonic villancicos in four parts and some Masses and other works. (Juan de Torquemada, *Los veintiún libros rituales y Monarchia Indiana, con el origen y guerras de los indios occidentales*, in Harrison and Harrison 1968, 6)

By the end of the seventeenth century only two Franciscans remained in the convent at Atitlán, as more advantageous ports had been found for the exportation of cacao and the focus of Spanish activity shifted elsewhere. After this period, as new sources of cacao replaced the local ones, Santiago Atitlán once again became isolated.

Pressure from Spanish and local ecclesiastical authorities to collect more revenue was brought to bear on the nontaxable monastic communities to cede their authority in mission towns to the taxable secular clergy, with the eventual result that Atitlán was secularized in 1756 (Aguirre 1972, 131). Secular priests were few in number, and in the eighteenth and nineteenth centuries the lake towns were often without resident clergy and were ministered to by a single priest who made only occasional visits to each town. The anticlerical movement that arose in Guatemala during the mid-nineteenth century led finally to the expulsion of the foreign clergy, leaving an even more greatly reduced number of priests in the country (O'Brien 1975, 20).

Both the Harrisons and Navarrete Pellicer partly attribute the survival of music from New Spain, which they documented, to a similar isolation that followed the disengagement of the church and commercial interests in each area. Speaking of the process in Santiago Atitlán, Robert Carlsen gives two reasons for this:

> First, a lack of significant readily exploitable natural resources in highland Guatemala correlated with scant Spanish interest in the region, particularly in the more peripheral areas. Second, in Santiago Atitlán the consequent limits on physical, social, and cultural contact limited the foreigners' capacity to control Atiteco behavior. (1997, 71)

Sometimes the measures taken to replace traditional beliefs with Catholicism were harsh, as occurred in neighboring San Pedro la Laguna during efforts to suppress the "Dance of the Tun" and seems to be occurring now in Atitlán. We have no evidence to help us imagine the sound of Tz'utujil songs before the conquest. As for instruments, only on one occasion did I hear a song accompanied by an instrument that pre-dates the Spanish contact, when during the "Song of the Rocking Cradle" (text on page 54 and audio file 1), the *c'unc'un* was played in the background while Nicolás Chiviliu sang. Whether the *c'unc'un* was played just at that time as an accompaniment to the ritual prayer and song being done at that moment, or was being played (as it is three times a day) to honor the sun, remains a question. In the songs, therefore, we find a Western musical style that became a vehicle for pre-hispanic K'iche'an poetic expression, and that contains Tz'utujil teachings considered to have originated at the beginning of the present creation.

Unlike liturgical music that would have been executed in public contexts like the church and the cemetery, the songs were sung and played on the *guitarra española*, which was regarded as a secular instrument. Therefore, the songs would have appeared, as today, in private and semiprivate contexts. The low volume of the guitar made it unsuitable for accompanying many voices in a large church, and later the institutional church frequently tried to restrict all instruments except the organ for use in church services. In 1565 the church ordered that singing and instrument playing were to be regulated due to the "harms and vices" of those brought up in the church as musicians (Orellana 1984, 203, footnote 65, originally from *Archivo General de Centroamérica* A1.2–4 *leg.* 2,195 fol. 214v. *Año* 1565). In the more private contexts of the *cofradías* or the home, songmen could have added their own texts to the melodies and rhythms that belonged to the repertoire of the *guitarra española*.

FINAL WORDS

THE COLLECTION OF TRADITIONAL SONGS of the Tz'utujil Maya called the "*B'ix rxin Nawal*" or "Songs of the Ancestors" is not unlike the water in a basin one might dip into the waters of Lake Atitlán. It contains only a taste, a shallow cupful of a great spring of ancient tradition, the depth and breadth of which are as yet unknown. Both the basin and the lake mirror the changing sky and the road Our Father the Sun has traveled since the root of time, but the picture in the basin is but a small snapshot of changing Tz'utujil culture captured at a brief moment in time.

The "Songs of the Old Ones" have their roots in pre-Columbian and Spanish colonial times and in the succeeding centuries, as evidenced by the content and style of their texts, the contexts of their performance, and their musical style. The poetics of the texts identify them as part of the tradition of the oldest written K'iche'an poetic literature that has survived from before the Spanish contact and continues a stream of Maya oral declamation and song performance that must flow from ancient times. These Tz'utujil songs constitute the oldest and largest known body of oral K'iche'an sung literature that exists in recorded form.

The rich mythological content of the texts and the ritual behavior they describe and in which they are performed enlarge the understanding of Maya cosmological time, especially of two key elements: the multilayered meaning of the metaphor of "the road" as the path through the life of each person that returns him or her to the Nawals, and the nature of dance as the currency of sacrifice and an agent of re-creation. The texts and their contexts allow a glimpse into Tz'utujil mores—the "Old Ways"—and suggest the identification of the deity "Old Mam" as a contemporary expression of the ancient Maize God of the Maya, whose rebirth is initiated by the movement of the dancing feet on the womb of the Santo Mundo.

The form and style of the music of the songs are survivals of forms popular in sixteenth- and seventeenth-century Spain, components of which have been preserved through oral transmission for more than three centuries. The guitar on which they are played is a descendant of the sixteenth- and early-seventeenth century *guitarra española*. In their musical structure, the songs belong to a body of music from the early decades of New Spain that has been found in other parts of the highlands of Guatemala and in Chamula and Zinacantán in Chiapas, Mexico, adding to the evidence of a vibrant Spanish musical life in this region of New Spain, both secular and sacred. Without a doubt, such songs existed—and may still exist as yet undiscovered—in other highland Maya communities.

Both their literary and their musical forms, in which variations on a theme is the predominant device used to express the Maya concept of cyclical time in which original models established at the beginning of the current creation by the Nawals repeat, not only in the linear sense (year after year), but also through the perception of time as metaphorical ("what happened at the beginning is also happening now"). Time with its repeating cycles of nature and human life can be described as a closed system; likewise the songs are a closed repertoire of melodies and content. The songs are the vehicle for the transmission of the original models, in some way contained in the Recibos created at the first festival. Together with the customary rituals, the songs serve as the major pedagogical tool for behavior according to the Old Ways of the Nawals.

The survival of the songs supports the understanding that, contrary to the long-held idea that Maya culture was overcome, "conquered," and essentially transformed by the Spanish presence, indigenous Maya culture actually survived, like Old Mam, in new clothing, especially when patterns in cultural behavior and perception were analogous to Spanish cultural forms. One example of this is the variation form found in Tz'utujil verse that was also characteristic of Spanish musical forms of the period. In the collision of the two cultures, this congruence of patterns must have found easy common expression in the parallel verse that Tz'utujil songmen were already creating for themselves. It was not a new style that was imposed, but a change of the musical vehicle that expressed it. For the Tz'utujils, however, the music of the Nawals is as old as the creation of Rilaj Mam, from the root of time, "at the beginning."

Songmen often said that the songs are "*de antes*" ("from before"), a phrase that meant "now disappearing" as much as "from the Nawals." Twentieth-century socioeconomic changes in Atitlán, especially the damage to the social fabric that has occurred since the onset of the civil war with its aftermath of division, together with sometimes hateful religious factionalism and fear, have now made the songs truly "*de antes*" in the sense that they are of decreasing relevance in today's Atitlán. Modernization and technology have changed the culture in ways that darken their deeper meaning beyond recognition. A multitude of churches now work in concert with local politics to suppress the Old Ways, continuing a process described in Mendelson's *Los Escándalos de Maximón* (1965). Robert Carlsen says that in the late twentieth century "a primary target of the anti-traditional agenda was the moral legitimacy of the cofradia system and the Old Ways, which came to be branded as evil" (1997, 125). The *cofradía* system and its customs are now regarded by many in just the way the sacred fruit warns in the "Song of the Fruit":

> You are garbage!
> You see me as if I were a stinking, dead horse
> or a dead chicken that reeks in the road.

The fruit, symbol of the fertile Santo Mundo, that once was cheered by the dancing of the boys-become-rain-men, today is "tired, an orphan, fallen in the dust of the road." A small community of those who practice the Old Ways continues the old customs, and, anxious to preserve and if possible recover them, has already asked for this collection to be made available to them. The commercialization of the customs for tourists has allowed remnants to survive, but pressures within the community to abandon them are very great.[1]

In 2011 I was introduced to José Cua Simaj, an *ajb'ix* who to our mutual surprise was the younger brother of Diego Cua Simaj, who I had recorded forty years earlier. I learned from him that the songmen I recorded, and whose songs are represented in this book, had all died, some in what is called *la violencia*, the twenty-year civil war. Several of those educated by MICATOKLA fell to the war as well, along with their pastor Father Stanley Rother. Others who helped me translate and write down the conversations and song texts, like Juan Mendoza Lacan, Diego Reanda Sosof, and Gaspar Culan Yataz, also died, some violently. That they loved the old customs was evident in the pleasure they took in explaining them to me, and in the pride they showed for the Old Ways. In 2011 I found a few songmen who still sing the *b'ix*, but except for José Cua Simaj, their songs were much simplified in music and text, with little variation or improvisation.[2]

In the 1970s I had employed Diego Pop Ajuchan to listen to my tapes and write down the texts, which he did with care and great interest. He listened to all the songs, conversations, and *cofradía* rituals I had collected, and he knew which songmen I had recorded. But there was one *ajb'ix* he wanted to take me to hear. Together we spent a full evening with songman José Sosof Coo' in the soft candlelight of his thatch-roof house, and after passing many hours honoring the Nawals with cigars, cane liquor, and the "*B'ix rxin Ojer*" ("The Songs of Yesterday"), José Sosof Coo's feelings, like ours, were overflowing. His heart was full of pleasure and satisfaction. He had heard his songs played back to him on UCLA's Nagra recorder, and he understood he was putting his songs, the Nawals' songs, "in a book." He had sung them all, he said, according to the old customs. Then he offered this "private song" to thank me:

Qui' Nuc'u'x   Sweet Is My Heart

nina nana nanana na   *nina nana nanana na*
na nana nana nana nana   *na nana nana nana nana*
na nana nana nana nana   *na nana nana nana nana*
la lala lala li   *la lala lala li*

Qui' nuc'u'xa, qui' nuc'u'x   Sweet is my heart, sweet is my heart
Qui' nuc'u'xa, qui' nuc'u'x   sweet is my heart, sweet is my heart

Enc'ola en powr   I am poor
pr majun ch'oj quimbanta.   but I do no quarreling.

ay ya yaya yan a dada da   *ay ya yaya yan a dada da*
ay ya yana yaya   *ay ya yana yaya*
ay ya dadada   *ay ya dadada*

aya yaya yana   *aya yaya yana*
Tak aqu'i nuc'u'x   So sweet is my heart
enc'ola awq'uin.   to be here with you.

ay aya yana   *ay aya yana*
Qui nuc'u'xa, qui'nuc'uxa   Sweet is my heart, sweet is my heart
pr, ATico, nkaj con jawra.   because, Diego, for a long time we have
                                                    kept these songs
Pr bonit jun kcostumbr nkaban,   because the customs we do are beautiful,
    ale.   dear.

Kgan kaban c'a cawra   With pleasure we do this
pr majun ch'oj nkabanta.   and we make no quarreling.

Quinya'c'a tzra.   I give you this song as a gift.

aya ya nana nana
yana na aya yana
ay di dada da
na nina nana na
nana nana nana nana
nana na nana nana na
nana na nana nana na

laila lala lu
lulu lulu lu
dada dada dadada
dada da dada dada

aya yana yan
Qui' ka'u'x, qui' kac'u'x
enc'ola awq'uin.

Qui' kac'u'xa, qui' kac'u'xa
a utza, utz
xkaban c'a cawra ajoj
pr kgan.
Majo'n xbi'na chka.

Kgan, kgan c'a, aleyan
kgan c'a, nute'.
Pr majo'n chic kate'
nko'ok'a camic.
[7.72.83, item 389]

aya ya nana nana
yana na aya yana
ay di dada da
na nina nana na
nana nana nana nana
nana na nana nana na
nana na nana nana na

laila lala lu
lulu lulu lu
dada dada dadada
dada da dada dada

aya yana yan
Sweet is our heart, sweet is our heart
to be here with you.

Sweet is our heart, sweet is our heart
it is good, good
what we are doing
with pleasure.
Nobody has made us do it.

With pleasure, with pleasure then, dear
with pleasure then, my mama.
But we don't have our mama anymore
and so now we are crying.

AUDIO FILES OF RECORDED EXAMPLES

Original recordings of these examples can be found at the University of Texas Press website (www.utpress.utexas.edu/index.php/books/obrien-rothe-songs-that-make-the -road-dance).

1. "Song of the Rocking Cradle" ("*B'ix rxin Cusul, Warbal*"). Nicolás Chiviliu Takaxoy, prayer-maker. [8.71.4A, item 40/077] (page 54)
2. "Song of Martín" ("*B'ix rxin Martín*"). Antonio Quieju Culan, songman. [9.72.94, item 424] (page 61)
3. "Song of the Drowned" ("*B'ix rxin Ajxe'ya*"). José Sosof Coo', songman. [8.72.83, item 388] (page 69)
4. "Sad Song of the Young Man" ("*B'ix rxin C'jol Triste*"). Diego Cua Simaj, songman. [8.71.10, item 78] (page 101)
5. "Song of the Young Girl Who Says Goodbye to Her Mother" ("*B'ix rxin K'poj*"). José Sosof Coo', songman. [7.72.82, item 387] (page 106)
6. "Song of the Young Girl Who Says Goodbye to Her Mother" ("*B'ix rxin K'poj*"). Gaspar Petzey Mendoza, songman. Recording by Joseph J. Gross. [11.66.V, item 12] (page 107)
7. "Song of the Young Girl Who Says Goodbye to Her Mother" ("*B'ix rxin K'poj*"). Gaspar Yataz Ramirez, songman. [7.72.28, item 169] (page 109)
8. "Song of the Young Men and Young Girls, of Insults and Ridicule" ("*B'ix cxin C'jola' K'poja Xyo'k'a Xtz'u'ja*"). Antonio Quieju Culan, songman. [9.72.92, item 416] (page 120)
9. "Song of the Old Maid" ("*B'ix rxin Rilaj K'poj*"). Juan Petzey Takaxoy, songman. [9.72.105, item 452] (page 123)
10. "Song of the Road" ("*B'ix rxin B'ey*"). Diego Cua Simaj, songman. [11.66.V, item 2] (page 179)
11. "Song of the Young Girl" ("*B'ix rxin K'poj*"). Antonio Quieju Culan, songman. [9.72.95A, item 426A] (page 128)

12. "Song of the Fruit" (*"B'ix rxin Sk'ul"*). Nicolás Coche Sapalu Damian, voice; Juan Petzey Takaxoy, guitar. [8.71.3, item 38F] (page 144)

13. "First, Second, and Third Recibos of Mam"; "First and Second Recibos of Santiago." Marimba Quieju Quieju. [8.71.7, item 090J]

14. "Third Recibo of Santiago: Sad Song of the Women" (*"Rxin Exki' Triste"*). Marimba Quieju Quieju. [7.72.121, item 504]

15. "First and Second Recibos of Mam." José Pop Ajuchan, songman. [7.71.16, items 142–144]

16. "Third Recibo of Santiago: Sad Song of the Women" (*"B'ix rxin Exki' Triste"*). Francisco Coche Yaj, songman. [7.72.109, item 469]

17. "Song of the Widows" (*"B'ix rxin Rilaj Exki'"*). Francisco Coche Yaj, songman. [7.72.107, item 459]

18. "Song of the Women" (*"B'ix rxin Exki'"*). José Pop Ajuchan, songman. [7.72.15, item 138]

NOTES

Introduction

1. "Tz'utujil" is pronounced "Tsoo-too-EEL" in Santiago Atitlán. With the exception of words adopted from Spanish, all Tz'utujil words have the accent on the final syllable. Vowels are as follows:

a: as *a* in *father*

i: as *ee* in *bee*

o: as *o* in *toe*

u: as *oo* in *boot*

y: as *ee* in *bee*

w: as *w* in *with*

An apostrophe following a letter represents a glottal stop, produced by obstructing the airflow of the voice. In English the *t* sound in *kitten* and *forgotten* is often glottalized, and the hyphen in *uh-oh*! represents a glottal stop.

Glottalized consonants:

b'

c'

ch'

tz'

k'

Other consonants are pronounced as in English with the following exceptions:

j: as English *h*

x: as *sh* in English

2. Carlin's evaluation that they sang without enthusiasm was probably a misperception that arose from his expectation that enthusiasm would be expressed in the same way as in American or Mexican music: a strongly accented beat and a fast-moving tempo. This western norm is quite different from the musical aesthetic of his indigenous congregation.

> Through daily rehearsal and performance, the new Mass [from Mexico] was taught by exclusively oral methods to the congregation. The *cantor*, who serves as organist and choirmaster, played harmonium accompaniment from a written manuscript. In the process of transmission some noticeable changes were made in the original. The Tzutuhil congregation tended to slow down the brisk meter, gradually substituting for it a sustained, unmeasured rhythm. This tendency was strongly emphasized by the cantor's harmonium accompaniment, and efforts to counteract it were altogether in-effective. Although he could demonstrate his ability to render the rhythm correctly, he was obstinate in refusing to teach it to the congregation. The mournful, wailing vocal quality in which the predominantly female congregation sang seemed to American ears inappropriate in sentiment for the liturgical celebration. It was also considered un-fortunate that the new music was not drawn from Tzutuhil musical traditions. A program was therefore initiated to develop a music for the liturgy, hopefully to be based on yet-to-be-discovered indigenous Tzutuhil musical styles. (O'Brien 1976, 379)

3. The Central American Church.

4. MICATOKLA is an acronym for Misión Católica de Oklahoma, the Catholic Mission of Oklahoma.

5. The Catholic Church had recently decreed a return to the vernacular languages of the people, and Carlin with his typical enthusiasm took on the project of translating the Latin Mass texts and scriptures into Tz'utujil, which was not yet a written language. In the much smaller neighboring village of San Pedro la Laguna (which had a population in 1966 of 4,000), Jim and Judy Butler of the Wesleyan Bible Group were developing an alphabet, grammar, and translations of scripture for the kind of Tz'utujil language spoken there. Locals in Santiago Atitlán call the dialect of San Pedro la Laguna "Pedrano" and insist that it is a form of Kaqchikel. Although closely related to the language of Santiago Atitlán, there are significant differences in vocabulary and pronunciation. One example is the pronunciation of the name of the people and their language: "Tz'utujil" (with an audible "h" for the "j") in San Pedro, and "Tz'utuhil" (with a silent "h") in Atitlán.

Because the dialect of San Pedro la Laguna has become the published academic standard in the field, the spelling "Tz'utujil" is used in this book. The insistence of Carlin's team of translators that the two are different, however, is substantiated by the fact that the dictionary and grammar published for the Tz'utujil language produced by speakers of Pedrano, has proved to be of limited use in clarifying translations of the texts in my collection from Santiago Atitlán. This is also ironic—and lamentable—because it was Ramon Carlin, together with Maryknoll's Ronald Lansing, who founded the Instituto Lingüistico Francisco Marroquin in Antigua, Guatemala, the school of Maya languages that much later produced the Pedrano Tz'utujil dictionary and grammar. The result is that in 2007 no literature or any textbooks for educational use were available for students in the Tzutujil of Atitlán (personal communication from the Director of Curriculum for the Department of Sololá, Fredi Montoya).

6. See Melville and Melville (1971) and Bonpane (1985) for a detailed account of the history of this movement in Guatemala.

7. In 1949 Humberto J. Castellanos noted:

Nuestros indígenas, como una característica idiosincrásica muy notable, no poseen canto, exceptuando desde luego el canto religioso cristiano. (Our indigenas, as a very notable and peculiar characteristic, do not possess song, except of course, religious Christian song.) (Castellanos 1949, 1375)

This sentiment is echoed in 1962 by Lise Paret-Limardo de Vela:

Y todas las voces que cantaban con el acento de la raza se han extinguido. Los indígenas no cantan ahora. (And all the voices that sang in the manner characteristic of their race have been extinguished. The indigenas no longer sing.) (7)

8. Jorge Murga Armas describes *Acción Católica*:

Acción Católica se inspira en el modelo de una nueva cristiandad pensado por Jacques Maritain, cuya característica fundamental es la creación de instituciones "temporales" cristianas (partidos políticos, sindicatos obreros y campesinos, etc.) y agregamos ahora que esa opción pastoral parte del convencimiento de que el cristianismo debe encarnarse en una cultura, en instituciones políticas y en una lucha por la justicia.(Catholic Action is based on Jacques Maritain's model of a new Christianity, that is fundamentally characterized by the creation of Christian institutions "of the temporal order" (political parties, workers' and farmers' unions, etc.), and we would add here that this pastoral choice arises from the conviction that Christianity must become incarnated in a culture, in political institutions and in a struggle for justice.)

See Murga Armas (2006) for further discussion of *Acción Católica* and the indigenous revolutionary movement as they were realized in Atitlán before and during the civil war.

9. Murga Armas (2006, 43) describes it:

A partir de los años sesenta la Iglesia Católica de Santiago Atitlán inaugura un programa pastoral que pone énfasis en el desarrollo social: en un breve período el padre Restituto Alonso trabaja en la formación de catequistas y el fortalecimiento de los grupos de Acción Católica ya existentes (jóvenes, coros, consejo de ancianos, etc.). Así, prepara el terreno a sus colegas norteamericanos Ramón Carlin, Thomas Stafford y Westermann de la Misión de Oklahoma, quienes a partir de 1963 y en visitas periódicas durante cinco años, harán un diagnóstico de la comunidad. Ellos, por lo demás, pondrán los mojones para que a partir de 1968 el padre Francisco Stanley Rother desarrolle el programa pastoral y social de la Iglesia Católica de Santiago Atitlán. (Beginning in the 1970s the Catholic Church in Santiago Atitlán inaugurated a pastoral program that emphasized social development: for a brief period Father Restituto Alonso worked to train catechists and build up the existing Catholic Action groups (youth, choirs, council of elders, etc.). Thus he prepared the ground for his northamerican colleagues Ramón Carlin [*sic*: Father Carlin was explicit that there were no accents in his name], Thomas Stafford, and [Robert] Westermann [*sic*: Westerman] of the Oklahoma Mission, who in 1963 made an evaluation of the community by making periodic visits over five years. They also lay the foundations for the development of a pastoral and social program by Father Francisco Stanley Rother beginning in 1968 in the Catholic Church of Santiago Atitlán.)

In fact the Oklahoma mission was established in the spring of 1964 by Fathers Carlin and Stafford, who began work there in March 1963. Robert Westerman came in 1965. From 1972 to 1975 Father J. Jude Pansini was pastor and directed the pastoral and social programs that had been developed. Stanley Rother took over as pastor in 1975 (personal communication from Ramon Carlin and Jude Pansini; see also Bonner 2008).

10. In Guatemala, the term *Ladino* refers to Spanish-speaking persons who have inherited or adopted hispanic culture, dress, and customs.

11. Consejo de Desarrollo Departamental, Sololá, 2008, 13.

12. These statistics were taken from a personal communication from anthropologist John Early, who also lived at the Catholic Mission when I was there.

13. Oklahoma diocesan fathers Ramon Carlin, pastor; Thomas Stafford and Robert Westerman, and Benedictine father Jude Pansini, OSB, assistant pastors; Marcella Faudree, RN, Rita Weil and Penny Gerbich, American Montessori teachers; and John Early, SJ, who was doing research in anthropology; and me. In 1968 Oklahoma's father Stanley Rother joined the staff.

14. A man by the name of Dexter Allen.

15. When I was still associated with the mission, I discovered that sixteenth-century manuscripts of music had been found in Santa Eulalia by Maryknoll Father Dan Jensen. At his request I transcribed a "Hymn to Santa Eulalia" into modern notation for his congregation to sing. These were later published by Robert Stevenson (1964), from whose extensive knowledge I would benefit at UCLA.

16. The term *ajcun* (also *ajkun*, *aj'kun*) denotes a ritual specialist whose function in the community is to offer prayers to the Nawals for the diagnosis and cure of illness, for good fortune, good crops, protection from danger or evil, and so on. *Ajcuns* are regarded as having specialized knowledge and spiritual powers. Common translations of *ajcun* in English and Spanish are healer (*curandero*), priest (*sacerdote*), and prayer-maker (*rezador*). Other terms like witch (*brujo*, *sanjorín*, or *sajorín*) and shaman carry connotations of charlatanism, evil, or trickery, and therefore they are not considered to be accurate translations of *ajcun*.

An *ajcun* who specializes in divination is also called *ajmes* (*mesero*, *adivino*), literally "man of the table."

17. I hope to soon make my entire collection available, including recordings, field notes, field journals, and photography, on a website yet to be established. The author can be contacted at 3tixel@gmail.com.

Chapter 1

1. Mendelson's informant told him there are six directions, the "four points, and above that *la gloria*, and below the earth, which makes six" (1957, 39).

2. *C'unc'un* is an onomatopoeic word for the musical instrument often called a "slit drum" (and often erroneously called a "split drum"). The *c'unc'un* is a ideophonic percussion tube made of a hollow log of hormigo wood that is incised in the form of an "H" to form two tonguelike keys that each produce a musical tone when beaten with a stick or antler. In Atitlán it is played only inside the *cofradías* on ritual occasions. In Mexico it is known by its Nahua name *teponaztli*, and in Yucatan as *tunkul*. It is also called *tun* or *tuntun* in Guatemala. Edmonson translates *tun* as "spine," as in *tun k'ixik* translating to "spiny magueys" (1971a, 95); *tun* may also mean "a year," "trumpet," and "ray of the sun."

3. Mendelson 1956, 40.

4. *Mam* is translated as "grandfather" by Christenson (2003a, n.p.), Kaufman (2003, 115), and Tedlock (2010, 310). *Titixel* (*tat ix eel*) also means grandfather and is used to refer to the progenitor deity, as in the creator couple of the *Popol Vuh*. Rilaj Mam was created—or revealed—by the Nawals, and is not the progenitor of the people, but the originator or author of Tz'utujil culture.

5. Even in the two years when I was associated with the Catholic mission, I came to know Nicolás Chiviliu through the work of Marcella Faudree, the nurse at the Oklahoma mission, who had gained the respect of the indigenous community for her healing skills. She was sometimes called to assist an indigenous midwife with a difficult childbirth. On one such occasion she invited me to accompany her to the *cofradía* San Juan where Chiviliu was the *alcalde*. The midwife had exhausted her means to help with the delivery, and appealed to Chiviliu for help. He came to the mission to ask Marcella to come and assist.

6. The orthography of written material in my collection was developed at the Summer Institute of Linguistics by Father Ramon Carlin and Tz'utujil Juan Mendoza Lacan, in 1966. Until that time, the dialect of Tz'utujil spoken in Santiago Atitlán was not a written language. Carlin developed lessons in reading and writing for his staff of Tz'utujils who were assisting him in translating liturgical texts, and for the Americans working at the mission, of which I was one. At the time of my original research (from 1966 to 1975), only the Tz'utujils who were on his staff had become fluent enough in writing their language to be able to assist me in transcribing the conversations, prayers, and songs on my recordings. All of my material was transcribed using this same orthography.

The orthography of Mayan languages used by scholars has gone through a series of permutations, but presently the Academia de Lenguas Mayas has established orthography that is now considered standard (Academia de Lenguas Mayas, 1988). It is different from Carlin's in some important ways.

I believe that the risk of a worse outcome should I attempt to update or correct the original orthography is considerable, so I have chosen to leave the Tz'utujil texts as my transcribers wrote them, with the occasional correction of obvious mistakes. The greatest differences between Carlin's system and current ones are as below:

O'Brien Collection orthography (Carlin's)	Academia de Lenguas Mayas orthography
k'	c' or q'
k	c or q
c'	k'
c	k

7. Hands and feet are the agents of movement and work, and are used to signify persons, here the Nawals. If one has big hands and feet, one has greater capacity to work and travel, i.e., great power.

8. Author's explanations are in square brackets. In the phrase "You carry it [*in your arms like a baby*]," the Tz'utujil word *alojden* is also used to mean "service in the *cofra-días*," because this service involves carrying the statues or bundles from place to place. Beyond the concrete level it means the same carrying of the world that the Nawals do by "holding everything carefully in their arms like a baby" or "like a basin of water."

9. The omission of words, phrases, or lines of prayers or songs because of deficiencies in the intelligibility of the recording is indicated by an ellipsis of three points within a line, and an ellipsis of four points for omissions between lines of the song or prayer. In citations of texts by other authors, the use of three points indicates the omission of a word, phrase, or a single sentence, and the use of four points indicates the omission of more than one sentence.

10. *Cap* means "cape," referring to the hooded capes the statues of the Santos are wearing, but this usage may also may be translated as "honey," or "sweet."

11. "In your hands justice was conceived" (*winkirwa*) refers to the K'iche'an concept of conceiving in the hand, which recalls the story in the *Popol Vuh* in which the maiden Lady Blood, conceives in her hand the Hero Twins Hunahpu and Xbalanque.

12. *Rmetr* means literally "your meters," and connotes kilometers, and here the far-reaching sphere of influence of the Nawals.

13. The Tz'utujil *c'a* ("then," "now," "though," "well") is used very frequently in songs and prayers. In songs it often provides an extra rhythmic beat. Translation into English is often omitted for easier reading, except when it adds meaning.

14. *Chipilín* refers to *crotalaria longirostrata*, an edible herb.

15. "8.71.4, item 39" is a collector's number that identifies an item in my field collection of recordings. The format of collector's numbers is month.year.tape reel number, item number. In this example, "8.71.4, item 39A" means "recorded in August 1971, on tape reel number 4; the 39th recorded item in the collection, the first half." Collector's numbers given in this book can be used to locate and listen to the sound recordings on the University of Texas website.

16. He used the term *ajitz* and the Spanish *brujo* for this. See discussion on page 126.

17. St. Bernardine is known in Franciscan lore for having used a sign that bore the single word "Jesus" in the center of a circle of golden rays of light, as a teaching device to the illiterate, telling them "Jesus is the only word you need to know to be saved."

18. Texts of the songs are arranged as far as possible so that each line of text corresponds to a musical unit. The ends of lines often correspond to a slight pause made

by the singer. Division into verses (strophes) was determined by the singer's pause or a guitar interlude.

19. "We will be regretful later" is the translator's guess for a text that is not clear.

20. Bill Douglas found that the word *suert* ("luck," "destiny") represents a complex idea that accounts for a person's character, abilities, calling, and ultimate fate and fortune. One's *suert* can be good at times, and bad at others. One also has some level of personal control over one's *suert* (Douglas 1969, 121–123).

21. That is, dawn to noon; noon to sunset.

22. *Atol* is a corn gruel of pounded maize flour, used as a ritual drink. Of these lines Diego Pop said, "This means the sun divides the sky into two parts, as we divide our cornfields, 'half for sunlight, half for *atol*' as half of the harvest might feed us, the proceeds from the other half might clothe us, or buy medicine, or atol, etc."

23. The warden, sentinel, witness, and watchman is Old Mam.

24. *Alguacil* is borrowed from Spanish and means "constable." *Alguacils* are young men who are minor officers in the *cofradía* system for one year. Most important among their many duties is participation in the rituals of Rilaj Mam during Holy Week. *Mayores* are senior officers or elders in the *cofradía* system with greater responsibilities for the Holy Week and other ceremonies.

25. The lords of nature can cast their spells on the earth (earthquakes, storms, and wind) and also undo them.

26. The meaning of this line is not clear.

27. *Espina* in the Tz'utujil text borrows the Spanish word for "thorn" and refers to the rays around the sun symbol carried by the statue of St. Bernardine.

28. Earlier in the song Diego identifies the sun with Manual de JesuKrista, whose statue is decorated with flowers, as are many of the Santos. Flowers represent the "Flowery World" of vegetation that produces food and cacao.

29. *Gloria* in Tz'utujil, borrowed from Spanish, means the sunlit sky.

30. "A poor man" can be a term of respect or confidence, meaning "a man who is just like me."

31. I had asked Juan Mendoza Lacán, Diego's neighbor, to tell Diego that I would record his songs when he was able to meet with me. He came soon afterward, bringing two friends, apparently to protect him from "Catholic magic."

32. "They were engendered" connotes something like "The Santo Mundo gave birth to them." It seems to mean here that if the Santo Mundo caused the Catholics from the mission to be born, they are probably not some type of dangerous spirits to be avoided. They are humans, again "just like me."

33. Diego was unsure whether there was the possibility that being at the Catholic mission might expose him to some spell or witchcraft, but he decided that it was not dangerous because the church, "the stopping place of Dio's," was next door.

34. The word *marimba* may refer to a single instrument, but also designates an ensemble that includes winds and percussion together with one or more marimbas, which in English might be called a marimba band. The instrument is found in several forms in Guatemala. It is popular and widespread among Mayas and Ladinos, and has been named the "national instrument" of that country.

The marimba is a xylophone that has a keyboard made of wooden bars suspended above a trapezoidal framework that holds resonating chambers (*cajones harmónicos*), originally gourds but now commonly wooden constructions made to resemble gourds, that correspond to each key. Near the bottom of each resonator is a small hole surrounded by a ring of black beeswax over which a membrane, usually of pig intestine, is stretched to form a mirliton that provides a much-desired buzzing or *charleo* when the keys are struck. The marimba is played with mallets (*baquetas*), the striking end of which is wrapped with strips of raw rubber to form a ball.

In the towns around Lake Atitlán the diatonic *marimba de tecomates* or "gourd marimba," the form that most closely resembles its African prototype, disappeared from use by 1975. The gourds have been replaced by wooden resonators, and some keyboards now include the keys of the chromatic scale arranged in two rows like the keys of a piano. A solo marimba is played by three or four players, to which a smaller "marimba tenor" may be added with two or three players. For *cofradía* celebrations in Atitlán one or two marimbas without wind instruments play the Recibos and other *sones* for dancing.

Outside the context of traditional rituals, popular music is played by bands made up of chromatic marimbas in ensemble with saxophones, trumpets, trap set, string bass, and percussion. See also Chenoweth (1964), Navarrete Pellicer (2005a, 2005b) and O'Brien-Rothe (1982, 1998, 2006, 2007a, 2007b).

35. *[El es] Santiago Apóstol Tz'utujil. Tz'utujil Acha' es, puro tz'utuj. Algunos dicen tz'utujal awan.* [Collector's number 9.72.110, item 474].

36. In Tz'utujil the names of men are preceded by "A" or "At," or for greater respect, "Ma." "Ya" precedes the names of women. I have been unable to discover a consistency in the orthography or capitalization for this title. APla's is sometimes written A Pla's, or Apla's (likewise Ma Pla's, MaPla's, and so forth). I have chosen to follow the orthography of my transcribers. APla's was often translated as "*señor.*"

Pla's is the Tz'utujil equivalent of Francisco. I recall that Father Stanley Rother, having just arrived in Atitlán, was mystified by the knowing looks and nods to each other of Tz'utujil friends when they learned his choice of name. They saw him as the re-embodiment of APla's Sojuel, the first among the ancestral Nawals who discovered Old Mam. Stanley lived up to their expectations by the courage he showed by remaining with the people during the horrors of the violence well after most other missionaries had left Guatemala. Stanley Rother was murdered at the mission by the military in 1981 during the violent civil war. The people petitioned that his heart remain in Atitlán, where it is now enshrined in the church.

37. *Cofradía* is often translated as "sodality." Because this organization is male-dominated, and because the etymology of *cofradía* is "brothers together," I prefer "confraternity" or "brotherhood" as its translation.

38. By 2007 all the traditional *ranchitos* had been replaced by cement block or wooden buildings.

39. *Cuxa* is homemade liquor made from sugar cane. Sold commercially in bottles it is called *guaro*, from *aguardiente* ("burning water").

Chapter 2

1. The *tz'ajte'l* (or in K'iche', the *tzité* tree), is also the sacred tree of the *Popol Vuh*. The *erythrina corallodendron*, also called "coral tree" or "pito tree," has bright red seeds

that are used by *ajk'ij* or sun priests for divination. A tree that I was told in the 1970s was the original one from which the figure of Old Mam was taken, stood on the hillside to the south of town behind the church. A great cleft in its trunk that appeared to be the result of a lightning strike, was said to be the cavity left after the image of Old Mam was carved out. This tree has since died and another in the vicinity has taken its place.

2. *Sones*, the plural of the term *son*, is used in Latin America to designate a musical form that varies from region to region, usually associated with a dance step. In Guatemala the *son* is usually in $\frac{6}{8}$ time, typically with some measures of hemiola, and is most frequently played by marimbas. In Atitlán the Tz'utujils use the term *son* to indicate the dance form that accompanies the traditional songs called *b'ix*, whether they are played on the guitar or the marimba or sung. The dance step of the *son* includes a *zapateado* or stomp often on the unaccented beat.

Because the spelling of *son* (a musical form) is the same as the English word "son" (male offspring), in this work the musical form is italicized.

3. I am grateful to Andrew Weeks, who introduced me to José Cua Simaj during my visit to Atitlán in 2007. At the end of an evening during which José sang many old songs I explained that I had recorded songmen years before, and I named them one after the other. Sadly, José confirmed that they had all already passed away. Finally I named Diego Cua Simaj, at whose name José brightened and asked, "Did you record Diego Cua Simaj? He was my younger brother. I learned the songs from him, and he taught me to play."

I returned in 2011 to record his songs, one of which is represented on page 41, the "Song of Francisco Sojuel."

4. In texts collected in 2011, I follow the contemporary orthography of my translator, Salvador Tziná Reanda, in which elongated vowel sounds are written with double letters: *aa, ee, oo,* and so forth.

5. *Tzojb'al* is what the Tz'utujils call their language, Tz'utujil.

6. Interestingly, in Tz'utujil "I dance" is often expressed as "I eat (guitar)" or "I eat (marimba)" (*quintej ctar, quintej mrimp*). Orellana points out that dancing in the presence of the images as tribute and sacrifice was probably common in the centuries before the Spanish conquest (1984, 100–101).

7. K'iche' and Tz'utujil are very closely related K'iche'an languages. K'iche'an languages include Q'eqchi', Uspantek, Poqomchi', Poqomam, K'iche', Kaqchikel, Tz'utujil, Sakapultek, and Sipakapense (Campbell and Kaufman 1985, 188).

8. I have not found Tz'utujil *sobsaj* in other Mayan language lexicons, but I believe both *sobsaj* and *slob* are contractions of *silob* from the common Maya root *sil*, for "move."

9. The patronymic alone is commonly used in Atitlán to refer to persons.

10. *Torij*, "to sing with power," has no exact equivalent in English. Part of its meaning is to sing without words, or to sing with nonlexical or onomatopoeic sounds, on an extended rolled 'r' [rrrr], for one example. It was described as the way birds sing, or the way women hum, or as soft whistling through the teeth. This type of singing has some kind of power to do something or make something happen. It also has the power to take away spells. "I will sing [*quintorij*] to you" is sometimes translated as "I will surprise you" or "I will scare you" and can imply a threat of some kind of witchcraft.

11. The entire prayer has 438 lines and a length of 16 minutes, 47 seconds.

12. "As they say" (also "so they tell it," or "as it is said," and so on), the Tz'utujil

cha', occurs frequently in songs and prayers. Translators explained that it means these words have been passed down from the Nawals. *Cha'* also occurs frequently in the *Popol Vuh*. Tedlock recognizes this word as a device the performer uses to remind the listeners that he is not using his own words, but is quoting from the ancient words or the ancient book: "Lest we miss the fact that they are quoting, they periodically insert such phrases as 'This is the account, here it is,' or 'as it is said.'" (Tedlock 1996, 30).

13. San Nicolás is a healer, and his statue depicts him holding a lance or obsidian blade that is used for acupuncture, called *chay*.

14. *Torij* means "wake you up, startle you." See note 10.

15. *Sale*, like *Balbe, Sabe*, and *Balver*, were explained as "old words no longer understood; perhaps the names of Tz'utujil kings or titles of great respect." *Chole* is probably from Spanish *chulo* ("handsome" or "cute," and also a term of endearment as "dear," "honey," and so forth) Translations of these words are mine.

16. This was explained as "your day [sun] was a true Martín-day [Martín-sun], a Martín-day [of] your birth."

17. *Dgo* is a nonlexical filler required by the rhythm of the melody.

18. *Royal box* refers to a box containing very old documents, possibly from colonial times.

19. This is Mendelson's *Los Escándalos de Maximón* (1965).

20. Among his other attributes, Old Mam was the archetypal trickster. I often heard people blame him for funny things that happened, and sometimes they were things that happened to me. On one occasion Nicolás Coche Damian took me to the *cofradía* Santa Cruz to show me the figure of Old Mam, who I was then calling "Maximón." I was carrying the Nagra recorder and a bag of recording tape and intended to record Nicolás' prayers to Old Mam.

Tuesday, September 12 [1972]: [Nicolás] knelt at the altar and prayed (first part of the recording). Then he knelt in front of the candles, facing the table, and prayed (recorded). Then he climbed up on the table and reached up to the rafters where a ladder lay across them. He brought the ladder down and rested its bottom on the table, and the top against a rafter, and climbed up to the rafters which had sticks [loosely laid] across them to form a sort of rustic "attic." I followed him with the Nagra and there, parallel to the altar with the Santos, on an iron frame bed with a mattress and covered with a typical Guatemalan blanket, lay Maximón, with his big shiny shoes sticking out at the foot of the bed and the outline of his mask with his cigar in his mouth showing in the candle light from below.

Nicolas began to pray—and I to record as quickly as possible. The new reel of tape I had just put on the recorder got hopelessly tangled, and though I tried two or three times to attach the free end to the empty reel to take up the slack, it was useless. I had to let it run all over the *petate* [straw mat], and it even slipped through between the logs of the rafters and hung down into the room below, so that the *xo'* [sitting downstairs] shouted up to Nicolás, "What is that coming down through the rafters?" I distinctly felt the Old Boy had played a trick on me—and could only gather up the whole reel of unwound of tape like so much dry pasta and stuff it in my bag. I recorded it all, though.

Then I watched Nicolás raise up the blanket that covered Maximon's feet and insert a yellow candle into each shoe, and put 25 cents (which he "borrowed" from me) under each foot, inside the shoes.

The candles were stuck into the instep side of the shoes, so that they were standing up almost straight, inside, between his feet. Then a few more words, a *despedida* [farewell] perhaps, and we descended the ladder and went down, after which Nicolás replaced the ladder in the rafters again. (O'Brien 1972b, 82)

21. The Tz'utujil word *warbal* means "hammock," often the place where babies are lain.

22. This was in June, 1973.

23. A coatimundi is a raccoonlike mammal.

24. Thanks to Stanzione (2003, 283) for correctly translating *nabeysil.*

25. The probable prototype for this song is the Litany of the Saints. The Litany is a series of invocations, each of which is addressed to a different saint, that is part of the Rite of Baptism in the Catholic Church and would also have been a part of the music of Easter in colonial times. Other survivals of the music proper to Holy Week and Easter form a major part of the repertoire of the music of JesuKrista, which is the domain of the Sacristanes.

26. One of the two priests who came to Atitlán in 1566 to be full-time permanent residents in Atitlán was named Diego Martín. The naming of the god of nature "San Martín" is possibly traceable to his influence. The name of Rilaj Mam as "don Pedro" may have a similar origin because in the 1580s fray Pedro de Arboleda became the director of the monastery in Atitlán (Orellana 1984, 119).

27. The sixth of eight medieval church modes for Gregorian chant is called the Hypolydian. The tone for psalm singing in mode six has the reciting tone a third below *do*, and a flat seventh (Benedictines of Solesmes 1952, 116).

28. A melisma is a musical phrase in which several notes are sung to a single syllable of text as a form of ornamentation. Melismatic denotes a melody that contains several melismas.

29. Another curious element of his song ties it to the tradition of Gregorian chant. At the end of the song Antonio sings a series of nonlexical vowels that sound like "a mo a e i al Mund." This may be a survival of an abbreviation, actually a mnemonic device, that appears in the modern *Liber Usualis*, the book that contains the collected chants for Catholic Liturgies. The words "*saeculorum. Amen*," are the final words of the "*Gloria Patri et Filio et Spiritui Sancto*." This doxology normally follows a variety of texts and is always sung as the final verse of a psalm. As a convenience, these words are not written in full in the *Liber Usualis*, but only their vowels, *a u o u a e*, which appear beneath the note on which each syllable is to be sung, providing an easy guide to the melodic cadence for the singer. Antonio's version is somewhat changed—but recognizable—by its survival in the oral tradition over a probable 350 years.

30. MaGalista: Ma is a prefix of respect for a saint or a Nawal. There is no equivalent in English, except perhaps "Mr." or "Sir."

31. *Osta suum* could be a remnant of a Latin prayer to St. Michael the Archangel, who is called "Prince of the Host of Angels." "*Hosta suum*" means "his host."

32. See Douglas (1969, 127–128) for discussion of illness caused by *xbijnim.*

33. Navarrete Pellicer found similar beliefs about the spirits of the dead and drowned in Rabinal and points out a continuity with the practices of the early sixteenth-century highland Nahua, who categorized their dead by cause of death so that the dead and the drowned were under the dominion of their own particular deity who had an annual feast day celebration (2005b, 32).

34. The town's electric generator was turned off at 10:00 p.m.

35. Doña Carmen Mordán operated a bar near the road leading up to the cemetery.

36. The *Administración* was a factory that made and sold *guaro* at the foot of the hill leading up to the cemetery.

37. The image is that of hundreds of people coming down the road from the cemetery, returning to town on the evening of all Saints' Day, November 1, the vigil of the Day of the Dead.

38. The *Baile de los Negritos* (Dance of the Black Men) is a group dance using grotesque masks that was performed during the yearly celebration of Corpus Cristi.

39. My translator Nicolás Coche Sapalu was studying divination with an *ajcun*. When he learned about my request for a prayer to find a husband, he wanted to show me that he also had some powers, so he demonstrated his own technique in the following way. This is an excerpt from my Field Journal:

> Yesterday I went to work with Diego [Pop, my transcriber] and Nicolás came to find me about 11 am, saying he had the *espada* [sword] for me. We went to my room, and he took out of his shirt a woven cloth with tassels on the four corners, about 8″ square, that I recognized as a blue and white tie-dyed *zut* [a ritual headscarf worn by men]. In this he had several (20?) pito [tree] seeds, a few (6?) corn kernels, two bits of candle wax, smoothly shaped, which he said he found at the pito tree too, one yellow, one pink and smaller, and a piece of costume jewelry in the shape of an Arabian scimitar, gold colored with a pin on the back. This, he said, was very special for divining, and would show me all kinds of things. He proceeded to demonstrate this by picking up three or four pito seeds, and putting them back in the zut he asked me "What color now?" to which I would reply "red" or "maíz" or "candela." He would dip into the zut and pick up something (not always what I had just said) until he had four in his hand. Then he would contemplate them and say "This is very interesting for you." He rolled a grain of corn around in his hand several times, blowing on his closed fist, then opening it. At times the kernel was standing, others lying down or on its side. My impression was that he was observing this [in detail]. After it (and he did all this maybe four times) he told me that Negro [a young Ladino man] has the [recently stolen] watch, and that if I want a husband, Maximón says I have to sleep five nights with a man before I go back to the USA or I'll never get married. [Nicolás tried to persuade me to secure my future husband by sleeping with him before I went home that summer. No deal.]
>
> He wanted to get in bed with me then and there, but I wasn't interested, so we parted for the moment. He said he would be back at 6:30 to go to record a former *telinel*. (O'Brien 1972b, 84)

Chapter 3

1. English translation by the author.

Estos caminos se refieren a una doble metáfora, por un lado son los espacios geográficos de un territorio, espacios míticos, llenos de leyenda, donde la naturaleza adquiere un significado sagrado en cada uno de sus accidentes: el lago, las montañas, los volcanes, las piedras, los ár-

boles, los manantiales; son lugares sagrados, sitios de entrada, de tránsito, de passage; pal b'al *les llaman en lengua tz'utuhil, ya que su principal característica es que comunican a los humanos con el otro espacio, el otro territorio, el otro mundo, el sagrado, el de los nawales, de los santos, los dueños de las cosas, los espíritus de los antepasados y los dioses mayas.*

Por otro lado, el camino también se refiere al proceso por el cual los humanos pueden llegar a convertirse en nawal, es decir, llegar a adquirir el conocimiento de los ancestros, para transitar por estos lugares sagrados y establecer comunicación con el otro mundo, el otro espacio, el otro tiempo, el de los nawales.

2. *"Del camino. Se trata de donde vamos a llegar con él or ella. También, si nos morimos o vivimos. No sabemos cuando y donde desaparecemos. Y no hay remedio. Dio's nos ayuda. Un día no hay tortillas para comer para mañana. Pero ahora hay tortillas. Bueno, la llamamos 'Del Camino', la llamamos 'Para el Camino', y por eso la llamamos así."*

3. The origin of the image of Mam in his present form as a doll-like figure is unknown. However, it is the spirit of Old Mam, not the figure, that it represents and localizes and that is understood to be powerful. When Nicolás Chiviliu told me about the attempt in the 1950s to eradicate the cult through a series of events that led up to the theft of the head or the mask of Old Mam, he commented, "They thought they took him, but they didn't get the real Mam, only the head of the figure."

4. Gaspar refers to the original hospital built by the Oklahoma Mission in the late 1960s, which was west of town. It was destroyed in a landslide and has been replaced by a new hospital on the east side of town.

5. Antigua Guatemala or Pank'an, the colonial capital of Guatemala, is about 55 miles over mountainous territory from Atitlán.

6. Sandra Orellana indicates that the sixteenth-century Franciscan missionaries to Atitlán introduced the fish called *mojarras* to the lake. Under colonial rule the Tz'utujils were sometimes ordered to take great quantites to the capital and other distant places, especially during Lent (1984, 161–162, citing Vasquez 1938).

7. Several of the translations of these names are from Stanzione (2003, 35) and from personal communications.

8. The use of names for Rilaj Mam by these two storytellers is significant because it shows the underlying attitudes of the speakers toward the divisive question of the cult of Rilaj Mam. Gaspar Culan Yataz was a young man from a traditionalist family that practiced the Old Ways. As a youth he joined Acción Católica and was attracted to Carlin's new openminded approach, which sought to unite the community by identifing commonalities rather than exacerbate divisions between traditionalists and Catholics. A thoughtful and idealistic person, Gaspar was conflicted by his respect for the cult of Old Mam, which was pivotal to the Old Ways adhered to by his ancestors and family, and for the Catholic teaching that identified Old Mam as a false god. Gaspar, who told me the story with obvious pride and pleasure, does not like the name "Maximón" because it is recent and not traditional, and because he is aware of its derisive connotations.

Juan Sisay was a highly politicized man around 50 years old, also raised in the Old Ways. His association with the Catholic Church included a period in the 1950s when he assisted the visiting priest in carrying out a plan to eradicate the cult of Old Mam by stealing its head and mask. He became alienated from the traditionalists, and associated himself with the very conservative form of Acción Católica of the 1950s, but was mistrusted by them also. Shortly after the mask-stealing events he made a trip to France to promote his career as a gifted primitivist painter. Talk at the Catholic Mission was that the trip was arranged for him as a reward for having helped the priest steal the head and mask. E. Michael Mendelson wrote about these events in *Los Escándalos de Maximón* (1965) and *Scandals in the House of Birds* under the pseudonym of Nathaniel Tarn (1997).

Juan's choice to use the name Judas Iscariot suggests his association with the opposers of the cult, especially in his identification of Mam with the effigy of Judas Iscariot that used to be constructed. For some reason in 1972 he volunteered—even seemed quite anxious—to tell me the story again with this change: "Maximón is not Judas Iscariot who sold the Lord Jesus as people say. Maximón was formed by a group of persons called the Nawals to heal people on earth."

9. A mask of Rilaj Mam is in the Louvre Museum. See Tarn and Prechtel (1997) for a more complete story of these events.

10. This tree still stood in 1975, but has since completely decayed. The place where it stood is still the site of prayer rituals.

11. The figure of Mam kept in the *cofradía* Santa Cruz is the one used during the rituals of Holy Week. Now there are other figures of Old Mam in private chapels also called *cofradías privadas* that are not part of the official *cofradía* system.

12. *Ali* is a term of endearment that is used for one's family members or friends. Translators gave the following meanings for this word: "mama," "dear," "cutie" (which in Spanish would be *chula*), "man," "mother-in-law," among others.

13. These lines referring to clothing suggest that Mam is the son of the primordial men and women who originated them.

The women's skirt is a straight length of cloth made by men on a foot-loom, using cotton yarns that are tie-dyed before weaving. This cloth is intricately patterned in colors and symbolic figures that identify the wearer's town of origin as Santiago Atitlán. Traditionally the men's shirts were also woven by men on foot looms, although as early as the 1960s they began to be replaced by western-style men's shirts that became easily available. Women's blouses or *huipils* and men's pants are woven by women on backstrap looms using white and purple cotton yarns that are woven in stripes. Those of the highest quality are heavily embroidered by the women using colorful silk threads to form figures of birds surrounded by leaves and flowers and other symbolic figures. The predominance of birds recalls an ancient name of Tz'utujil rulers, the *Ajtz'ikinajay*, or "Men of the House of Birds."

14. The four corners of the earth, the intercardinal points of the compass that converge at the cross in the center of town.

15. *Palb'al* is a sacred place where there is a special tree on which Ángeles come to stand and rest, like a bird.

16. *Jo'k* is a corn husk that serves as toilet paper. This and "garbage," "dog," and other words suggest that Old Mam can be anywhere in a form that no one will even notice.

17. The Tz'utujil *biana* is not clear, but may mean "half," referring to the short stature of Mam.

18. The final vowel does not have gender significance in Tz'utujil as it does in Spanish.

19. This is one of the first songs I recorded. At that time I did not request a transcription of the Tz'utujil, but only the translation into Spanish.

20. In pre-hispanic times, indigo dye obtained from molluscs was used to obtain a deep purple color. "Molluscan indigoids are still used sparingly today by Central American and Japanese dyers" (McGovern, Lazar, and Michael 1990, 23). The cultivation of a plant that produced indigo later became an industry of the Spanish colonists in the highlands of Guatemala.

21. A very beautiful natural red dye made from cochineal was formerly used for red stripes that were added to the purple and white ones of the Tz'utujil costume. McLeod describes the production of the much-desired cochineal during colonial times and the grueling labor of its cultivation and harvesting that was forced on the indigenas (MacLeod 1973, 172). Today red dye is no longer natural and is inexpensive, and regarded as the color used by someone who is poor.

22. Thanks to Vincent Stanzione for the connections to Ix Chel and Ix Chebel Yax (2003, 23).

23. *Finca* refers to large plantations on coastal lands where Maya peasants are forced by economic necessity to work for very low pay, usually involving abandoning their families for long periods. Conditions are very difficult, often deplorable, unhealthy, and abusive.

24. This text is the first part of the song only; the rest has not been not transcribed. The whole song is about 15 minutes long.

25. The root word *poknak* was used in another context that reveals something of its meaning. When Ramon Carlin asked for the Tz'utujil translation of "Lord, have mercy on us," after much discussion he was given "*Kajawal Dio's, tpoknak kawach*" (Lord Dio's, our face is fallen in the dust of the road). Rilaj Mam is called *poklaj ala'*, "the dust boy."

26. I give the translation of *xeñora* as "lady" (it also means *señorita ladina* ["Ladino girl"]). He calls her this, referring to the light color of her skin.

27. "Who says goodbye to her mother" is part of the extended title that was always given to me in Spanish ("*que despide a su mamá*").

28. *Mangash*, from the Spanish *manga* ("sleeve"), is a longsleeved coat of black wool used by traditionalist men who are part of the *cofradía* system. (This endnote is not in Mendelson's original.)

29. I was told that a girl might also sing the "Song of the Young Girl," though it is not common to hear this in the *cofradías* anymore. Women do sing *tristes* (laments), lullabies, and songs to the Nawals for help in childbearing.

30. This line is spoken by her mother.

31. "The hands and the feet" is used here to mean the actions of a person, things they do with their hands and feet.

32. As explained previously, the Tz'utujil word *k'ojom* is the specific term for the big drum used in the town for processions for funerals and for other rituals. The word is also used for a smaller drum, a marimba, or a guitar, even though the latter two are also called specifically *mrimp*, and *ctar* or *quitar*. Here marimba may be indicated for dancing in the *cofradías* when one has been hired to play, but it could also mean a guitar played by a songman in the *cofradía*, which might happen any time.

33. *Ndta'* is literally "my father," but here she means "a husband."

34. The meaning here is "you beat me to teach me how to work."

35. She will go to live in the *sitio* that belongs to the boy's parents, because her sister and her husband will come to live with her parents.

36. In these lines her mother comments that the boy's parents have not yet sent anyone to initiate the process of asking her parents for their daughter.

37. *Kas c'ota rsquerment* means literally "who has a sacrament," meaning some kind of religion, something moral or spiritual.

38. These lines mention local herbs.

39. "Boy" and "man" in this and other courting songs usually address Old Mam, the guardian of human sexuality, whose presence is always felt during the courting process.

40. My translator explained that this means the girl is begging the boys to hurry up and marry her, so she won't have to suffer from the insults of courting for very long.

41. The boy is too poor for cloth with purple stripes or embroidery on his clothing; they are made of plain white cotton.

42. *Choni* and *Chona* are nicknames for Concepción.

43. *Xpaxij bis* means to pour out sadness, as when a pot breaks and the contents spill. It is also to break, take away, or leave. Here, the drink made the sadness pour out and disappear.

44. It is understood that Nicolasa spoke ill of the boy and gave her advice not to marry him.

45. This was the case with a woman who was trained at the mission to teach in the Montessori preschool that was established to help Tz'utujil children acquire the basic skills they would need to be successful in the local public school. Her name was Concepción Ajuchan Pop, a very beautiful woman whose face was chosen to appear on the Guatemalan 25 cent coin. (For this privilege the government paid her with a framed photograph of herself.) She was a gifted teacher's assistant in the school, but by 1975 she was in her mid-twenties, too old—and too educated—to be desirable to a Tz'utujil man. In 2007 she was a very poor and lonely childless widow, not having married until she was well into her fifties. She passed away in 2011. She has since been memorialized by her people with a statue that stands in the central plaza of the town.

46. Douglas 1969, 161.

47. Long pants are worn by Ladino men, as opposed to the knee-length pants of the typical Tz'utujil costume.

48. Bill Douglas (1969, 98–101) also describes Tz'utujil beliefs about *isom*. Folktales about *isom* (called *characoteles* or *naguales* in the literature, but rarely in Atitlán) are recorded by Butler (1969), Sexton (1999), and Orellana (1975).

49. The episode referred to here tells how the father of the Hero Twins, One Hunahpu, is tricked by the Lords of Death and murdered by them. They place his head in a calabash tree, which attracts the virgin princess Xquiq (Lady Blood). When she comes near, the head spits into her hand, impregnating her with the Hero Twins Hunahpu and Xbalanque.

50. It is common for a mother to call her son "papa," and her daughter "mama."

51. *Mo's* comes from Spanish *mozo*, a Ladino headman or boss. It means powerful and handsome.

52. A large nose is considered an attractive feature.

53. "Boy" in this context refers to Old Mam.

54. Here the son calls his father "my boy."

55. This and the following lines refer to a fight between Diego and María. The mother justifies her son's actions.

56. It is not clear who asks Diego this question.

57. *Metz* means "eyebrows," and in this context a term of endearment.

58. The meaning is not clear; this translation is a guess.

59. "My namesake" is translated as *c'sel* or *c'xel*. Here Elena refers to her grandfather, whose land she has inherited, illustrating the concept that children are reborn as the replacements of their grandparents. This is the idea of *c'ex* (*k'ex* in standard orthography) as explained by Carlsen (1997, 50–57).

60. Orellana mentions that traders brought back fragrant white flowers from the coast, citing Ocaña. These remain important as part of the the Holy Week rituals (1984, 165).

61. This translates literally as "you washed my head."

62. For many of the details and interpretation of the *alguacil*'s journey I have relied on Stanzione (2003).

63. Now that the *cofradía* Santa Cruz has become a major destination for tourists to visit, the figure of Old Mam is no longer hidden but on display, not on the altar with the Santos, but on a separate table where it can be examined and touched.

64. "There [Nicolas and I] talked a while, inspired by the drinks and our mutual interest in the esoteric. During that conversation he told me about the '12 stars, 12 locks, 12 screws' being in the sky, pointing out the Pleiades as the '12 stars' and saying that the 12 *candados* (locks) hadn't risen in the sky yet. (It was 12:30 or 1:30 a.m. on Sept 10, 1972.) He was surprised when I asked him about these things, saying, 'Where did you hear about that?' And then he answered me. He also told me that they are part of Maximon's body" (O'Brien 1972b, 81).

65. Translation by Christenson (2007b, 16–19.)

Chapter 4

1. Of the approximately 330 *b'ix* I recorded, about 226 are instrumentals by guitar, marimba band, or cane flute and drum, and about 104 were sung. Fifty-two have very short or repetitive texts, and fifty-two others have significantly long poetic texts. (Numbers are approximate because songs were sometimes strung together, or recordings are incomplete fragments, or my cataloging is less than accurate.)

2. Allen Christenson recounts the history of the manuscript in his introduction to the *Popol Vuh*:

Ximénez's manuscript lay forgotten in parish archives until the Guatemalan Civil War of 1829 when all religious orders were expelled from the country. Books and papers formerly housed in convents and monasteries were subsequently transferred to public libraries, government repositories, or the collections of private individuals. Ximénez's copy of the *Popol Vuh* manuscript apparently ended up in the library of the University of San Carlos in Guatemala City. An Austrian traveler named Carl Scherzer saw it there in 1854 and had a copy made to take with him back to Europe. In part, Scherzer commissioned this copy to be made due to the poor condition of the manuscript. He described it as having been "written in such light ink that the original might very well become illegible and useless in a few years" (Scherzer 1856, 9). Lamentably, this faded copy of the Ximénez transcription of the *Popol Vuh* has since vanished from public records. Scherzer published Ximénez's Spanish version of the text in 1856, the first time the *Popol Vuh* had appeared in print. The book was greeted with a great deal of excitement in Europe and America, where interest in ancient cultures was widespread.

In 1861, four years after Scherzer's book, the Quiché version of the *Popol Vuh* was published for the first time, along with a rather flowery French translation by Father Charles Etienne Brasseur de Bourbourg. This publication was based on yet another copy of the Ximénez transcription which Brasseur had obtained from a Quiché man, named Ignacio Coloch, who resided in the town of Rabinal. This manuscript is of supreme importance because it is the oldest known Quiché version of the *Popol Vuh* text which has survived. Ximénez was in charge of the parish of Rabinal from 1704–1714, immediately following his years in Chichicastenango. It is unknown whether Ximénez prepared the "Rabinal Manuscript" during this period of his ministry or brought it with him from Chichicastenango. (2007a, 40–41)

3. Insertions in brackets are mine.

4. These lines mention local herbs.

5. A vocable is a nonlexical syllable or word, that is, a "nonsense" syllable or word. It is made of syllables valued for their sound rather than their meaning, for example, "*e-i-e-i-o*," or "*lala la.*" Some vocables are onomatopoeic, and sound like what they imitate, like "plink plink."

6. Elision marks (‿) indicate the union of two adjacent vowel sounds to produce a single syllable, so that "*xintz'u'ja‿anen*" is pronounced "*xintz'u'janen.*"

7. The *bandurria* is a flat-bodied plucked chordophone imported into the New World from Spain during Colonial times. It exists in several different regional forms in Latin America. Its use in Atitlán in the past is not documented and it is not now among the instruments now used for traditional music there. However, songman Gaspar Reanda Ramirez told me, "No, I don't play the guitar very often because of my age. Before, yes, I played and I also played the *bandurria*. Do you know it? It is a small guitar, a *primera.*"

8. "Give me one who wears a vicuña hat . . . sandals," means one who has money. Vicuña hats were expensive, and only some of the more affluent men wore sandals. At that time most Tz'utujil men and almost all women and children went barefoot.

9. As mentioned, I had the impression that most people know these stories. All of my transcribers of the texts (from the Tz'utujil of the recordings, to written Tz'utujil, to Spanish) were associated with Acción Católica, because at that time they were the only group who could write Tz'utujil. All of them knew the extended titles of the songs, although none was a songman nor attempted to sing them.

10. Navarrete Pellicer found that in Rabinal the ability to improvise within a given structure of memorized prayers was a required skill for one to become an *abogado* or prayer-maker (2005b, 40).

11. To clarify this, an example may be helpful. The following is a scansion of the first lines of verses 1 and 2 of a well-known song. In the first verse, there are two unstressed syllables on beat 1 ("-ny comes"), whereas in the second verse there is only one unstressed syllable on the same beat 1 ("church"). Yet, the rhythm and the number of beats (underlined) remain the same.

First verse, line 1:
Whĕn *JÓhn*-ny comes *march*-ing *home* a-*gain* [9 syllables, 4 beats]
    beat 1   *beat 2*   *beat 3* *beat 4*

Second verse, line 1:

Thĕ *Óld* church *bell* will *peal* with *joy* [8 syllables, 4 beats]
    beat 1   *beat 2*   *beat 3*   *beat 4*

12. In discussing the patterns of wording that display parallel verse, Tedlock mentions that K'iche' singers "augment the prayers of a less eloquent daykeeper with chants or songs together with further prayers" but offers no examples of the texts of songs (Tedlock 1987, 146).

Chapter 5

1. These forms are the prototypes of the Baroque *chaconne* and *sarabande* before they became formal and stylized.

2. The Harrisons (1968) and Navarrete Pellicer (2005b) identified the relationship to the *chaconne* and *zarabande* in the music of the highland Maya communities they studied.

3. *Bombas* were balls of string and glue—the size of large softballs—wrapped around a core of gunpowder. After lighting the wick the *bomba* was dropped into a two- or three-foot upright metal cylinder. The ejection of the *bomba* from the cylinder created a deafening "bang." Once I discovered an unexploded *bomba* just above the ceiling of my bedroom.

4. These transcriptions are presented in A Major for purposes of comparison.

5. See also O'Brien (1975, 77). Other survivals of liturgical music in Latin are still sung for *cofradía* rituals in Atitlán. Until recently the singing of three-part Latin psalmody in *fauxbourdon*, a style that was used during the early renaissance, survived in Atitlán as part of the music of Tenebrae services of the last three days of Holy Week. In this style, formulaic psalm tones are harmonized in three parts on the second inversion in parallel six-four chords. In 2007 the Sacristan in charge of this traditional ritual complained to me that the resident Catholic pastor would no longer allow them to sing anything in Latin. The adaptation of the old music and its Latin texts to a Spanish translation has presented insurmountable difficulties for the Sacristans and probably guarantees the loss of this tradition.

6. I am grateful to Joseph Gross for this recording.

7. In the 1960s TGW broadcasted music from a very large collection of recordings of regional rural music of Guatemala that was part of its archives. It is likely that no comparable document of its kind was made. If it still exists, it is a valuable treasure of the music of Guatemala.

8. I was told but did not verify that these were made by prisoners in El Salvador. At the Terminal Market there were several among the many styles of guitars for sale in the 1970s, but not in 2011.

9. The five-course guitar from Spain was brought to its highest development and popularity in Italy, where it acquired its name *guitarra española*.

10. For studies of the development of the five-string guitar see Bellow (1970), Esses (1992), and Turnbull (1991), among others.

11. Although the tuning is not explicit in Fuenllana's publication, both Turnbull (1991, 14) and Bellow (1970, 79) agree that the compositions imply the A–D–G–B–E tuning.

12. *"Las fuentes históricas atribuyen dos significados a las zarabandas: el de un evento social, donde la gente bebe y baila con la música de sones dentro de las fiestas de cofradía, en las velaciones de niños o en los ranchos pajizos y tabernas, y el de un baile particular entre hombres y mujeres que se efectuaba durante las celebraciones de cofradía y, por inferencia, la música de ese baile. Las zarabandas eran, pues, una forma popular de expresión religiosa considerada pagana por las autoridades. En Rabinal se usa la palabra para referirse a un evento social con música de marimba de sones, baile y alcohol. En el vecino departamento de Alta Verapaz, existe actualmente un grupo instrumental formado por un arpa, una guitarrilla y un rabel identificado por Sáenz Poggio (1997: 81) en 1877 como una especie de orquesta llamada zarabanda (escúchese pista 15 en el disco compacto)."* [The translation is mine.]

13. See Harrison and Harrison (1968, 14–18) and Stevenson (1962, 1963) for more extensive discussion of the probable origins of the *zarabanda*.

14. *"Para gozar, solamente, para quedar contentos. Sí, es como una zarabanda, pues."*

15. For details of the impact of the cacao industry on local communities, see MacLeod (1973).

16. *"Los naturales deste pueblo son de buen entendimiento dociles y bien ynclinados para entender y deprender todas aquellas cosas de que son enseñados, en especial los que tratan en la iglesia que son los cantores los quales saben leer y escrevir y cantar. An tomado bien el canto y organo, sirben de oficiar las misas, vísperas y otros oficios divinos. Saben tocar los ministriles como son organo, trompetas, flautas, sacabuches y cheremías y otros instrumentos que ay en la iglesia para el servicio y ornato del culto divino. Ay una escuela donde los niños del pueblo acuden a deprender la Doctrina Xristiana en su lengua materna y a deprender a leer y a escrivir y en esto tienen gran quenta el guardian y religiosos, los quales tienen señalado y nombrado un yndio natural y principal deste pueblo quien es el maestro de loa niños el qual es muy diestro para ello, con facultad de la real abdiencia y se le paga salario de los bienes de la comunidad. . . .*

Los dichos religiosos dieron orden como en este dicho pueblo ubiese escuela para los niños para que deprendiesen a leer y escrevir y cantar y oficiar las misas y oficios divinos por canto llano y de organo en lo qual el dia de hoy son dóciles." [The translation is mine.]

Final Words

1. When in 2007 I gave presentations in the secondary schools of Atitlán that included recordings of the music of the Nawals, and slides of the village and the old customs in the 1970s, the response from the predominantly Tz'utujil students was a surprising silence. In six presentations, only three young men timidly came up afterwards and quietly thanked me, anxious to have a CD or some photos to take home to their parents.

2. In my journal for 2011 I entered this comment after a session with a songman:

There were no candles or libations or drinks passed around. His house is not on the earth of the Santo Mundo, but on a concrete slab—difficult for libations. His guitar style and singing show lots of acculturation from popular music, even a *"tropicál"* style of singing. He plays a six-string guitar from which he has removed the low E, but it has two bass strings, because he didn't replace the A with a lighter gauge and raise it an octave, like the old tuning.

GLOSSARY

Acción Católica (**Catholic Action**): a movement within the Catholic Church prevalent in Latin America in the twentieth century, characterized by its mandate to create Christian educational and political institutions that are appropriate to local culture, and by its dedication to the promotion of social justice

ajb'ix: a Tz'utujil ritual musician, literally "a songman"

alcalde: mayor, or headman of a *cofradía*

ajcun: a ritual specialist who is a prayer-maker and healer

ajitz: a ritual specialist who is a witch

ajmes: a ritual specialist who uses divination

alguacil: literally "constable"; a young male initiate into the *cofradía* system

APla's Sojuel: Francisco Sojuel, the youngest of the twelve Nawals who found the tree that contained the spirit of Old Mam

Atiteco(a): a man or woman from Santiago Atitlán

Atitlán: the abbreviated name of the town Santiago Atitlán; also Lake Atitlán

atol: a drink made of corn gruel and other flavorings or alcohol, often used in rituals

b'ey: road, street, path; one's destiny, luck, or life's journey that optimally will lead one to becoming a Nawal

b'ix: music, song, and dance, specifically the songs of the Nawals in Santiago Atitlán

Catequistas: the group of Tz'utujil leaders in the Catholic Church who are reformists opposed to the inclusion of any indigenous elements in Catholic rituals, and whose intent is to break the power and influence of the *cofradías*

chacona (***chaconne***): a musical form consisting of continuous variations on a theme, possibly originating, like the *zarabanda* (sarabande), in sixteenth-century Mexico

characotel: see *isom*

chirimía: a simple shawm or double-reed wind instrument

chromatic: in this context, a marimba keyboard that includes all the semitones of the musical scale

cochineal: an insect that lives on cacti and from which a crimson dye is made *cofrade*: a man who does ritual service to the *cofradías*; a *cofradía* member

cofradía: a hierarchical religious fraternity or brotherhood; refers both to a prayer-house and to the group of men and women who perform ritual services to the *cofradía* system, such as preparing the calendric celebrations of the traditional indigenous religion

c'unc'un: a musical instrument often called a "slit drum," (and erroneously a "split drum"); an ideophonic percussion tube made of a hollow log that is incised in the form of an "H" to form two tonguelike keys; in Mexico it is known as *teponaztli*, in Yucatan as *tunkul*, and elsewhere in Guatemala it is called "*tun*" or "*tun tun*"

cusul: "rocking cradle"; the box that contains the ritual bundle for women in the *cofradía* San Juan

cuxa: homemade cane liquor

diatonic: in this context, a marimba whose keyboard contains the tones of the major scale

Dio's: a major Tz'utujil deity

Gregorian chant: the medieval liturgical chant of the Roman Catholic Church

guaro: commercially made cane liquor

guitarra española: a five-course guitar developed and popular in Spain and Italy in the late sixteenth century

Hero Twins: Hunahpu and Xbalanque of the K'iche' epic, the *Popol Vuh*

Holy Week (*Semana Santa*): the Monday through Saturday preceding Easter Sunday

huipil (**sometimes spelled *güipil*):** the traditional indigenous woman's blouse made of decoratively embroidered woven cotton

isom (**Spanish *characotel*):** a transforming witch or shapeshifter who at night may take the form of an animal such as a dog or cat to perform an evil deed

jawal: a Spirit-Lord

JesuKrista: a major Tz'utujil deity syncretized with Jesus Christ

Ladino: (1) a Spanish-speaking person of mixed parentage (Spanish-Indigenous) who follows a non-indigenous way of life (in Mexico such a person is called a *mestizo*); or (2) an indigenous person who has abandoned indigenous culture and adopted Ladino dress, customs, and Spanish language, in an effort to join the Ladino community

maize: corn

Marias: the ancestral women; the female Nawals

marimba: the national instrument of Guatemala, a xylophone that has wooden plates or keys and resonators, originally gourds, below each key; "marimba" is used to signify a single instrument and also an ensemble of two or more marimbas that often includes saxophones, drums, and other instruments

Martín bundle: a sacred bundle kept in a chest in the *cofradía* San Juan that contains items related to the fertility of nature

Martíns: the Spirit-Lords of nature

MICATOKLA: *Misión Católica de Oklahoma*, the Catholic Mission of Oklahoma in Santiago Atitlán

mirliton: a membrane (in Guatemala usually of pig intestine) attached to the resonators of a marimba, that produces a buzzing sound called *charleo* when activated by striking the keys

nabeysil: the rain priest in Santiago Atitlán, attached to the *cofradía* San Juan

Nawals: in Santiago Atitlán, the original ancestors of the Tz'utujil people

Old Mam: *see* Rilaj Mam

Old Ways: the traditional customs and belief system of the Tz'utujil Mayas

Popol Vuh: the origin story of the K'iche' Maya

punteado: the technique of playing the guitar by plucking with the fingernails on a single string

rasgueado: the technique of playing the guitar by drawing the nails or fingers across several strings

Recibos: "Reception Songs," six musical pieces attributed to Old Mam that are the vehicles for the transmission of the teachings of the Old Ways of the Nawals and the apparent origin of the melodies and the style of the *b'ix*

Rilaj Mam: "Old Mam" or "Old Grandfather," a principal deity of the Tz'utujils

Sacristánes: singers whose service in the *cofradía* system is the music of JesuKrista, in Latin or Spanish

Santo: a Catholic saint who has been identified as a Spirit-Lord and adopted into the pantheon of Tz'utujil deities

sitio: a family compound consisting of several houses and other buildings, such as a *temescal* or steam bath, on a single property

son, sones: in Atitlán the dance form that accompanies the traditional songs called *b'ix*, and the songs themselves whether they are played on the guitar or the marimba, or sung

susto: fright that is believed to cause illness and distress, both mental and physical

telinel: a priest of Old Mam

tixel: a woman who serves in a *cofradía*

triste: "sad," used in the title of certain songs

zarabanda **(sarabande):** a musical form consisting of continuous variations on a theme, possibly originating, like the *chacona*, in sixteenth-century Mexico

WORKS CITED

Academia de Lenguas Mayas
1988   *Lenguas mayas de Guatemala: Documento de referencia para la pronunciación de los nuevos alfabetos oficiales.* Guatemala: Instituto Indigenista Nacional.

Aguirre, Gerardo G.
1972   *La cruz de Nimajuyú, historia de la parroquia de San Pedro la Laguna.* Guatemala: Litoguat.

Alvarado, Pedro de
1924   *An account of the conquest of Guatemala in 1524 by Pedro de Alvarado.* Edited by Sedley J. Mackie. New York: Cortés Society.

Bellow, Alexander
1970   *The illustrated history of the guitar.* Rockville Centre, NY: Franco Colombo Publications.

Benedictines of Solesmes
1952   *The Liber Usualis.* Tournai and New York: Desclée.

Betancour, A. P., and Fray P. de Arboleda
1964   *Relación de Santiago Atitlán, año de 1585, por Alonso Paez Betancor y Fray Pedro de Arboleda. Anales: Sociedad de Geografía e Historia de Guatemala,* vol. 37, 87–106. Guatemala: Tipografía Nacional.

Bonner, Jeremy
2008   *The road to renewal: Victor Joseph Reed and Oklahoma Catholicism, 1905–1971.* Washington, DC: Catholic University of America.

Bonpane, Blase
1985   *Guerillas of Peace: Liberation theology and the Central American Revolution.* Lincoln, NE: toExcel.

Butler, James
1969   *Tasiq'uij ja chiste pa katzobal (Cuentos folklóricos).* Instituto Lingüístico de Verano, Guatemala.

224

Campbell, Lyle, and Terrence Kaufman
1985   "Mayan linguistics: Where are we now?" In *Annual Review of Anthropology*, vol. 14, 187–198.

Carlsen, Robert S.
1997   *The war for the heart and soul of a highland Maya town*. Austin: University of Texas.

Castellanos, J. Humberto
1949   "El 'son' en Guatemala, danza y melodía." In *Estudios CentroAmericanos*, vol. 4, no. 36, 1372–1387. San Salvador: Universidad Centroamericana "José Simeón Cañas."

Chenoweth, Vida
1964   *The marimbas of Guatemala*. Lexington: University of Kentucky.

Christenson, Allen J.
2001   *Art and society in a highland Maya community: The altarpiece of Santiago Atitlán*. Austin: University of Texas.
2003a   *K'iche'-English dictionary and guide to pronunciation of the K'iche'-Maya alphabet*. http://www.famsi.org/mayawriting/dictionary/christenson.
2003b   *Popol Vuh, Volume II*. Winchester, UK: O Books.
2007a   *Popol Vuh: The sacred book of the Maya*. Norman: University of Oklahoma.
2007b   *Popol Vuh: Sacred book of the Maya, electronic database*. Provo: Brigham Young University.

Consejo de Desarrollo Departamental
2008   *Planificación de desarrollo municipal con enfoque territorial. Municipio de Santiago Atitlán, Sololá*. Santiago Atitlán, Guatemala: Municipalidad de Santiago Atitlán.

Douglas, Bill Gray
1969   *Illness and curing in Santiago Atitlán, a Tzutuhil-Maya community in the southwestern highlands of Guatemala*. PhD diss. Palo Alto: Stanford University.

Edmonson, Munro S.
1971a   *The book of counsel: The Popol Vuh of the Quiche Maya of Guatemala*. Middle American Research Institute, publication 35. New Orleans: Tulane University.
1971b   *Lore: An introduction to the science of folklore and literature*. New York: Holt, Reinhart & Winston.
1986   *Heaven born Merida and its destiny: The Book of Chilam Balam of Chumayel*. Austin: University of Texas.

Esses, Maurice
1992   *Dance and instrumental diferencias in Spain during the 17th and early 18th centuries*. Stuyvesant, NY: Pendragon Press.

Feld, Steven
1990   *Sound and sentiment: Birds, weeping, poetics, and song in Kaluli expression*. Philadelphia: University of Pennsylvania.

Freidel, David, Linda Schele, and Joy Parker
1993   *Maya cosmos: Three thousand years on the shaman's path*. New York: William Morrow.

Geertz, Clifford
1983   *Local knowledge: Further essays in interpretive anthropology*. New York: Basic Books.

Gross, Joseph J.
1997   *Domestic group structure in a Mayan community of Guatamala.* PhD diss. Rochester, NY: University of Rochester.

Harrison, Frank, and Joan Harrison
1968   "Spanish elements in the music of two Maya groups in Chiapas." In *Selected Reports in Ethnomusicology*, vol. 1, no. 2, 1–44. Los Angeles: Institute of Ethnomusicology, University of California at Los Angeles.

Hudson, Richard
2001   "Sarabande." In *The New Grove dictionary of music and musicians*, edited by Stanley Sadie. London: Macmillan.

Hull, Kerry M., and Michael D. Carrasco
2012   *Parallel worlds: Genre, discourse, and poetics in contemporary, colonial, and classic period Maya literature.* Boulder: University Press of Colorado.

Kaufman, Terrence, and John Justeson
2003   *A preliminary Mayan etymological dictionary.* Foundation for the Advancement of Mesoamerican Studies, Inc. www.famsi.org/reports/01051.

Keller, Angela
2009   "A road by any other name: Paths, trails, and roads in Maya language and thought." In *Landscapes of movement: Trails and paths in anthropological perspective*, edited by James E. Snead, Clark L. Erickson, and J. Andrew Darling, 133–157. Philadelphia: University of Pennsylvania.

Looper, Matthew G.
2009   *To be like gods: Dance in ancient Maya civilization.* Austin: University of Texas.

Mace, Carroll Edward
1970   *Two Spanish-Quiché dance dramas of Rabinal.* New Orleans: Tulane University.

MacLeod, Murdo J.
1973   *Spanish Central America: A socioeconomic history, 1520–1720.* Los Angeles: University of California.

McBryde, Felix W.
1947   *Cultural and historical geography of southwest Guatemala*, no. 4. Washington, DC: Institute of Social Anthropology, Smithsonian Institution.

McGovern, P. E., J. Lazar, and R. H. Michael
1990   "The analysis of indigoid dyes by mass spectrometry." In *The Mass Spectrometric Analysis of Indigoid Dyes*, vol. 1, no. 1, 22–25. Philadelphia: Museum of Applied Science Center for Archaeology, University of Pennsylvania.

Melville, Thomas, and Marjorie Melville
1971   *Whose heaven, whose earth?* New York: Alfred A. Knopf.

Mendelson, E. Michael
1956   *Religion and world-view in Santiago Atitlán.* PhD diss. Chicago: University of Chicago.
1957   *Religion and world-view in Santiago Atitlán [Long Text].* Collection of Manuscripts on American Indian Cultural Anthropology 52 (microfilm). Chicago: University of Chicago Library.
1965   *Los escándalos de Maximón: Un estudio sobre la religión y la visión del mundo en Santiago Atitlán.* Guatemala: Tipografía Nacional.

Mendieta, Fr. Gerónimo de.
1993   *Historia eclesiástica indiana.* México, DF: Editorial Porrúa.

Murga Armas, Jorge
2006   *Iglesia católica, movimiento indígena y lucha revolucionaria (Santiago Atitlán, Guatemala).* Guatemala: n.p.
Navarrete Pellicer, Sergio
1999   *The meanings of marimba music in rural Guatemala.* PhD diss. London: University College.
2005a   *Los significados de la música: La marimba Maya Achí de Guatemala.* Mexico, DF: Centro de Investigaciones y Estudios Superiores en Antropología Social.
2005b   *Maya Achi marimba music in Guatemala.* Philadelphia: Temple University.
O'Brien, Linda L.
1972a   "Paradigm for research." Unpublished manuscript.
1972b   "Field journal." Unpublished manuscript.
1975   *Songs of the face of the earth: Ancestor songs of the Tzutuhil Maya of Santiago Atitlán, Guatemala.* PhD diss. Los Angeles: University of California at Los Angeles.
1976   "Music education and innovation in a traditional Tzutuhil-Maya community." In *Enculturation in Latin America: An anthology,* edited by Johannes Wilbert, vol. 37, 377–394. Los Angeles: University of California at Los Angeles, Latin American Studies.
O'Brien-Rothe, Linda
1982   "Marimbas of Guatemala: The African connection." In *The World of Music,* vol. XXV, no. 2, 99–104.
1998   "Guatemala." In *The Garland Encyclopedia of World Music: South America, Mexico, Central America, and the Caribbean,* edited by Dale A. Olsen and Daniel E. Sheehy, vol. 2, 721–737. New York: Garland Publishing.
2006   "Dos canciones de Faz-de-la-Tierra." In *Tradiciones de Guatemala,* vol. 66, 11–20. Guatemala: Centro de Estudios Folklóricos, Universidad de San Carlos de Guatemala.
2007a   "Marimbas de Guatemala: La conexión africana." In *Tradiciones de Guatemala: Etnomusicología en Guatemala,* edited by Matthias Stöckli and Alfonso Arrivillaga Cortés, no. 66, 141–146.
2007b   "Guatemala." In *The New Grove Dictionary of Music and Musicians.* London: McMillan.
2011   "Field notes (1966–2011)." Unpublished manuscript.
Orellana, Sandra
1975   Folk literature of the Tzutujil Maya. In *Anthropos,* vol. 70, 839–876.
1984   *The Tzutujil Mayas: Continuity and change, 1250–1630.* Norman: University of Oklahoma.
Paret-Limardo de Vela, Lise
1962   *Folklore musical de Guatemala.* Guatemala: Tipografía Nacional.
Pérez Mendoza, Francisco, and Miguel Hernández Mendoza
1996   *Diccionario Tz'utujil.* Proyecto Lingüistico Francisco Marroquin. Antigua Guatemala: Cholsamaj.
Prechtel, Martin
1999   *Long life, honey in the heart.* New York: Jeremy P. Tarcher–Putnam.
Sahagún, Fr. Bernardino de.
1956   *Historia general de las cosas de Nueva España.* 4 vols. México, DF: Editorial Porrúa.

Sexton, James D., ed.
1999   *Mayan folktales from Lake Atitlán, Guatemala.* Albuquerque: University of New Mexico.

Sodi, Demetrio
1964   *La literatura de los mayas.* Mexico, DF: Editorial Joaquín Mortiz.

Stanzione, Vincent
2003   *Rituals of sacrifice: Walking the face of the earth on the sacred path of the sun.* Albuquerque: University of New Mexico.

Stevenson, Robert
1962   "Sarabande: A dance of American descent." In *Inter-American Music Bulletin,* no. 30, 5–6. Washington, DC.
1963   "The Mexican origins of the sarabande." In *Inter-American Music Bulletin,* no. 33, 7. Washington, DC.
1964   "European music in sixteenth-century Guatemala." In *Musical Quarterly,* vol. 50, no. 3, 341–352.

Tarn, Nathaniel, [E. Michael Mendelson], and Martín Prechtel
1997   *Scandals in the house of birds: Shamans and priests on Lake Atitlán.* New York: Marsilio.

Tedlock, Dennis
1983   *The spoken word and the work of interpretation.* Philadelphia: University of Pennsylvania.
1987   "Hearing a voice in an ancient text: Quiché Maya poetics in performance." In *Native American discourse: Poetics and rhetoric,* edited by Joel Sherzer and Anthony C. Woodbury, 140–175. Cambridge, MA: Cambridge University.
1996   *Popol Vuh.* New York: Simon & Schuster.
2010   *2000 years of Mayan literature.* Los Angeles: University of California.

Turnbull, Harvey
1991   *The guitar from the renaissance to the present day.* Westport, CT: The Bold Strummer.

Vallejo Reyna, Alberto
2001   *Por los caminos de los antiguos Nawales: Ri Laj Mam y el nawalismo Maya Tz'utuhil de Santiago Atitlán, Guatemala.* Guatemala: Fundación Cedim y Norad.

Ximénez, Fr. Francisco
1857   *Las historias del origen de los Indios de esta provincial de Guatemala.* Edited by Carl Scherzer. Vienna: Imperial Academia de las Ciencias.

Discography

Alderson, Richard
2004   *Bats'i Son: The music of the highlands of Chiapas, Mexico.* Chicago: Latitude/Locust Music.

INDEX

Page numbers in italic indicate figures. Page numbers in bold indicate text of songs. Page numbers in bold italic indicate examples.

Weavers, 57
Westerman, Robert, 202n9
Wind-Men, 57
witchcraft, 25, 126–127
womb, Santo Mundo as, 18. *See also* childbearing
women: breast-shaped cacao representing, 57, 146–147; collecting water from Mam's clothing for fertility, 149; duties of a wife under Old Ways, 97; songs sung by, 47–52, 170, 213n29; *xo'* (head-woman of *cofradía*), 20, 35. *See also* childbearing; courtship
Woods, William, 4
"World-Face of the Earth" (*Mund-Ruch'lew*), 18

xajoj ("to dance"), 44
Xbalanque. *See* Hero Twins (Hunahpu and Xbalanque)
xbijnim ("big fright," Sp. *susto*), 64
Xbinel (Spirits-that-frighten), 64
Xe'cjol Ak'om ("The Place or Root of Medicine"), 83
Ximénez, Francisco, xv, 155, 215–216n2
xjowik ("to move"), xvii
xo' (head-woman of *cofradía*), 20, 35
xocomil (south wind), 64
Xquiq (Lady Blood), 204n11, 214n49
xul (cane flute, general name for male instruments), 32, 36, *151*

"Ya" (preceding female names), 206n36
YaLen Botrán, 119–120
YaMri'y CastilYan (wife of Old Mam), 146
YaMri'y Iyom (Maria Midwife, who delivers Old Mam), 140, 143
YaMriy Canon (Maria Serpent or Yellow), 82
YaMriy Ch'ejquem (Maria Warp-Beams), 82
YaMriy Q'uir (Maria Small Heddles), 82
YaMriy Quemo' (Maria Thread-Beater), 82
YaMriy Skaj (Maria Large Heddles), 82
YaMriy Tzitzu' (Maria Small Thread-Beater), 82
Yataz Ramirez, Gaspar: courting song, **63**; Mam making things move, 93; "Song of Mam," 90–92; "Song of the Young Girl Who Says Goodbye to Her Mother," 63, **109–113**, 113, **113–114**, 175–176, *177*; as translator, 26
YaXep Bitz'bal (Josepha Spindle), 82
YaXper (Midwife goddess), 150
Yurchenko, Henrietta, 4

zarabanda/sarabande, 168, 184–186 (*184*), 217nn1, 2
Zinacantán, 185